9.95
(1)

Europe in 1914

A note for the general reader

Total War and Social Change: Europe 1914–1955 is the latest honours-level history course to be produced by the Open University. War and Society has always been a subject of special interest and expertise in the Open University's History Department. The appeal for the general reader is that the five books in the series, taken together or singly, consist of authoritative, up-to-date discussions of the various aspects of war and society in the twentieth century.

The books provide insights into the modes of teaching and communication, including the use of audio-visual material, which have been pioneered at the Open University. Readers will find that they are encouraged to participate in a series of 'tutorials in print', an effective way to achieve a complete command of the material. As in any serious study of a historical topic, there are many suggestions for further reading, including references to a Course Reader, set book and to two collections of primary sources which accompany the series. It is possible to grasp the basic outlines of the topics discussed without turning to these books, but obviously serious students will wish to follow up what is, in effect a very carefully designed course of guided reading, and discussion and analysis of that reading. The first unit in Book 1 sets out the aims and scope of the course.

Open University students are provided with supplementary material, including a *Course Guide* which gives information on student assignments, summer school, the use of video cassettes, and so on.

Total War and Social Change: Europe 1914–1955

Book 1 *Europe in 1914*
Book 2 *The Impact of World War I*
Book 3 *Between Two Wars*
Book 4 *The Impact of World War II*
Book 5 *Retrospect: War and Change in Europe 1914–1955*

Other material associated with the course

Primary Sources 1: World War I, eds Arthur Marwick and Wendy Simpson, Open University, 2000

Primary Sources 2: Interwar and World War II, eds Arthur Marwick and Wendy Simpson, Open University, 2000

Secondary Sources, eds Arthur Marwick and Wendy Simpson, Open University, 2000

Total War and Historical Change: Europe 1914–1955, eds. Clive Emsley, Arthur Marwick and Wendy Simpson, Open University Press, 2000 (Course Reader)

J. M. Roberts, *Europe 1880–1945,* Longman, 2000 (third edition) (Set Book)

Book

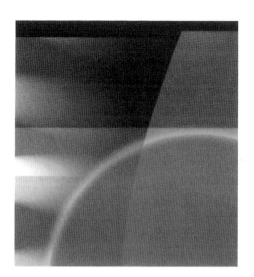

Europe in 1914

Arthur Marwick, Clive Emsley and Annika Mombauer

The Open
University

This publication forms part of an Open University course: AA312 *Total War and Social Change: Europe 1914–1955.* Details of this and other Open University courses can be obtained from the Call Centre, PO Box 724, The Open University, Milton Keynes MK7 6ZS, United Kingdom: tel. +44 (0)1908 653231, e-mail ces-gen@open.ac.uk

Alternatively, you may visit the Open University website at http://www.open.ac.uk where you can learn more about the wide range of courses and packs offered at all levels by the Open University.

To purchase this publication or other components, contact Open University Worldwide Ltd, The Berrill Building, Walton Hall, Milton Keynes MK7 6AA, United Kingdom: tel. +44 (0)1908 858785; fax +44 (0)1908 858787; e-mail ouwenq@open.ac.uk; website http://www.ouw.co.uk

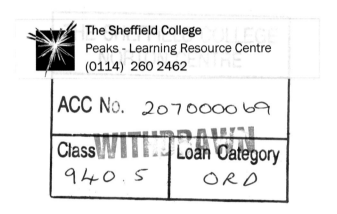
The Open University, Walton Hall, Milton Keynes MK7 6AA

First published 2000. Reprinted 2002

Edited, designed and typeset by The Open University

Printed and bound in the United Kingdom by The Alden Group, Oxford

ISBN 0-7492-85540

Cover illustration: poster by E. V. Kealey, *Women of Britain say – 'Go',* 1914, Imperial War Museum, London

1.2

28380B/aa312b1i1.2

Contents

Acknowledgements

Grateful acknowledgement is made to the following sources for permission to use material in this book:

Text

Holton, S. S. (1986) *Feminism and Democracy*, Cambridge University Press; Macmillan, J. F. (1988) 'World War I and women in France', and Reid, A. (1988) 'World War I and the working class in Britain', in Marwick, A. (ed.) *Total War and Social Change*, Macmillan Press Ltd; Hardach, G. (1977) *The First World War 1914–1918*, Allen Lane. Copyright © Deutscher Taschenbuch Verlag GmbH, translation copyright © Ross, P. and Ross, B. 1977; Marwick, A. (1974) *War and Social Change in the Twentieth Century: A Comparative Study of Britain, France, Germany, Russia and the United States*, Macmillan Press Ltd; Anderson, R. (1977) *France 1870–1914*. Routledge & Kegan Paul; Clark, M. (1984) *Modern Italy 1871–1982*. Longman Group Limited. Sheehan, J.J. (1978) *German Liberalism in the Nineteenth Century*. The University of Chicago Press.

Tables

Table 2.4: Moeller, R. G. (1986) *Peasants and Lords in Modern Germany*, Unwin Hyman Ltd; *Table 2.5:* Blum, Jerome, *The End of the Old Order in Europe*. Copyright © 1978 by PUP. Reprinted by permission of Princeton University Press; *Table 2.6:* Price, R. (1981) *An Economic History of Modern France 1730-1914*, Macmillan Press Ltd; *Table 2.8:* Woodruff, W. (1976) 'The emergence of an international economy 1700–1914', in Cipolla, C. M. (ed) *The Emergence of Industrial Societies, Part 2*, The Fontana Economic History of Europe, Volume 4, The Harvester Press Ltd. © William Woodruff 1971, 1976; *Tables 2.9, 2.10 & 2.11:* Pearson, R. (1983) *National Minorities in Eastern Europe 1848–1945*, Macmillan Press Ltd;

Every effort has been made to trace all the copyright owners, but if any has been inadvertently overlooked, the publishers will be pleased to make the necessary arrangements at the first opportunity.

Unit 1 INTRODUCING THE COURSE

ARTHUR MARWICK

Open University students of this unit will need to refer to:

Course Reader: *Total War and Historical Change: Europe 1914–1955*, eds Clive Emsley, Arthur Marwick and Wendy Simpson, Open University Press, 2000.

1   THE COURSE TITLE EXPLAINED

This is the first book in the Open University history course AA312 *Total War and Social Change: Europe 1914–1955*. The first part of the course title brings out that particular emphasis will be placed upon the two 'total' wars of 1914–1918 and 1939–1945, with questions being raised about the significance of war in twentieth-century European history; the first part of the title also indicates that we shall have a special concern with 'social change'. The second part of the title indicates that it is a course in twentieth-century European history up to about 1955. It would have been possible to construct a course which was more simply a general history of Europe between 1914 and 1955, much as the textbook by J. M. Roberts, *Europe 1880–1945* (the set book for this course) is a general history of Europe between the two dates contained in its title. Roberts's aim is, within the space at his disposal, to cover anything that is of importance in understanding the development of Europe in the period he is concerned with. Inevitably, he emphasizes certain topics at the expense of others, but he has chosen his topics in order, firstly, to give as fair and comprehensive a coverage as possible and, secondly, because he believes the topics he has chosen to be the most important in explaining the development of modern Europe. Naturally he discusses the two major wars ('total' wars as we shall be calling them in this course), but he does not give any special emphasis to them. Our course (while making great use of Roberts's excellent book as a basic secondary source) *does* give a special emphasis to the two total wars. This is partly because we believe that a history course is more likely to arouse and maintain your interest, and is more likely to be effective as teaching material, if it sets up some central questions and issues to be discussed, and partly because there actually is quite a good case (perhaps greater than Roberts allows) that it is impossible to understand twentieth-century European history without being fully aware of the various implications of the two total wars. You do not have to agree with this proposition: the course encourages debate and argument over it. Indeed, you could say that there is a third reason for designing the course in this way, which is that among historians and students of twentieth-century history everywhere this debate is considered a most important one, as shown, for instance, by the fact that 'war and society' courses now exist in a number of other universities.

As a teaching course *Total War and Social Change* differs in other ways as well from a general textbook such as that by Roberts. In a very skilful way, and at a quite advanced level, Roberts presents his readers with information, ideas, interrelationships, causes, consequences, comparisons and contrasts: he presents a balanced, carefully structured account, involving narrative, analysis and description. But our course encourages you (the student and reader) to be active. It seeks to help you to develop and practise some of the skills of history. It seeks to show you how to discuss important historical issues relevant to the course, how to develop these arguments in properly written essays. It seeks to develop your understanding of the nature of the primary source materials upon which all historical writing is based, and of how to analyse and use such sources. It seeks to help you master many of the problems involved in historical study and to understand the differences between the 'professional', 'source-based', 'non-metaphysical' approaches of the Open University History Department (and most other University History Departments) and the more theoretical approaches of, say, Marxists and postmodernists. (Britain's leading Marxist historian is Eric Hobsbawm. Marxist approaches have been vigorously defended by the late E. H. Carr and John Tosh. Keith Jenkins is a useful guide to postmodernist approaches. I deal with the main issues in a number of publications. See 'Further reading'.) Most of this introductory unit will take the form of an elaboration and discussion of the following six aims:

1   To enable you to argue in an informed way over the nature, extent and causes of social change within and across the main European countries 1914–1955, which are defined for the purposes of this course as Russia, Austria–Hungary (up to the aftermath of World War I only), France, Germany, Italy and the United Kingdom (with references, after 1921, to Ireland); Turkey and the Balkans, Central European, Scandinavian and other European countries will feature only with regard to specific events and topics.

2   To help you to understand the nature of total war and how it differs from other kinds of war, and to help you to discuss in an informed way the relationship (if any) between total war and revolution.

3   To enable you to discuss the causes of the two total wars, evaluating 'structural' (that is to say 'concerning economic and demographic imperatives') forces against ideological and institutional ones and those of geopolitics, nationalism, human agency, and contingency.

4   To enable you to argue in an informed way about the role of total war with respect to social change, and in particular to evaluate the significance of the two total wars relative to structural, ideological and institutional, forces, and to enable you to discuss the relationship of the wars to the major geopolitical changes.

5   To assist you in developing skills learned at Arts Level One and Level Two in:

   (a) the critical analysis and interpretation of primary source materials, including written documents, as well as literary and artistic materials, film, radio and the artefacts of popular culture;

   (b) understanding the differences between the 'professional', 'source-based', approach to historical study, and the more theoretical approaches of Marxists, Weberians, postmodernists, and some (by no means all) feminist historians.

   (c) dealing with such problems as periodization and historical semantics; and

   (d) writing history essays of Level 3, or BA (Honours) standard.

6   To take further your understanding of the nature of historiographical controversy (a matter first raised in the Arts Level 1 course, dealt with further at Level 2) and to enable you to arrive at informed judgements on the issues and debates presented within the framework of the course.

2   THE SIX AIMS OF THE COURSE EXPLAINED

Aim 1

Essentially this aim serves two purposes: it indicates that a major concern of the course is social change, and it spells out firmly which countries we shall be dealing with.

To grasp how important the topic of social change is, just reflect for a moment on how different Europe was by the middle 1950s from what it had been in 1914. The changes are quite staggering. But it is not just a matter of knowing what changes took place. It is also a question of puzzling out *why* these changes came about. This course is very much concerned with problems of historical explanation.

It is a platitude that history is concerned with both continuity and change. Aim 1 brings out that our emphasis is on change, the idea being to highlight issues for discussion and debate. If one looks rigorously and systematically for change, one will automatically reveal starkly the areas in which there was little or no change. Note that Aim 1 speaks, as does the title of the course, of social change. Here it is time to pause, in order to help you to be sure that you know what is meant by social change.

Exercise   Three potentially useful ways of pinning down what is meant by 'social change' would be:

1   to write a direct definition of the term;

2   to write down examples of social change;

3   to identify other types of historical change which are not *social* change.

I now want you to try to do each of these things. I suggest that after a quick shot at a definition you move on to the other two tasks. After dealing with them you may find it possible to attempt a fuller answer to the first one. ■

Specimen answers and discussion   For an initial definition you may have said something like: 'social change is change taking place in human societies', or 'social change is change affecting everyday life'. I hope you then went on to give such examples as living conditions, social welfare, social structure, beliefs, customs and attitudes. For other types of historical change I hope you thought of political, constitutional and economic change; perhaps also administrative, technological, scientific and intellectual change and change in international relationships. ☐

Social change may include, or be related to, some of these, but it is not identical to any of them. I'd offer a definition something like this: 'Change in the institutions, ideas and behaviour of society; change affecting human lives as they are actually lived, change directly affecting everyone in society, or large sections of it.' By that sort of definition, social change is not rigidly distinguished from other sorts of historical change, but is indeed seen as embracing, or being closely involved with them. Thus when we say this course is primarily concerned with 'social change', it is a matter of *emphasis* rather than precise content. A change of government would conventionally be regarded as a political change. But quite possibly it would be preceded by social change inducing significant numbers of voters to change their voting preferences; quite probably it would be followed by social change as the new government introduced new social legislation.

Briefly, there is not, in my view, a great deal of value in arguing over what precisely is 'political' and what 'social'. It will be much more useful to you if I now list the ten overlapping areas of social change on which we shall concentrate in this course.

Ten areas of social change

1   *Social geography*

    This concerns population (including, for instance, rises and falls in birthrates), population movements (including from agricultural to urban areas), and the environment in general. It concerns those matters affecting society as a whole which, as the heading suggests, might traditionally be associated with the discipline of geography, that is to say the distribution of people, of town and country, of housing and communications. Such matters are absolutely basic to any study of social change.

2   *Economic performance and theory*

    Here we are already into overlap. Economic performance, that is to say the building of factories and the production of commodities, will obviously affect social geography. But here the emphasis is on relative efficiency, productivity, and so on. Also included are questions of the levels of exploitation of science and technology, and the impact of these (very important social questions), and the related question of the nature of work (something which affects very large numbers of people). It can well be argued that upon levels of economic performance depend all other matters such as standards of living and welfare benefits. As indicated, the concern too is with the theories lying behind, or alternatively themselves being affected by, economic activities: for instance, theories of free trade or private enterprise and *laissez-faire* or, on the contrary, of state regulation and intervention.

3   *Social structure*

    This area also is a strong contender for being considered the central one in all questions of social change. It refers to the way in which societies divide up in hierarchical fashion into 'classes', 'estates' or 'social groups'. In the eyes of most non-Marxist historians, 'classes' are a feature of industrial rather than non-industrial societies (of which there were many in Europe before 1914); Marxists accord a special importance to 'class' (as they understand the term) throughout all periods of history.

4   *National cohesion*

    As I have just suggested, individual countries divide up into 'estates' or 'classes'. Very many, especially in pre-1914 Europe, divided up into different ethnic groups as well. Religion was often a highly divisive factor. We shall look at the extent to which different countries were nationally cohesive (or unified), and the extent to which they were divided up ethnically.

5 *Social reform and welfare policies*

This is a very obvious aspect of social change, and probably one of the ones you thought of immediately in answering the first exercise. It covers such matters as Old Age Pensions, Family Allowances, National Health Services.

6 *Material conditions*

Material conditions are central to social life in the most obvious sense of that term. Specifically they concern housing, diet, nutrition, health and sanitation, and relate also to conditions of work.

7 *Customs and behaviour*

Here we come to an area which would almost certainly have been neglected in traditional accounts of political, constitutional or economic change. We come to the very heart of the most 'advanced' kind of social history. There is, of course, some overlap with material conditions, and even more overlap with the next three headings (particularly 'Role and status of women', and 'High and popular culture'). None the less this is a useful heading for fixing attention on such matters as rural folk customs (such as feast days, festivals and important fairs) and questions about what happened to these in urban society, on costume and dress, eating and drinking habits, hours of work and recreation, and attitudes towards such authorities as monarch, local nobility, church and family.

8 *Role and status of women*

Clearly the role and status of women is a very important issue in social change (some would say, the most important one). A more fashionable heading would be 'gender', which, however, would take us into theoretical discussions as to how far differences between men and women are 'culturally constructed'; discussions perhaps best avoided in a general history course. Since that is a contentious point, the matter is touched on again in Unit 3.

9 *High and popular culture*

Culture, as is well known, is a difficult word with several shades of meaning. Here it is taken to mean what our newspapers often refer to as 'the arts and entertainment', together with leisure activities in general. To avoid direct overlap with 'Customs and behaviour', the emphasis is very much on art, literature, music, film, and radio. By and large, 'high' culture is the culture of the élite, always a minority in any society – it includes 'classical' music, and the work of artists and writers considered to be 'great' or, at least, whose work was accorded attention by serious critics. Historians (and history students) usually avoid high culture like the plague. One of the many pioneering features of this course is that we include it in our analysis of the many ramifications of total war. Popular culture refers to the entertainment and leisure activities of the mass of the people. In itself it has two aspects (a) culture created *for* the masses (by rich newspaper proprietors, film producers, and so on); (b) culture created *by* the masses (for example, folk songs, traditional village football games and carnivals).

10   *Values and institutions*

Are we going beyond the boundaries of social change here? One can't in practice discuss 'changes affecting everyone in society, or large sections of it' without considering those institutions which do, indeed, impinge on ordinary lives: town and village councils, parliaments and their correlatives, the possession, or non-possession, of the right to vote. Still more important are questions of values: do people accept the pre-conditions of liberal democracy, that the majority have the right to rule, but that the rights of minorities must be respected? Is religious 'truth', or national solidarity, or obedience to the monarchy, ranked more highly than liberal democracy? Is socialism regarded as a high ideal or a sinister threat? These are all important questions intimately related to other aspects of social change.

Concluding words on the ten areas of social change

We shall be studying politics, as relevant, but the thrust of this course is towards *social* change. Clearly major political upheavals (both revolutions in government, and those changes in national frontiers which we shall term 'geopolitical changes' – that is, changes which are both geographical and political) arising from, or at the very least coinciding with, the two total wars, did affect the lives of whole societies and vast numbers of people. This important aspect is taken up in Aim 4.

It would be widely agreed that in most, if not all, of the ten areas I have just identified, noteworthy changes did take place between the first decade of the century and the 1950s. However, in serious historical study broad generalizations about 'noteworthy' or 'important' changes are not enough. As Aim 1 spells out, this course is concerned with 'the nature and extent of social change', that is to say we have to establish answers about how much social change there was in the different areas, we have to distinguish between areas in which a lot changed, and areas in which not very much changed.

Having established the basic way in which social change will be treated in this course, I must add that some historians would prefer to define social change in rather broader terms: in terms, indeed, of shifting patterns of dominance, of changing structures of power, of groups and classes overthrowing or replacing or reaching accommodations with each other, of, perhaps, a bourgeois class replacing a landed class and then, say of the bourgeois class skilfully fending off the claims of a 'rising' working class. Such approaches are not ruled out, though they do take us towards the Marxist, the Weberian, the theoretical.

Countries to be studied in this course

The central and inescapable point about the geographical coverage of this course is that it concerns Europe; the focus is on changes across Europe, and on comparisons between the different European countries. There is no emphasis on Britain, but in order to set clear limits somewhere, there is an overwhelming emphasis on what would usually be agreed to be the 'major' European countries. In our case, this means Russia, Germany, Italy, France and Britain (and Ireland). The Austrian Empire (Austria–Hungary) was a major power, until it was pulled apart in World War I; thus it figures prominently in Books 1 and 2. One highly troubled area before 1914, and the location of the actual crisis which brought about war, was the Balkans, where the once triumphant imperial power, Turkey, was in a state of retreat and collapse. The Balkans and Central Europe (largely the states which had formerly made up the Austrian Empire) continued to be sources of international friction and the site of German ambition in the inter-war years: thus, although these countries do not figure consistently in all parts of the course, they do have to be brought in from time to time. The course, in other words, concentrates on those countries which were directly involved in the two total wars of the twentieth century: after all, one of our major concerns is to discuss the effects of these two wars.

Exercise   I have listed the ten areas of social change the course deals with. You will be introduced to arguments that the experiences of war had important effects in bringing about changes in most or all of these areas. Yet such arguments could be said to have a fatal weakness if they concentrated solely on the countries engaged in the two wars. What is this weakness? ■

Specimen answer   If it could be shown that neutral countries (for example Denmark in World War
and discussion   I, Sweden in both wars) had shared broadly in the same social changes as the other countries, this might cast doubt on the idea that change was brought by war.

It can indeed be maintained that, in many ways, the Scandinavian countries are models of progressive social change. Thus, although we make no consistent study of the neutral countries, references to them will have to be made. □

Let me make it absolutely clear what your workload responsibilities are: with regard to the main countries identified, you will be expected to read the course units, J. M. Roberts *Europe 1880–1945* (the set book), *Total War and Social Change in Twentieth-Century Europe*, edited by Clive Emsley, Arthur Marwick and Wendy Simpson (the Course Reader) and also the two volumes of primary sources and the volume of secondary sources when you are referred to them; with regard to other countries you need not go beyond the references made to them in the course units themselves.

Aim 2

The French philosopher Raymond Aron wrote of the twentieth century as 'the century of total war' (1954). We do not need to worry about the precise meaning of the term 'total war': it is widely accepted in both academic and popular usage as being an effective description of the two major wars of the twentieth century, the wars we are concerned with in this course. The implication is that the term does not apply to earlier wars, or to some wars since (for example, the Korean War or the Falklands War): World War I was the first total war. Later you will be asked to read the article on 'Total war' by Ian Beckett in the Course Reader, which brings out that the distinctions between the twentieth-century wars and earlier wars are not as clear-cut as often thought. Nevertheless the essential distinction remains that earlier wars were in essence fought by the armed forces, without civilians directly participating in the war effort (though they were often affected by the devastation of war), while total war, the war of mature industrialized societies, entailed direct involvement of civilian populations (because of the need for munitions, the need to organize the workforce in the most effective way, and so on) and attempts by governments to control whole societies, rather than purely strategic and military aspects. Thus, total war has been seen as affecting society in almost all its aspects in a way in which previous wars did not: this idea provides a good deal of the subject matter for this course.

We know the dates of the declarations of war by the various powers (the dates vary somewhat for different countries, of course: Italy was not involved in World War I until 1915, Russia in World War II until 1941) and we know the dates of the armistices and of the peace settlements. We can, therefore, define the periods of what, whatever the qualifications that have to be made, I shall now call the two total wars. But towards the end of World War I in Russia (to take the most striking example), total war developed into revolution, and then into civil war ('Whites' versus 'Reds', with the active interference of the Western powers on the side of the former), and then into a long period of violence and heavy loss of life within Russia, which was certainly not international war, but nor was it really civil war (in the sense of there being two clearly identifiable 'sides' fighting against each other): this phenomenon, in which an indisputably established government was in violent conflict with a section of its own population (basically the 'kulaks', defined by Stalin as the peasants who resisted collectivization) is best described as one of 'internal war'. Thus, you should keep the following categories in mind: international war (as in the Balkan wars which preceded World War I), total war, revolution, civil war, and internal war. We are concerned with the other types of war only in so far as they are directly related to one or other of the total wars.

As Aim 2 indicates, this course takes a close look at the relationship between war and revolution. It is common knowledge that the closing stages of World War I in Russia were accompanied not just by the February (leading to parliamentary government) and October (leading to Bolshevik one-party dictatorship) revolutions, but also by revolutions in Germany, Austria–Hungary, and Turkey, which if limited in character, certainly brought the end of imperial rule. To Marxists at the time (and to some today) revolution is an inevitable stage in historical development. At the extreme that line of argument would hold the war to have been irrelevant. A less extreme position might be that the war provided the actual crisis which provoked revolution at the precise moment it occurred. An extreme position at the other end would be that it was war alone (or most specifically, failure in war) which brought the collapse of the existing regime, and therefore the revolutionary situation.

Exercise   Are there any other elements you would expect to find in the bringing about of a revolution? ∎

Specimen answer and discussion   There are several things one might say, such as conditions of extreme deprivation, possibly a strong sense of national resentment among an oppressed people, but the (arguably) more universal element I was thinking of was a strong revolutionary leadership. □

You might see strong revolutionary leadership as operating independently of war, or you might see the war as giving such leadership its ideal opportunity. You can see how there are a number of different arguments, and your task will be to try to develop a position on the influence, or lack of it, of war with regard to the main revolutions we shall be studying.

Further questions arise relating forward to Aim 4: what are the interconnections, if any, between war, revolution and social change? In Russia, in Germany and in Czechoslovakia (formerly incorporated in the Austrian Empire) there were various social reforms in the years after the war. Were these a direct result of revolution, or of the war, or of both, or of neither? I have mentioned the period of 'internal war' in Russia in the 1920s: was that directly an outcome of the revolution, or of the war, or was it perhaps a calculated decision by Russia's rulers? You can see the sorts of problems we shall be trying to tease out in this course.

Aim 3

It would be a strangely incomplete course that discussed the consequences of war without first examining their causes. Unit 5 is wholly devoted to bringing together the arguments about the causation of World War I, and Unit 19 serves a similar function with respect to World War II, but longer term causes of the war are discussed in other units. Aim 3 (and 4) introduces some words which need explaining.

Structural

Marxists have long argued that the wars in essence were the inevitable outcomes of capitalist struggle for markets and industrial and commercial supremacy – the causes are essentially economic and, perhaps, demographic. That is one type of 'structural' argument: political and diplomatic decisions or bungles, for instance, are played down compared with long-term economic, or 'structural' factors. Many non-Marxists would give precedence to similar (though not quite identical) arguments, particularly with respect, in the case of World War I, to the expansionist drives said to be inherent in German economic and commercial development in the years before 1914.

Ideological

'Ideological' in this context simply means 'relating to ideas, beliefs and attitudes'. Among educated liberal opinion in the West there was deep hostility to Tsarist Russian autocracy and in Britain, at least, some of this sentiment emerged in the form of a generalized hostility towards Russia among the population at large. However, in the event, Britain, as well as France, fought on the same side as Russia. Ideological forces may be thought to be more important with respect to the origins of World War II, when German National Socialist ideology aroused much fear and loathing. Yet one has to tread cautiously in noting that the war began with Germany in alliance with Soviet Russia, and then continued with the Western democracies in alliance with that power though many in the West who disliked (and some who didn't dislike) Nazi ideology felt a greater loathing for both Soviet ideology and Soviet practice, and had therefore supported appeasement and opposed war against Germany. If we consider the broadly shared attitudes and assumptions of European rulers (and probably most of their subjects too) in 1914 we alight on the point stressed by many historians that going to war in support of national interests was a perfectly normal act: this particular 'shared ideology' may be a large part of the explanation of the events of 1914.

Institutional

Institutional forces or circumstances are generally more important in domestic and social developments than in international ones – I am thinking of different institutions of government (monarchies, parliaments, etc.), different forms of trade union, or of religions, organizations, etc. In 1914 there were few international institutions (the International Court at the Hague being the most significant one) – basically international relations were dominated by traditional diplomacy and alliance-making. After World War I there was a League of Nations, but as an institution it had many weaknesses.

Geopolitical

More traditional non-Marxist historians have always tended to stress geopolitical considerations: fears in Germany of being encircled by a powerful ring of hostile powers, Russia in the East, Britain and France in the West, and fears in the West of a potential German dominance of (or hegemony over) the European continent. There is a long tradition of maintaining that Britain entered World War I to 'maintain the balance of power', and Germany's continuing preponderance in Europe can be seen as the underlying cause of World War II.

Nationalism (a sub-set of 'Ideological', but a particularly important one)

Few historians have found it possible to discuss the origins of World War I without some reference to the problems of nationalism: Serbia wishing to unite within her frontiers fellow southern Slavs still living within the boundaries of Austria-Hungary, Russia seeing herself as the champion of the Slav populations both inside and outside Austria-Hungary, and various subject nationalities having aspirations themselves towards separate nationhood.

Contingency

'Contingency', as I have used it here, means something like 'chance event or occurrence'. Arguably no event occurs completely by chance (all human beings are, and are known to be, mortal; assassins, however crazy, usually have some political purpose). However some events are chancier than others, and may certainly be brought about by a highly unpredictable convergence of longer term forces and immediate circumstances. As is well known, the event which touched off the series of threats and counter-threats, and orders for mobilization, which brought war as an actual fact, was the assassination on 28 June 1914 of the Austrian Archduke Franz Ferdinand and his wife by a Serbian nationalist. It needs no profound historical skills to see nationalism as a deeper force behind this 'chance event'; historical investigation has made clear that powerful persons in Austria-Hungary were only too happy to have an excuse to intimidate or crush Serbia. Yet, had the assassination attempt not taken place, had it failed (as it very nearly did), the way things actually happened would have been different, though how different it is nearly impossible to say.

Psychological

There is another aspect of this sort of approach which might reasonably be termed 'psychological'; the argument that there was already in 1914 a widespread expectation of war (possibly a fear of war, possibly a desire for war) which helped to facilitate war as an actual happening.

Political and diplomatic

Some historians would still continue to pay a great deal of attention to the detail of political and diplomatic arrangements, particularly the system of interlinking alliances built up before World War I which resulted, it has been argued, in all of the powers being pulled in one after the other in support of their allies.

Conclusion

I hope you can begin to see the kind of evaluation of causes, as between different circumstances and trains of causation, that we shall be concerned with.

Aim 4

This aim links with Aim 1 and together the two aims encapsulate what is absolutely central to this course, historical change and the question of the relationships to it of the two total wars. Aim 1 deliberately concentrated on social change, since that is where the major emphasis of the course lies. What I did mention then was that, even if one's main concern is with social change, it would be impossible to ignore the ramifications of geopolitical change. So Aim 4, in its concluding phrase, indicates that we shall be giving careful attention to the redrawing of national frontiers as a result of war, with the disappearance of the Austro-Hungarian Empire (would this have come about eventually anyway, as a result, in particular, of the forces of nationalism? We must in this course consider all the options with an open mind); the emergence after World War II of Russia as a superpower (would this have come about anyway? Was it simply a restoration of the position Russia had enjoyed before 1914?). We shall need to give careful consideration to the processes of peacemaking, the actual details of peace settlements (while wars leave certain geopolitical consequences which simply cannot be gainsaid, statesmen of strong character can influence at least the detail of the drawing of boundaries, and the allocation of territories and resources).

Nowhere in this course is it argued that war is the most important, still less the only, cause of major social change: the task is to evaluate the significance of war as against all the other possible factors. For convenience these factors can be discussed under four headings: 'structural', 'ideological', 'institutional' and 'political'. Unit 4 goes into more detail, bringing out that these headings are not totally distinct from each other, but explaining the ways in which they may be used. In the major historical debate over whether or not the two total wars were of importance in bringing about social change, the most frequently found line of divide is over the weight to be attached to structural forces. Very many historians, both non-Marxist and Marxist, would contend (and it does indeed seem very difficult to disagree) that the great changes of the twentieth century – higher living standards for the mass of the people, expanded welfare provision, greater (if still circumscribed) freedom and new roles for women, a key position in society for the mass media, and so on – are essentially the product of long-term economic, demographic and technological processes. Some would also stress the importance of such ideological movements as liberalism, democracy, socialism and feminism. A relatively small number of historians (though they have been increasing in number in Britain in recent years) put a major emphasis on the importance of individual politicians, political parties, pressure groups or political activists. The sorts of question this course sets out to explore are: did certain developments come about in the *way* they did and *when* they did because of the experiences of war? Did the necessities of war, as it were, force the hands of politicians at certain times? What exactly is the relationship, with regard to particular issues, between long-term trends (structural and ideological), the pressures of war, and the calculations (or perhaps even eccentricities) of politicians?

I am now going to give you some examples from secondary sources of what historians have written in connection with these issues, in order to see if you can identify the various approaches being taken. (Note 'tertiary sector' – see extract (c) – is that embracing the service trades – shops, banks, etc; the 'primary sector' is agriculture, the 'secondary sector' industry.)

Exercise   Comment on each of the following extracts from secondary sources, saying what position they take with regard to the significance of World War I in bringing about historical change relative to the other causes of change (in particular, structural, ideological, institutional and political).

Extract (a) (refers to Germany)

Wars are usually considered as periods of accelerated change, if not as birth-places for new social formations. Certainly World War I had a far-reaching impact on the social fabric in Germany, even though in the end the forces of continuity proved stronger than those of change. However, in socio-economic terms the exigencies of the war appear not to have initiated anything altogether new; rather they resulted in a considerable acceleration of those processes of change in economy and society which had already been under way for a considerable time, but which so far had been moderated by a variety of political and economic factors which under the conditions of the war lost their momentum.

(W. J. Mommsen, 'The social consequences of World War I: the case of Germany', 1988, p.27)

Extract (b) (refers to Britain)

It seems reasonable to argue that British suffragists might fairly have expected to have gained the vote by 1918 if a Liberal government had been returned in the expected general election. It is even possible that there might have been a limited measure of women's suffrage under a Conservative government. All this must significantly modify those interpretations which stress the advent of war as the decisive factor in the eventual winning of the women's vote. It might even be that the war postponed such a victory. What can be confidently asserted is the importance of women's suffragists' own efforts, especially the efforts of the democratic suffragists, in securing the strong position enjoyed by their cause at the outbreak of war. Women's war work may have been important in converting some former opponents, or providing others with a face-saving excuse to alter their positions. But even before this, the political alliances the democratic suffragists had formed in support of their demand had ensured that women would have to be included in any future reform bill.

(Sandra Stanley Holton, *Feminism and Democracy*, 1986, p.130)

Extract (c) (refers to France)

Contrary to popular belief, the war had not led to exciting new opportunities for women in the world of work. Both the war and the demobilisation involved distortions and disruptions which sometimes obscured the broader pattern, which is best discerned by comparing pre-war figures with the census data of 1921 and 1926. Overall, *fewer* women were employed in industry than in 1906. More than a quarter of a million women disappeared from the textile industry between 1906 and 1921 – a drop of 18 per cent. The clothing industry *shed nearly* 55 000 women workers in the same period, and another 162 000 between 1921 and 1926. Domestic service lost 86 000 women between 1911 and 1921, with another 12 000 following suit over the next five years. At the same time as women were abandoning jobs in the traditional 'feminine' sectors, they began to be taken on in newer industries such as chemicals, electricity, and light engineering, and in the tertiary sector ... The tertiary sector employed 344 000 women in 1906; 855 000 in 1921; and 1 034 000 in 1936 (by which latter stage it accounted for nearly a quarter of the entire female work force outside of agriculture). The war, therefore did not increase the number of women at work but formed part of a process whereby women were redistributed in the labour force.

  The drift away from older occupations into new jobs was clearly visible before 1914. The trend towards the tertiary sector was especially marked and had its roots in pre-war technological change and in the expansion of the bureaucracy. The numbers of state schoolteachers tripled between 1866 and 1936; likewise employees at the Ministry of Posts. Fewer than 410 000 civil servants in 1866 had become more than 600 000 in 1906 and over 900 000 in 1936. Women gained particularly from the invention of the typewriter, the telegraph and the telephone and from the advent of the big department stores and the multiplication of banks. In 1866 they formed only 25 per cent of employees in the commercial sector: by 1911 this had risen to 40 per cent. The feminisation of office work was well under way when World War I broke out. Likewise, at the higher level of the professions, the decisive battles to open up careers for women in, say, medicine and law, had been fought and won before 1914. Julie Chauvin became the first woman to graduate from the Law Faculty of the Sorbonne in 1890, while some 578 female students were registered to read medicine in 1914. Professional women were still a long way from achieving equality with men (in 1929 there were still only a hundred women enrolled at the Paris Bar) but World War I was not a turning point in their struggle.

  (James F. McMillan, 'World War I and women in France', 1988, pp.9–10)

Extract (d) (refers to Britain)

... how are we to explain the important legislative and political changes which occurred in its [World War I's] immediate aftermath? Here it seems the answer is that Arthur Marwick was quite right when he drew attention to the importance of the 'military participation ratio'. That is, the larger the proportion of the population which is involved in a national war effort the more likely it is to be accompanied by major social reforms, or, to re-state it in other terms, the further down the social hierarchy this involvement goes the more egalitarian the social consequences are likely to be. Whatever the objections to Stanislav Andreski's original formulation of this idea (that he stressed the military aspects too much, or that his use of the word 'ratio' implies an unwarranted degree of precision) the emphasis on the social and political consequences of mass participation is a valid one. Put in the crudest terms, this is because of the demand for labour: even if that labour was of much the same type and quality as before war broke out the removal of large numbers of young workers into the armed forces and the increased demand for labour in war industries would strengthen the position of the less advantaged and less powerful groups in the nation ...

Understanding the impact of World War I on British society in terms of an improved bargaining position for the working classes offers an explanation of why the war had significant social consequences even though it affected the quality of social relationships so little.

(Alastair Reid, 'World War 1 and the working class in Britain', 1988, pp.21–3)

Extract (e) (refers to Europe in general)

There are turning-points in history whose significance is at once economic, social and political. That the Great War undoubtedly qualified as such was already recognized by contemporary observers, a view which the intervening years have done nothing to change. On the other hand certain structural elements in the international economy were at most only temporarily, and never more than superficially, affected by the Great War ...

Least of all did the Great War crystallize the inner social tensions in the industrial capitalist nations. On the contrary, being an imperialist war, it brought the proletariat's class consciousness more nearly into accord with their objective class condition than had previously been the case. Where the ruling classes sought to reduce increasing pressure by means of concessions, there might appear to be a trend towards the harmonization of class relations. This forms the point of departure for the theories evolved by Andrzejewski [Andreski] and others to the effect that a positive correlation exists between the mobilization of large masses for war on the one hand and, on the other, social change tending towards the harmonization and stabilization of social relations, as exemplified in the 'welfare state'.

The foregoing is explicitly based on the British experience which in no way admits of generalization. On the Continent, the critical year 1917 had already demonstrated that, under increasing pressure from the 'left', a bourgeois society might react, not with concessions, but equally well and even for preference, with a move to the 'right'. Looked at in this way, the rise of fascism after the First World War is not surprising, although it may at first be distasteful to see 'liberalism' and 'fascism' ranged alongside each other as alternative forms of bourgeois rule. In conclusion, attention should once more be drawn to the fact that the exacerbation of social tensions gave rise to the socialist October revolution in Russia and hence to the polarization of the world economy into a socialist and capitalist camp. The Russian Revolution and its consequences, whose epoch-making significance largely escaped contemporary observers outside Russia and the revolutionary labour movement, is now perhaps generally acknowledged to be the most important consequence of the First World War.

(Gerd Hardach, *The First World War, 1914–1918*, 1987, pp.283, 293–4)

Extract (f) (refers to Britain, France and the USA)

The women's success story in the First World War is well known; in Britain women over the age of thirty, who were themselves householders, or whose husbands were householders, were given the vote in 1918, and the various states of the Union granted votes for women throughout that, and the two following years; in each country including France, there was a spate of legislation affecting the social position of women. It is important to be clear first of all how much these successes depended on the participation in the war effort, not of women, but of men. It was this, obviously, which provided the first employment opportunities for women; and, in the end, it was because a drastic reform in the franchise for men was being contemplated in Britain, so that those men who had never had the vote, or who had actually lost their residence qualification by going out to fight, might be rewarded for their part in the war effort, that the question of women's suffrage also became a pressing issue. Although voting rights for women in France were widely predicted as early as 1915, French women did not get the vote at the end of the war. Partly this was because traditional attitudes about the roles of the sexes were stronger in rural, Catholic France. But two other factors, particularly significant with regard to this question of *participation*, are also relevant: *all* French *men* already had the vote, so in this case there could be no question of men's efforts helping to open the door for women; and, secondly, the French labour movement, being weaker than the British, was less able to push anyway. A third point brings the United States into the comparisons and contrasts: it was in the United States first, then in Britain, that the Women's Rights movements were strongest before the war. Due weight must be given to the unguided forces of change: yet in history, as elsewhere, those are helped who help themselves.

But once all differences are stated, the process by which women's participation in the war effort brought considerable social, economic and political gains can be traced in a very straightforward manner. The first issues to stress this time are again strengthened market position and the desire of governments to offer rewards for services rendered. But two further changes are also critical: the increased sense of their own capacity and increased self-confidence on the part of women themselves; and, on the other side, the total destruction of all the old arguments about women's proper place in the community, which both men and women had previously raised against any moves towards political and social equality for women (in France both changes appear only in a much weaker form). In the political story what is most striking in Britain and the United States is the way in which one after another all the old leading opponents of the idea of votes for women recant, and declare that since women have played such a vital part in the national effort, of course they must be allowed to share in the politics of their country. However, political rights are only one side of the story. Women also gained a measure of economic independence. And, whatever the intentions of law-makers, they had gained a new self reliance and new social freedoms.

(Arthur Marwick, *War and Social Change in the Twentieth Century*, 1974, pp. 76–7) ∎

Specimen answers and discussion

Extract (a)   Quite clearly and explicitly this passage gives overriding priority to long-term forces ('forces of continuity') and it is clear that what is intended here is what I have called 'structural forces' ('processes of change in economy and society which had already been under way for a considerable time').

At the same time Mommsen does fully recognize that World War I 'had a far-reaching impact': however, he sees this impact in terms of 'acceleration' of existing structural forces, rather than in terms of the initiation of anything new.

I will just add that I find something unsatisfactory about the notion of 'acceleration', a metaphor drawn from the physical sciences. Beware of such metaphors: they may possibly *describe* what is happening, they certainly do not explain it. If it is true that wars accelerate existing trends (and this has to be demonstrated), then we need to know *why* this happens. Some suggestions will be made during this course.

Extract (b)   This extract stresses the importance of political forces, in particular the efforts of the women's suffragists *before* the war. It is also suggested that in ordinary circumstances a Liberal government, or perhaps even a Conservative one, would in any case have been inclined to concede a measure of women's suffrage. So, perhaps ideological forces are being stressed as well: a general 'democratic' trend towards extending the franchise, particularly in the direction of women. In this passage, the war is not seen as at all important: indeed, it is even suggested that the war may have postponed votes for women.

Extract (c)   This passage denies that the war had any effect on employment opportunities for women: what is stressed is the long-term structural process 'whereby women were redistributed in the labour force'.

Extract (d)   The author of this extract recognizes that the war itself did have important consequences though he puts limits on these by saying that 'the quality of social relationships' was altered little (by this he means that people did not suddenly become equal with each other, women with men, workers with employers – which is certainly true enough). He draws attention to an explanation that is related entirely to the war itself, not to structural, ideological or political factors. As he mentions, it is an idea which I have used myself and which I originally got from the sociologist, Andreski. The idea is an important one and you will find it cropping up quite often in this course (though you do not, of course, have to agree with it). Basically it is that when under-privileged groups (for example, the workers, or women) participate in the war effort, this very participation tends to improve their social position: in essence, as Reid puts it, they have 'an improved bargaining position'. I will just add here that I personally, as Reid suggests, dislike the full phrase 'military participation ratio': I prefer to talk simply of 'participation', arguing that such participation, generally in domestic industry, rather than in the military effort in the narrow sense, does produce social gains for the participants.

Extract (e)   While recognizing that the war had economic, social and political significance, essentially the author of this passage stresses that structural elements were basically unchanged. As I hope you noted, the approach is Marxist, referring to such other long-term structural factors as the inner 'social tensions' held to be inherent in capitalist society, and the advance of 'the proletariat's class consciousness' nearer to congruence with 'their objective class condition'. (Incidentally, it could be noted, with regard to our earlier discussion of Aim 3, that the causation of the war is seen as structural; it is an 'imperialist war'.) Hardach then goes on to refer to the military participation theory we have already encountered (he gives the original Polish version of Andreski's name), but comments that if it is relevant at all, it applies only to Britain. In traditional Marxist vein he argues that under pressure from the Left a bourgeois society is quite likely to react with a move to the Right. Thus, he suggests, rather than progressive social change, a main consequence of World War I was fascism. His general line is the Marxist one of the increased social tensions provoked by war resulting in polarization: on the one side, fascism, and on the other, Soviet Russia, in his view 'the most important consequence of the First World War'.

Extract (f)   This clearly gives weight to the significance of the war, contrasting with the views of Holton and McMillan, and chiming in with those of Reid. (Note, incidentally, that there are references to the United States as well as to France and Britain – when you are doing your work for this course you will have to ignore such references.) Like Reid the author makes the argument about 'strengthened market position', but also adds that governments themselves desired to reward those who had participated in the national effort, and that through their war work women gained an 'increased sense of their own capacity and increased self-confidence'. It also maintains that women's war work brought about 'the total destruction of all the old arguments about women's proper place in the community'. This is much too extreme a comment, as I would now confess, though I would maintain that a significant number of opponents of votes for women did change their views because of women's war work. The passage reveals the important factual point that women in France, unlike those in Britain, did not actually get the vote at the end of the war. Obviously this is very important in any general assessment of whether wars tend to bring change or not. The passage brings in other long-term and short-term forces. It suggests that traditional attitudes (ideological forces, we might call these) played a part in preventing French women from getting the vote. It is also pointed out (a matter of contingency, or immediate political circumstances) that the participation at the battle front of men who had not previously had the vote meant that there had to be franchise reform anyway – this, it is being said, provided the *occasion* for votes for women as well. Finally, like Holton, the author does point to the importance of the women's movement itself ('those are helped who help themselves'). □

That has been just a brief scattering of different ways in which historians have addressed the question of the relationship between war and social change. If you read each author in full, paying attention to all of their qualifications and detailed arguments, I think you would find that their overall accounts do not clash as much as they may seem to do at first sight. Good historians who have done their work well will generally agree on the main developments; their differences are essentially matters of emphases within the complex of forces which bring about social change.

Aim 5

Our first four aims have been concerned with content, what problems you will be discussing, what countries you will be studying, and so on. Now we turn to the other important dimension of the course (and the one which would not be treated in a straightforward textbook, such as the book by Roberts), that of methods and skills.

Aim 5(a)

Absolutely fundamental to all serious historical study is the question of the critical analysis and interpretation of primary sources; it is a simple truism that without primary sources there could be no history. A historian producing a learned article or a major new historical work seeks out the sources in archives and libraries, as indeed does a PhD student. You as an undergraduate will, of course, simply be studying the extracts from various primary sources (always translated into English) which we have selected for you. None the less you will be applying the basic principles of source criticism, and I now want to discuss with you the sort of documents exercise we will be setting you in order to test whether you have mastered these principles. What we will give you will be a substantial extract from one of the documents, usually at least a paragraph in length, and we will set this question:

> Comment on the following extract, saying what the document is, setting it in its historical context, commenting on specific points in the text, and summing up the extract's historical significance for the study of total war, and social change, 1914–1955.

In the *Introduction to History* in the Open University's Level 1 course *An Introduction to the Humanities* I stressed that no real working historian tries to interpret a document without already knowing a good deal about the historical context. It is from your general reading in the course that you will be able to say what the document is (and therefore, what strengths and weaknesses it has), and give the historical context (that is, what circumstances brought it into being, what events were taking place at the time, how it fits in with other aspects of the topic it is related to). In order to interpret a document, historians need to be sure that they have fully understood particular phrases and technical terms within it. We ask you, again calling upon your general reading, to comment on specific points and phrases in the extract. The final task, summarizing the historical significance of the document, is the most important one. The significance of a document always depends on what subject is being studied: here we ask you, naturally enough, to pin down the significance with regard to some aspect of the topics studied in our course – not war and social change in general, but the specific issue to which the document is relevant.

Given the background knowledge which is needed, it would be unfair to expect you at this stage to do a full commentary on a document. None the less, it would be fruitful if now you did begin to think about the sort of response you might make.

Exercise   I want you to jot down any thoughts you have about writing a commentary on the extract that follows. My specimen answer will actually take the form of a fully rounded exam answer to this kind of question. Here I will give you a little bit of the contextual information which normally you would have to acquire from your wider reading in the course. As a break from the earlier discussions and exercise, this one concerns World War II.

In March 1944, more than two months before D-Day, France was under German occupation, against which clandestine warfare was being waged by various resistance groups. After the Liberation many Resistance leaders participated in the first Liberation government, which was responsible for a number of economic and social reforms, including votes for women, nationalization of the leading banks and insurance companies, the coal mines, many major companies (for example Citroën), and also welfare legislation. Resistance groups included right and centre elements as well as socialist and communist ones; however, many historians have argued that there is a connection between the struggles of the Resistance against the rule of the Nazis and those who collaborated with them, and social reform after the war.

Now attempt a commentary on the extract that follows (observing the rubric for an exam question set out above):

> United as to the goal to be attained, united as to the means required to achieve this goal, the speedy liberation of the country, the representatives of the movements, groups, parties and political tendencies joined together in the CNR, proclaim their decision to remain united after the liberation …
>
> In order to promote essential reforms:
>
> (a) Economic plan:
>
> – the establishment of a true economic and social democracy, involving the expulsion of the great feudal combines of economics and finance from the direction of the economy;
>
> – a rational organization of the economy assuring the subordination of private interest to the general interest and freed from the direction of employment instituted in the images of the fascist states;
>
> – an increase in national production in accordance with the plan to be issued by the state after consultation with everyone involved in such production …
>
> (Programme of the National Council of Resistance [Conseil National de la Résistance, CNR], 15 March 1944) ∎

Specimen answer   This is an extract from the Programme of the National Council of Resistance which, as the extract itself tells us, joined together various different resistance groups, which from other sources we know to have been right-wing and centrist, as well as socialist and communist. As is clear from the way the programme is phrased it is intended as a statement of policies to be followed by government immediately 'the speedy liberation of the country' has been achieved. It is an accurate record of these intended policies, though it cannot, of course, tell us whether the policies were actually carried out. At the time when the programme was issued, France was still under German occupation, though there was optimism at this stage of the war that German power was on the wane. In fact the Allied landings were just over two months away, so one could say that this very precise statement of reforms was being issued in good time for the expulsion of the Germans and creation of an independent French government. In sum, the document is a programme for peace, promulgated in the later stages of the war.

The necessities of war and the overriding need to defeat the common enemy, and perhaps also the sense of having shared, whatever one's own political opinions, in common dangers for a common cause, are the mainspring behind the declarations of unity, which open the document and are clearly intended as its keynote. The intention was almost certainly genuine, though it has to be noted that once the enormous danger was over, and once the country was faced with the problems of reconstruction, political unity began to break up. The next part of the extract sets out 'essential reforms': obviously the feeling was that the France which had collapsed in 1940 had been much in need of reform. The first reform in part reflects the belief held by Centre and Left that France in the 1930s had been run by a 'wall of money', 'the 200 families'. The use of the word 'feudal' is noteworthy – *France must modernize*. It is a moot point whether the Liberation government achieved 'true economic and social democracy', but certainly the great combines *were* nationalized as stated here. The second reform develops the idea of combining private enterprise and the idealistic notion of 'rational organization' (always argued for by socialists and communists); it also reflects the current experience of control of labour in the fascist 'image'. The idea of central planning is developed in the third proposed reform. The emphasis on *increased* production may represent the view of more traditional and conservative elements, but also, again, the widespread feeling that pre-war France had been commercially stagnant (recent research has shown that this was not entirely true). Consultation with the workers indicates, in a remarkable way, the consensus achieved in the Resistance: hard-line left-wingers traditionally envisaged a total take-over by the workers. Post-war France was marked very much by rigorous economic planning and, to a much lesser degree, worker participation.

Thus much of what is proposed here was put into practice. The significance of the document is that it shows the experience of war (specifically of Resistance) engendering ideas of consensus on behalf of progressive economic and social planning. Because of the prestige of the Resistance, and because of the feeling that defeated France had been a flop, many of these proposals were put into practice after the Liberation.

Discussion   I don't expect you to have achieved anything like that, many of the points I make simply being unknown to you at this stage. But I hope you see now how all information (some of it from the document itself) is incorporated in a systematic analysis. Note the precise use of *brief* quotations from the document itself. □

Aim 5(b)

No primary source is a simple, straightforward statement of 'truth'; analysing a primary source (or 'document') and bringing out its significance for whatever topic we are working on requires knowledge and skill. No secondary source – article or book – is a straightforward statement of truth either (though, of course, there is an obligation on historians to be as accurate as they can, and as faithful to the sources as possible). That is why it is important to have an idea of the different sorts of approach lying behind the various books and articles you will be encountering. This is not an easy matter to deal with in a brief space, and in an introductory fashion. So I am going to take it stage by stage.

Stage I

Let us ask ourselves a big question, a question which everyone involved in university-level work should ask:

Why do we think we know what we think we know?

Most historians would answer: 'Through the critical study of the primary sources'. However, certain non-historians (philosophers, perhaps), and maybe some historians as well, might answer: 'Because there is a general theory, or a series of general laws, governing the development of human societies'.

In our history courses we incline strongly to the former *assumption*. This word 'assumption' is a very useful one and worth keeping in the foreground of your mind. Professional, source-based, non-metaphysical history is based on the assumption that we can actually produce knowledge about the past if we follow the critical methods of professional historians. Other (more-theoretical) approaches, often critical of professional history, are based on different *assumptions*. No one can *prove* that our assumptions are more valid than those, say, of the postmodernists. All we can do is set out our assumptions unambiguously. Perhaps adding that professional history has been remarkably successful in illuminating the past, and in providing training in the analysis of evidence and writing of balanced, well-substantiated reports.

History is an intellectual discipline, and historians deploy theories (if not one overarching theory) and concepts. But another of our claims is that we teach you to be cautious and reflexive in your use of concepts. 'Gender' is a useful concept in drawing attention to the way in which differences between men and women may be created by society rather than biology. It may be less useful when it is used to imply that no differences are due to biology. 'Class' is an indispensable concept: but it may be that the definitions of Marx or Weber are not actually the most useful ones (see 'Further reading' for my discussion of this topic).

Stage II

Let us now ask a slightly smaller question, one which all interested in history should ask:

Why do historians disagree with each other?

We have just seen that with respect to the causes and the consequences of World War I different historians present different interpretations. I suggested then that on closer examination the differences might turn out not to be as pronounced as they seemed at first sight – save, perhaps, with respect to Hardach whose approach was uncompromisingly Marxist. Apart from Hardach, the differences might well be explained under one or more of the following headings:

1   Primary sources are complex, fragmentary, and difficult to interpret: therefore it is perfectly possible for historians, being as systematic and conscientious as possible, still to interpret them in different ways.

2   History is concerned with human beings in society, that is to say, with attitudes and values: it is perfectly legitimate for me, Arthur Marwick, to say. 'Look, the evidence is overwhelming that in most countries the status of women was higher after the First World War than before', and it is perfectly legitimate for another historian, James McMillan perhaps, to say, 'Come on now, the change is pretty pathetic when judged against the standard of true equality'. So, really it boils down to what standards you are applying, and there is no problem.

3   Problems of causation in history are extremely complex. Sandra Holton might possibly agree with me that women's status had changed for the better, but then she argues that the cause is not the war, but the work of the suffragists before the war. That's a tough one to resolve, and much of this course is concerned with just such tough problems.

4   Political differences between historians. In my view, this rather simplistic one is much overdone. It may apply with old-style political history, though even here I believe that the competent historian ought to be able to rise above political prejudices. With regard to the big issues of the causes and consequences of wars, it's difficult to see what a 'tory' line ought to be, and how that would contrast with a 'socialist' one. Perhaps Sandra Holton was motivated by her feminist beliefs; personally I prefer to see her book as a very scrupulously researched piece of professional history – I find myself in much greater agreement with it than there was room to explain in a brief exercise.

And that comment takes me to one of my key points with regard to your attitudes when you are referring to some book or article:

remember that what the historian is doing is putting forward, as honestly as possible, his or her interpretation, based on scrupulous research in the sources, but that this is only a *contribution* to knowledge, and will be subject to evaluation and criticisms by other historians.

Eventually a balanced view should appear in the textbooks (such as Roberts), or in a course such as ours. But even then we, and Roberts, do have our preconceptions; and in any case new research is going on all the time.

Stage III

I want now to add two further justifications for what I am doing in this subsection.

The first is most easily explained by making an obvious reference to the game of football. Even non-players and non-fans will understand that the footballer who stands out is the one who, as we say, 'puts his foot on the ball', slows things down, looks around, knows exactly what is going on; this contrasts with those who put their heads down and simply 'kick and rush'. Well, the metaphor applies to academic work. It's no good tearing into every book you can lay your hand on, copying out whatever information you find there. Frankly, some books are much more reliable, or relevant than others; it helps if you can make some kind of assessment about the author, and, perhaps, the approach he or she is following. Here is a very simple example: in the course reader we have brought together for you a marvellous collection of articles relevant to this course – but do, for Heaven's sake, read first what Clive Emsley and I say about the articles and their authors in our introduction. Often in tutorials I hear students saying 'they' said this, and 'they' said that. The reference is to some anonymous author or some anonymous book the student had rushed at. That is not good enough; you must be aware of individual authors, and you must try to form some idea of what their stance or approach is. Is it fundamentally based on the primary sources, or is it governed by some grand theory? Both sorts of approach, based on different assumptions, may make important *contributions*, but they'll be different sorts of contributions.

My second further justification is even more relevant to many of you as Open University students. It is highly likely that you will already have taken courses in the social sciences, or in other arts subjects such as literature or art history. Personally, I think it is a great advantage if history students have taken courses in other subjects but I think it is desperately important to say absolutely openly and explicitly that these other subjects have their own ways of going about things (and quite right too), and that these ways are often crucially different from the ways in which we go about things in history – the point can be particularly crucial when these other subjects become involved, as they inevitably must, with the historical dimension. Some academics argue that there is but one approach valid for all arts and social science subjects. On the whole historians believe in specialization, and that the skills of the historian are difficult enough, and should not be confused with those (very properly) taught in other disciplines, though, as I shall explain in a moment, historians should always be ready to learn from other disciplines. If you, in *this* course, want to use some of the concepts you have acquired in other courses, that is perfectly acceptable (all Open University historians believe in openness and pluralism) provided (a) that you do show that you have understood why we believe in our methodology, and (b) you explain clearly what you are doing – i.e. do not assume that the concepts you use (such as, for example, 'patriarchy' or 'ideology') are automatically to be taken as unchallengeable. We *do* give you clear guidelines in your TMA booklet on how *history* essays are to be written – you are strongly advised to follow them.

Stage IV

It is fundamental to your study of history that you must understand that many of the most important words you will be using have several different meanings. There is nothing we can do about this, so the important rule for all historians is to be absolutely clear which particular meaning is intended each time the word is used. This matter of 'historical semantics' was expounded in A103 *An Introduction to the Humanities*, 'Introduction to history', and developed further in the Level 2 history course, A221, *State, Economy and Nation in Nineteenth-Century Europe*, and is taken up in the next subsection, Aim 5(c). Typically difficult words are 'state', 'culture', 'class'. Usually historians use such words as 'ideology', 'narrative', 'discourse' in a straightforward, 'neutral' way. When, earlier, I was talking of ideological factors, I simply meant 'factors relating to sets of ideas'. Without wishing to go into unnecessary complexities here, let me just alert you to the point that in Marxist, postmodernist, cultural theory, and some feminist writings, 'ideology', 'narrative' and 'discourse' are used in special ways related to the notion of a wicked bourgeoisie manipulating power. If you wish to use these words in that sense, be sure you know what you are about. Now a most important word:

History

In ordinary discourse we often say 'history' when, for precision, it would be better to say 'the past'. History, as professional historians would define it, is:

> The study of the (human) past, through the systematic analysis of primary sources and critical use of secondary ones, and the bodies of knowledge which arise from that study (I say bodies, because history covers so many periods and so many cultures that one unified body of knowledge is impossible). In short, 'history' is the knowledge about the past produced by historians (just as the sciences are the bodies of knowledge about the natural world produced by scientists) – it is not the past itself.

However, certain of the more theoretical approaches (such as those of Mayer and Maier in your Course Reader, where there is fuller discussion of these issues) take the view that 'history' actually has a 'real' existence as the process which links past to present to future, and that the basic structures of this 'history' (classes in conflict, discourses in conflict, patriarchal oppression, etc. etc.) are already known. To non-metaphysical historians, on the contrary, the past, while it definitely did have a 'real' existence, is now gone for good; all we have are the relics of that past, the primary sources, and it is out of these that we produce our knowledge of the past, 'history'. (I say 'non-metaphysical historians' – or 'non-philosophical', if you like – because it would be quite wrong to call professional, source-based historians 'non-theoretical' – no intellectual can avoid theorizing).

Conclusion

This has been a preliminary introduction to large issues whose relevance will become particularly clear during the course, specifically where you discuss gender and class, and the ideas of Mayer and Maier. Summarizing very complex issues has not been easy; I quite understand if you are feeling a little dazed – but do keep in mind the illuminating notion of the different assumptions which underlie different intellectual approaches. In this course we are primarily concerned with the assumptions and practices of professional, source-based, non-metaphysical history.

Aim 5(c)

Periodization

Periodization simply refers to the way in which historians divide history into, say, 'The Renaissance', 'The Eighteenth Century', 'The Revolutionary and Napoleonic period', 'The Victorian period'. This is partly done for convenience, but also, more importantly, because historians feel that they can distinguish particular characteristics which do give a 'period' genuine unity. But there are no absolute rules governing the selection and definition of historical periods. In our course, we wanted, at the outer limits, to include both the origins of World War I and the consequences of World War II. We also, as with the listing of the countries to be included, wanted to set firm limits on what ground we were asking you to cover. Clearly some of the deeper origins of World War I go back into the nineteenth century and, quite certainly, the consequences of World War

II do not suddenly cease to have any effect in 1955. The period covered by your set textbook, J. M. Roberts, *Europe 1880–1945*, is different at both ends. If you glance inside the book at the list of other volumes in the same series, you'll see that the choice of dates by Roberts was at least partly dictated by a need to fit into the series.

Exercise   However, on the back cover there is an attempt to pin down the sixty-five years, 1880–1945, as constituting a coherent period. What is the essence of this period as stated on the back cover?■

Specimen answer   It is the period of 'the apogee of European power'. It is the period when Europe's political and economic domination of the globe came to a climax – and then crumbled. □

If you look at Roberts's table of contents you will see that he does not break his main period up explicitly into a number of smaller periods. His book steadily moves forward, mixing narrative with analysis and description: chapters 1–8 cover the period before 1914, only chapter 9 deals with World War I, then chapters 10–15 deal with the inter-war years, with just chapter 16 dealing with World War II. We, on the other hand, have divided our course up into five separate books, the first four suggesting a kind of periodization: *Europe in 1914; The Impact of World War I;* Between Two Wars; The Impact of World War II.

Such sub-periodization might well be considered excessive; but it does parallel the very strong sense that many ordinary people in the twentieth century have had of each of the total wars being a historical watershed. It is one of the functions of a serious academic course to examine carefully such popular ideas, which may well turn out to have little real foundation. Certainly the lines of critical change will vary in different parts of Europe. For example, the break between pre-1914 and post-1918 probably was quite sharp in those parts of East and Central Europe where there was both a change in regime and a new contact with Western ideas and behaviour. Pause just for a moment to reflect on your own (for the moment preliminary) notions on periodization. Is it your impression that the inter-war years were a very different era from the years before 1914, or that the years after 1945 were very different from those before 1939? By the end of the course your thoughts should have been refined and clarified.

Historical semantics

'Semantics' means 'concerned with the meaning of words'. Language is such an important issue that, apart from lower level courses such as A103 and A221, I've already touched on this matter in mentioning some of the more theoretical approaches towards studying the past.

Among the most abused terms in historical writing are 'bourgeois' and 'middle class'. On any common-sense reckoning, the 'middle class' ought to be the class in the middle, that is to say between the upper class above, and the lower or working class below. On this reckoning it is, in the twentieth century, a highly miscellaneous class, ranging from elementary school teachers, small shopkeepers, and clerical workers at the bottom to successful business and professional people at the top. However, 'middle class' is often used as translation of 'bourgeois class', implying a dominant position, rather than one in the middle.

For effectively the whole of the period we are studying, every European country except Britain had a substantial peasant class. Disabuse yourself immediately of any connotations the word 'peasant' may have in colloquial English. In fact the nearest translation for the French *le paysan* or the German *der Bauer,* always rendered as 'peasant', is really much more like 'farmer', save that that term can suggest attitudes and values alien to the 'peasant'. The core peasantry owned and cultivated their tiny smallholdings; some were quite prosperous but many were no more than landless agricultural labourers. There were many degrees of dependency in between. It is salutary, and perhaps even helpful (for potential tourists!) to note that any dish in Germany with the label *Bauer* in it will be large, rich and satisfying.

I have already said something about total war. A similar sounding word which also first came into use in 'the century of total war' is 'totalitarian' (*totalitario* in Italian). One of the earliest recorded uses in English occurred in November 1929 when *The Times* wrote of a 'reaction against parliamentarianism ... in favour of a "totalitarian" or unitary state, whether Fascist or Communist'. Broadly the term connotes a state which attempts to control all aspects of political and social life in the interests of one political philosophy or ideology and which suppresses all dissent. Parliamentary government implies the existence of at least two competing political parties, totalitarianism indicates the existence of only one.

Now, finally, consider this collection of words: 'nation', 'country', 'society', 'state', 'government', 'power'. Several of these words have more than one meaning, and most overlap in meaning. The word 'power', as in the phrase 'the great powers', is usually used with reference to a country in its international aspect and implies a combination of strong and efficient government, a relatively stable society, and a strong economy. It is the word 'state' which has had most attention in recent years, in part because of Marxist arguments that the state is simply an expression of the power of the dominant class. Wilhelmine, Weimar and Federal West Germany were all divided into a number of separate 'states', as of course was the Federal United States of America. That is a particular usage of the word 'state'. In its more general sense the word connotes the entire apparatus of decision making, administration and, as necessary, coercion within an individual country. One can, in parliamentary democracies, make a distinction between *governments,* which may change with elections, and the *state* which only changes with a thorough-going revolution. You will most often meet the term in this course in such phrases as 'state control', or 'the extension of state powers'. Examples are state control of, say, the coal mines or new state regulation governing the sale of alcoholic liquor. It is not just one government doing these things; all relevant agencies of the state are involved in the control or regulation. Bernard Shaw's aphorism may be useful here: 'the government has no more right to call itself the state, than the smoke over London has the right to call itself the weather'. The allegation against totalitarianism is that it merges together government, state and large sectors of society as well.

The essence of the semantic issue is that it is not possible to rule absolutely that words must be used only in a certain way. Words do shift in meaning; you have to be clear at any particular time which meaning is intended.

Aim 5(d)

This sub-aim concerns assisting you to develop the skills of writing history essays of BA (Honours) standard. The writing of history is the critical activity of the historian. The historian who spends years in the archives, making the most exciting discoveries, but who never communicates them to his or her colleagues or the wider world, is not really contributing to historical knowledge. An undergraduate essay, of course, is somewhat different from the research-based writings of a professional historian. Still, as I have already suggested, the basic principles are the same. Thus, one of the most important activities of the student of history is the writing of history essays. These should demonstrate the following skills:

• the ability to *find* and *select* relevant material, basically from secondary sources, though also probably using the volumes of extracts from primary sources which we are supplying you with – thus, in a rather elementary way, an exercise in 'research';

• the ability to address precise problems and to develop balanced and well-substantiated arguments, presented in a coherent and well-organized essay, written in English prose of an acceptable standard, and setting out quotations, references and bibliography in the approved manner.

The only truly effective way of learning how to write history essays is by actually writing them and then having them thoroughly criticized and commented upon by your tutor. For students on this course, that is what will happen. The writing of essays is not simply, or even mainly, a means of assessing you: it is a means of helping you to develop important historical skills. Here I can do no more than offer a few tips on the skills itemized above, and offer you one exercise designed to help with the crucial problem of planning and organizing your essays. The skills of filing and organizing the information you will be collecting long preceded the invention of the computer, but a computer will greatly facilitate the process, as long as you remember that it has no independent brain of its own. The older methods described here will serve very well.

   All the single essays can be done from the course materials; but for the double TMA you will be using books available at summer school. If you are aiming to do a really decent essay, it is important that you collect as wide a range of evidence and opinions as you can. It is not expected that you will read the whole, or even necessarily a large part of any one book. It is important to learn to get quickly from each book just what is relevant to your particular essay topic; to do this make use of the table of contents and the index. Develop the skill of skimming pages very quickly, stopping to give full and careful attention every time you come across something that relates directly to the essay you are writing. When you first start you may, quite understandably, have some difficulty in being sure what is going to be directly relevant to the essay and what is not. You may have to read around the subject a bit to begin with. But force yourself to start thinking as early as possible about the sorts of argument you will be wanting to make; it's actually easier and lazier to do a lot of general reading to no great purpose than to do the hard thinking that is necessary in order to begin to plan out what you will need for your essay and what you will not need. The more thought you put in (after doing any necessary preliminary reading), the less likely you are to take loads of notes which will in the end turn out to be useless.

It's not necessary to take notes on cards; practically any sort of paper will do, provided it is loose, so that you can shuffle your pages around in organizing the plan of your essay. The one golden rule is to take notes on one side of the paper only, so that there is no risk of overlooking something when you do come to plan out the essay. Be sure to note carefully where exactly you are taking each piece of information or quotation from (author, date, title and place of publication, publisher and page reference). Be completely clear whether you have taken a direct quotation from the book, or simply your own summary.

By the later stages of your 'research', ideas and arguments relative to the precise question you are dealing with should be beginning to form. But, in any case, go through all of your notes carefully. Then, on a separate blank sheet of paper, work out a plan, and a plan that is not simply a despairing set of arbitrary headings, but a plan that will enable you steadily to develop coherent arguments directly relevant to the topic set. If you number each section of the plan, you can then attach numbers to your notes, indicating where in the essay each idea or piece of information will fit in.

The first thing to do with an essay (or, for that matter an exam) question is to read it very carefully to make sure you understand exactly what is being asked. Often there may be more than one question requiring to be answered, there may be several issues needing to be resolved, there may be problems of definition. Often it may be best to start by breaking the question down into separate components (what social classes are involved, which countries, what topics or debates, and so on). You should attempt this before you start on your reading ('research'), though further reading may reveal complexities in the question not apparent at first sight. You should not attempt to draw up a plan until you have done a fair amount, or preferably all, of your reading.

Exercise
Imagine you are writing an essay on: 'In what ways, if any, did the experiences of World War I increase the political rights and raise the consciousness of women in Britain and France?'

1   There are actually four components to this question, which immediately give rise to four separate questions which need to be answered. Identify (a) the four 'components', then (b) the four questions.

2   What matters of definition have to be settled and what other issues, implicit in the question as a whole, have to be discussed before you can attack the essay question satisfactorily as a whole? ■

Specimen answers and discussion
1(a) The four components are: women in Britain, women in France, political rights, and consciousness.

(b) The questions are:

What effects, if any, did the war have on the political rights of British women?

What effects, if any, did the war have on the political rights of French women?

What effects, if any, did the war have on the consciousness of British women?

What effects, if any, did the war have on the consciousness of French women?

2   You need to explain 'political rights' – the right to vote, and the right to be elected to parliament or national assembly. You also need to explain 'consciousness' – self-confidence, women's belief in their own capacities, and a willingness to speak up for themselves.

Before it is possible to answer the question as a whole, you would need to establish whether political rights *were* increased (a) in Britain, (b) in France, and in the same way whether consciousness *was* raised. Where you did feel that you could detect changes you'd have to ask how far they came about for other reasons (structural, political, and so on) rather than the war. All this has to be sorted out if you are to give a clear, balanced answer to the question 'In what ways, if any ...'. In this essay it would be difficult to avoid the disagreements between different historians and you'll certainly have to explain clearly where you stand as between the different views. □

Exercise   Now let us draw up a plan. This is a slightly artificial exercise since there isn't time here for you to do all the necessary reading. However we can simulate some of the preliminary reading if you, first, re-read the relevant extracts set out in the exercise you did in connection with Aim 4 (particularly extracts (b) by Holton, (c) McMillan and (f) Marwick),and then read the following extracts.

Extract (g)

The calling of this Speaker's conference [on franchise reform] had been a response to political problems created by the war. Though it had been agreed to suspend party-political conflicts at the beginning of hostilities, this truce was constantly an uneasy one. At any time the government might have found itself called upon to seek a new mandate at a general election. Even after the formation of an all-party government in May 1915 the dissolution of parliament was repeatedly extended with the agreement of the opposition, but only for short periods at a time. In the event of a general election being called, the voting registers themselves promised to become the focus of considerable dispute and unrest. With the dislocations that attended the war, these registers no longer recorded the possible electorate at all adequately. In particular, men overseas on active service would effectively have been disenfranchised. Moreover, many presently hazarding life and limb at the front had never been enfranchised at all. These issues became particularly contentious with the extension of compulsory military service in May 1916. Arthur Henderson, the Parliamentary Labour Party leader, who had joined the all-party government formed the previous year, used the occasion to raise once more the general issue of franchise reform, including women's suffrage, in cabinet. He was supported in this by another minister, Sir Robert Cecil, the leader of the Conservative women's suffragists in parliament. Meanwhile other Unionists like Sir Edward Carson were waging a vociferous campaign for the 'soldiers' vote'. Franchise reform, then, had again become a live issue in 1915, and a pressing one by early 1916. The government attempted a series of initiatives during this period to resolve the more immediate issue of the voting disqualification of men at the front, but all were rejected in the House of Commons. The setting up of an all-party Speaker's conference in the autumn of 1916 was intended to resolve this impasse by identifying a compromise programme of franchise reform that would be acceptable to all sides.

While these debates had focused only on how to protect the rights of existing voters, especially the troops at the front, women's suffragists had kept merely a watching brief. But once it became clear that some more fundamental reform might come under consideration, campaigning for votes for women began anew. This campaigning was, of course, to take place in a quite different context to that of the prewar period. The war had brought significant changes to women's lives. The most central of these was the extension of work opportunities, temporary though most of it proved to be. Women had been given a prominent place in the war effort, first in keeping going existing services and industries, but perhaps even more significantly in the massive manufacture of munitions required in twentieth-century warfare. Many, like the women's suffragists' former arch-enemy, Asquith, used such developments to explain their change of heart on votes for women. It remains a matter of dispute whether such longstanding male prejudice was significantly undermined or only put aside for practical reasons during this time. But certainly there were a number of well-publicised 'conversions' to women's suffrage among prominent public figures in the war years, while the rationale of many of the old antisuffragist arguments was effectively undermined by wartime requirements.

Modern warfare needed the mass mobilization of women as well as men for its execution. Ironically, the ideology of separate spheres lost much of its former legitimacy as women provided essential support in this way ...

When the Speaker's conference report was published it advised full adult suffrage for men on a residential qualification. It then recommended a measure of women's suffrage based on age and property qualifications. Women over thirty or thirty-five should be qualified to vote if they or their husbands were on the local government register, then based on an occupier franchise. As we have seen, suffragists had themselves advised MPs on such a means of limiting the women's vote. Nonetheless it was to be a source of further discord among suffragists. It was pointed out that the young women munition workers, for example, would be excluded by such a franchise. Democratic suffragists in the North Riding and Manchester federations made use of their remaining EFF [Election Fighting Fund] resources to begin a campaign against such limitation of votes for women. The National Union leadership subsequently agreed to run similar campaigns wherever there were munition works. Yet all their parliamentary advisers stressed the danger of the full adultist [that is, all women over 21] demand. Consequently Mrs Fawcett advised working to lower the age limitation but to take care not to upset the whole basis of the compromise that had been achieved. On these grounds the National Union executive resolved to welcome the Speaker's report, while expressing the hope that the House would improve on the recommendations.

(Sandra Stanley Holton, *Feminism and Democracy*, 1986, pp. 144–5, 148)

Extract (h)

By the end of the war working-class women, as we have seen, had gained far more than a limited right to vote. For years now, in their menfolk's absence, many had reared a family, and found in the responsibility a new freedom. Women were more alert, more worldly-wise. Yet the liberty won, some felt they would have to fight hard to retain once the warriors returned. But with surprise they discovered that husbands, home again, were far less the lords and masters of old, but more comrades to be lived with on something like level terms. Women customers in the shop commented on this change time and again. Life had broadened in scope; a certain parochialism had gone for ever. Food illiterates – husbands who had left home the bane of a wife's existence over what they could and could not eat – came back permanently cured; their taste, often enough, widened by army food. Customers remarked on it with amusement and relief – 'They'll try anything now!' Boys in their war-time waywardness warned by mothers of what would happen when the ruler of the house returned were often surprised to find father good-humoured, indifferent to minor misdeed, understanding, even; a human being, not a tin god. Grown children, remembering the authority that clothed him in pre-war years, felt indignant at the liberties now bestowed upon the 'spoiled' younger end. Disciplines steadily eased all round. The gulf that had stood so long between parent and child began to narrow at last.

(Robert Roberts, *The Classic Slum,* 1971, p.174)

Extract (i)

The continuing exclusion of married women from the world of work suggests that the revolution in social attitudes forecast for the post-war years was as chimerical as the revolution in job opportunities. The non-appearance of any new deal for women in respect of their lack of civil and political rights points to the same conclusion. Despite all the rhetoric and confident predictions of the war years and their immediate aftermath, married women continued to be denied the right to full legal capacity and all women were denied the right to vote. A few minor changes in the law, such as the temporary right to assume the paternal power (1915) or the right to guardianship of orphans (1917) did not alter the more important fact that, in the eyes of the law, married women were treated as persons unfit to act in their own right. The Civil Code still obliged wives to be obedient to their husbands, to reside where they chose to live and to recognise their full control over the children. Full legal capacity came only in 1938.

Nor did French women become fully-fledged citizens of the Republic. The auspicious vote in the Chamber in 1919 notwithstanding, French women did not receive the right to the suffrage until after World War II. The bill passed by the Chamber was thrown out by the Senate in 1922. Arguably, far from emancipating women, the war was 'actually a setback for the women's suffrage movement in France'. [This quotation is identified by McMillan in a footnote; it is from a book on women's suffrage in France by S. C. Hause and A. R. Kenney, 1984.] It cut short a campaign which had been building up promisingly on the eve of the war and dispersed its leading figures and organisation. In the words of Hause and Kenney:

The war also buried women's rights under a host of other problems to which politicians accorded primacy, such as economic recovery or the diplomacy of French security. Such problems created a national mood in which the foremost desire seemed to be a return to the halcyon days of a lost *belle époque* rather than to further the transformation of French society.

(James F. McMillan, 'World War I and women in France', 1988, pp.11–12)

1   How does extract (h) differ from extracts (g) and (i)?

2   Now try to draw up at least two (and preferably more) plans for the essay, that is to say list the main headings (and, if you like, sub-headings) for the different sections and paragraphs of your essay, keeping in mind how each section will link with the next one. If you do manage more than one, please say which plan is the best and explain why. ■

Specimen answers and discussion

1   *Extract (h)* is a primary source, an autobiography in fact (the give-away is the personal reminiscence 'women customers in the shop': you wouldn't find that in secondary sources like extracts (g) and (i).

2   *Essay plans*

Example I (This is the very barest of plans, arising out of our earlier discussion.)

1   *Political rights in Britain*
Definition, then account of what happened with evaluation of the significance of war as against other factors.

2   *Political rights in France*
Definition, then account of what happened with evaluation of the significance of war as against other factors.

3   *Consciousness in Britain*
Definition, then account of what happened with evaluation of the significance of war as against other factors.

4   *Consciousness in France*
Definition, then account of what happened with evaluation of the significance of war as against other factors.

5   *Conclusion*

Example II (This is a more elaborate version of Example I which reserves space for the other issues raised in our earlier discussion.)

1   *Introduction*
(a) Explanations of political rights and consciousness.
(b) What actually happened and the historians' debate. (Significant political rights in Britain, effectively none – despite Assembly vote whose significance is calculated differently by McMillan and Marwick – in France. Some debate among historians over raising of consciousness – you'd have to offer some firm conclusions for each of Britain and France.)

2 *Long-term forces tending towards political rights and higher consciousness in both Britain and France*

   (a) Long-term change in women's role in the economy.

   (b) Ideological forces and the women's movement.

3 *Political rights in Britain*

   (a) Discussion of the significance of the women's suffrage movement.

   (b) Discussion of actual course of events during war evaluating contribution of war experience as against other factors. Firm conclusion stated. (Did war actually obstruct women's rights?)

4 *Political rights in France*

   Depending on what line you'd established in 1(b) you'd say: (i) war had no effect; (ii) war obstructed women's rights; (iii) war had some effects (that is, removing prejudice in National Assembly). Again state a firm conclusion.

5 *Consciousness in Britain and France*

   (a) Discuss arguments of, for example, Roberts, Holton and Marwick. Your conclusions here will depend on how highly you rate these, but remember also to refer as necessary to points made in 2, in order to offer a careful evaluation.

   (b) Similar discussions for France, bringing out any comparisons and contrasts if there are any.

6 *Conclusion*

   Can be very brief since you will have been producing arguments and conclusions as you worked your way through.

Example III (This example puts heavy emphasis on the questions raised by the essay being matters of historical debate.)

1 *The historical debate*

   (a) The various views on the war and political rights in Britain and France.

   (b) The various views on the war and consciousness in Britain and France.

2 *Developments in Britain, 1914–c.1921 (rights and consciousness)*

   Discussion of different factors: your conclusions.

3 *Developments in France, 1914–c.1921*

   Discussion of different factors: your conclusions.

4 *Conclusion*

Example IV (This is a variation on Example III.)

1 *The argument that war did not have any effects or was negative in its effects*

   (a) Political rights in France.

   (b) Political rights in Britain.

   (c) Consciousness in Britain.

   (d) Consciousness in France.

2   *The argument that war did have positive effects*

   (a) Political rights in France.

   (b) Political rights in Britain.

   (c) Consciousness in Britain.

   (d) Consciousness in France.

3   *Conclusion*

Example V

1   *Long-term forces possibly affecting political rights and consciousness (Britain and France)*

2   *Political forces possibly affecting political rights and consciousness (Britain and France)*

3   *Effects of war experiences possibly affecting political rights and consciousness (Britain and France)*

4   *Conclusion*

Many variations on these basic examples would be possible. Very probably you thought of other basic models. I hope anyway you came up with at least one reasonable attempt.

I don't know whether you did manage to distinguish between your best plan and other possible plans (quite a difficult task). Of my five plans I think Example II is best, in that it leaves room to explore all the different issues involved in the question sufficiently. It would be perfectly possible to write good essays based on the other plans (provided that the various ramifications were gone into along the way), but in so far as they are rather basic and simple, I'd see them as plans for exam answers rather than for the more expansive and detailed format of an essay. A good plan is vital, but naturally the standard of the essay will finally depend on how well you write it up. □

There is not, obviously, scope for highly original work in your own essays, where you're drawing most of your information and ideas from our course materials, or, in the double TMA, from other people's books. Still, you will usually find that the course materials and books do not directly address the question asked or the topic set in your TMA. The task for you is to *use* what you have found out in order to address in a systematic and informed way the actual question set.

One of the requirements I mentioned was for a 'balanced' argument. This means that you must consider all relevant information and arguments, though in the end you must make it clear what line or conclusion you are opting for. It is here that the requirement for being 'well-substantiated' becomes particularly important. Explain why you are opting for one line of argument rather than another; at all times cite reasons and evidence for your contentions.

The great test to apply to an essay is to check each individual sentence and to ask of it what contribution it is making to your overall argument. Satisfy yourself on this point with each single sentence. Do not leave in sentences that do not, as it were, 'pull their weight'. Beware of sentences beginning 'It is interesting to note that ...': this nearly always means that you're not really very clear what the significance of the point you are about to make is in your general argument, but that you vaguely thought you ought to stuff it in anyway. Quite often it is not a matter of dropping a sentence that doesn't seem in itself to be contributing much; sometimes you need to add another sentence or phrase bringing out how what you are saying contributes to the development of your overall argument.

Don't overload your essays with direct quotations, certainly not long ones. Remember that the phrase 'scissors and paste' when applied to an essay, is a very severe criticism, implying that all you have done is pasted together bits and pieces from different books without really working out any coherent argument of your own. Quotations from primary sources are, of course, more to be welcomed than quotations from secondary sources. Be sparing with the latter and check carefully to see whether a direct quotation is really necessary. Often you can convey the information or opinion in your own words, simply making a reference to the secondary source. In all quotations the golden rule is to quote the minimum amount necessary to make your point. Be sure that the point is clear to your reader. Don't just leave a quotation to 'speak for itself'. Just as you have to justify each sentence that you write, you have to justify every quotation that you make.

References are not for show, but to serve the highly functional purpose of indicating to the reader where you have got a particular point or quotation from. Bibliographies are there to give a general sense of the sources on which your work is based. The vital question that readers should always be asking, whether they are students reading a book by an academic, or an academic reading an essay by a student, is 'how does he or she know that?' The good historian always satisfies his or her readers on that point (and that, of course, is the primary function of references or footnotes).

Good writing comes easier to some people than to others. It's a matter on which people are often sensitive: there is no substitute for careful correction by a tutor. Unfortunately face-to-face discussion and correction is not generally possible within the Open University situation. My own procedure when I used to discuss badly written sentences face-to-face with individual students was to ask them to explain to me directly what it was they were trying to say. If you're not clear in your own mind what it is you're trying to say, then you will not write a clear sentence. So that is the first point to think about. Sometimes, however, students can express verbally perfectly clearly and simply what it is they are intending to say. The lesson here is always to aim at simplicity. Don't feel that because you are writing a university essay you have to aspire to some highfalutin' or elaborate style. Be very careful with long words. Don't just use them because you like the sound of them or think they will sound good. Be absolutely sure that you really do know what their correct meaning is. There are lots of platitudes and clichés in historical writing which historians who ought to know better often use themselves. One can't, therefore, make too much of a fuss about this. I also recognize that for students who have difficulty in keeping their writing going at all, it is often helpful just to fall back on well-worn, if often rather meaningless, phrases (it is for this very reason that serious academics, fearful sometimes of 'drying-up' themselves, make use of such phrases). Still, avoiding clichés and tired phrases is an objective well worth aiming for even if, like most of the rest of us, you can't always live up to it. The secret of dealing with this one actually is not to worry too much about tired phrasing and clichés in the first draft, but to make a big effort to get them out, or replace them with something more elegant when you go through again polishing up your arguments and your style.

Here are examples of the kind of weary phrase I am thinking of: 'spectrum of opinion', 'climate of ideas', 'tool of analysis', 'frontiers of knowledge', 'spectre of defeat'. Worst, of all, in my view, is the routine use of 'dramatic', which presumably ought to mean something like 'with the force and emotion of a drama': but in standard, unthinking, historical writing, we seem never to have a rise in prices, nor a fall in stocks, never a religious revival nor a political recovery, but each must be 'dramatic'. Whenever you feel yourself reaching for this word, ask whether 'big', 'large', 'major' or 'significant' might not better serve your purpose.

The use of metaphor can greatly enhance historical writing. But the exaggerated use of metaphor can often indicate that a student is really trying to cover up for the fact that he/she doesn't have anything very clear or straightforward to say. The protracted metaphor is usually to be distrusted: the causes of a war may, if the writer has a liking for particularly hackneyed metaphors, be equated with a long fuse leading to a powder keg, or to runaway trains set on a collision course, but it will be unwise to force every single circumstance or development to fit the metaphor.

Exercise Say what, if anything, you find wrong with this short extract from a secondary source:

> 'All the cards in the hand of France's post-liberation destiny', says Mr. R. Mathews in his *The Death Of The Fourth Republic,* 'had been dealt by April 1945; it only remained for time to play them'. Such a view, though exaggerated, does contain a modicum of truth.
>
> (Gordon Wright, *History of Modern France*, 1959, p. 529) ∎

Specimen answer and discussion First of all, it seems to me, the metaphor within the quotation from Mr R. Mathews is high-flown and not really terribly helpful. Presumably it means that everything which governed the history of France from April 1945 until the end of the Fourth Republic (in 1958) was already settled before April 1945. Once spelled out, the idea, which for a moment did sound quite striking, seems rather absurd. Surely there were other developments of importance after April 1945 – Marshall Aid, the onset of the Cold War, to mention but two of the best known. The comment by the principal author seems even more feeble. What precisely does it mean to say that a judgement is 'exaggerated', and precisely how much is a 'modicum'? What the main author is trying to convey is something like this:

> Many of the circumstances which determined the history of France from the Liberation to the end of the Fourth Republic were already settled by April 1945, though these circumstances alone are not sufficient to explain what happened in the years which followed.

Instead, the author reached for the lazy approach of sticking in an apparently striking (but actually rather silly) quotation from another author, tacking on to it a rather weary qualification. It is always best to work out for yourself exactly what you mean, then to say it in the simplest and most direct way. □

The skill of writing balanced, well-argued, properly-substantiated, carefully structured reports is one of the most important learning outcomes of doing a history degree. You will find what I am saying here summarized and amplified in 'Guidance on History TMAs' in your TMA booklet.

Aim 6

Historiography is the study of the way history is written, of the different kinds of interpretations and arguments that historians put forward.

Exercise   We have already encountered one major historiographical debate. Say what it was, and mention some of the main points made in the debate. ■

Specimen answer   The debate is over the consequences of World War I. We looked at:

two extracts (one Marxist) stressing the effects of long-term structural forces over those of war itself;

two extracts arguing that the war had little or no effect on the changing status of women;

two extracts which did suggest that the participation element in war was an important factor for social change. □

Exercise   You might say, as many people have said, that if historians themselves can't come to some agreement, why should anyone else study history. Can you see any value in historiographical debate and controversy of this sort? ■

Specimen answer   It can clarify issues. It can force historians on different sides of the argument to reconsider their own arguments. It can enforce a re-examination of the evidence or a search for new evidence. As long as historians don't simply dig themselves into entrenched positions, historiographical debate can actually further historical knowledge. □

It is historical knowledge we are concerned with, not the relatively minor details of which historians said what. Still you do have to be aware (particularly when you come to write your own essays) that no history book is a neutral repository of knowledge. To a greater or lesser degree historians will be taking up personal positions: you will have to take this into account when seeking out information for your essays. You have already learned something of my own attitudes, and you can learn more from what Beckett says about me in his article on total war in the Course Reader (Chapter 1). You may well, therefore, in reading my units in this course, want to be on guard in case I tend to exaggerate the effects of war. It is pretty clear, on the other hand, from the period Roberts chooses to study, and from the layout of his chapters (only one chapter each to the two wars), that he does not see war as a particularly potent influence for change. You might want to bear that in mind too. To know your history, sometimes, it is important too to know your historian.

Revisionist/revisionism

These are words you will encounter when historiographical debates are being discussed. There is no one 'revisionist' approach to history in the way in which there is a Marxist or a feminist approach. Whenever the word 'revisionist' is used, it must refer to one specific historical controversy. And you must always bear in mind that historians are forever revising and qualifying each other's work. Scientists do this as well – this is how knowledge is advanced. But sometimes something like a consensus forms over a particular topic, over the origins of World War I, for instance, or over Soviet Russia as a prime example of totalitarianism. Then the consensus is challenged – and so we speak of 'the revisionist view of the origins of World War I', or 'the revisionist view of Stalinist Russia'. But do not use the words 'revisionist' or 'revisionism' yourself unless you are absolutely sure about how you are using them.

3   CONCLUSION: THREE THEMES

The aim of this unit has been to give you a clear idea of what is involved in this course. There are twenty-nine units still to go and obviously at this stage you cannot really have learned anything of any significance about the issues we shall be discussing. None the less, in order to return from the questions of how one writes and studies history to the questions of content, I am going to present here three themes which form another way of summarizing what in essence the course is about. At the end of the course there will be a whole unit on each of these themes, designed to sum up for you the material we will have covered by that time. The themes are:

1   The nature and causes of war
2   The processes of change
3   The impact of total war

The following questions relate to each of these themes.

The nature and causes of war

Exercise   1   Comment on this statement, saying whether you agree or disagree with it, and why. Try to suggest what approach to history the statement might represent.

'Societies are constantly at war; it is impossible to say when war ends and peace begins.'

2   Attempt to answer this question:

Were the causes of World War II very different from the causes of World War I, or were there many causes common to both wars? (We, of course, are concerned only with the European aspects of World War II.) ■

Specimen answers   1   World War I was preceded by the Balkan wars, and succeeded by civil and
and discussion   internal war. Within societies there was much conflict. A Marxist approach might well argue that war, in the form of class war, was in operation continuously. On the other hand, there were firmly dated declarations of war and peace settlements, which do separate out war from peace. More critically, the two world wars were characterized by enormous devastation and loss of life. This, one could reasonably argue, does quite distinctively single them out from periods of peace.

2 I don't know how much you felt able to say on this one. There is the argument about German expansionism and ambitions being the causes of both wars. There is the rather obvious point of wars being caused because of the willingness of powers to use war as an instrument of policy. It has been said that World War I came about because everybody prepared for war and then stumbled into it, whereas World War II was caused because the Western powers weren't sufficiently prepared to resist Hitler. Maybe you simply contented yourself with the idea that in the causation of all wars there are structural, geopolitical, ideological, and diplomatic and political factors. For detailed analysis you'll have to wait until Unit 19. □

The processes of change

Exercise   Just one question this time:

In the period of the course, 1914–1955, which has had greater significance, social change or geopolitical change?
(I'll comment on this after I have asked a question on the third theme.) ∎

The impact of total war

Exercise   Here also there is just one question:

By 1955 women in practically all of the European countries had the vote, the European empires were in sharp decline, all governments claimed to recognize the interests of the masses, all countries had advanced welfare legislation. Would these circumstances have been roughly the same had there been no total wars? ∎

Specimen answers and discussion   *Theme 2* If your concern is with change that affects the lives of ordinary people, you will probably come down on the side of social change. But even there, it is not as simple as all that. The extent to which the Poles, the various southern Slav nationalities, the Czechs and the Slovaks threw off the rule of the Russian and Austrian Empires was of considerable importance to them. The division of Europe into East and West at the end of World War II is obviously also of profound general significance. The emphasis of this course, as you know by now, is on social change, and I think it is reasonable to argue that this is what is most important; but we must not ignore the geopolitical changes.

Theme 3 Well, as I hope you will have already gathered, the answers will depend on how one estimates long-term structural and ideological forces, as against what happened during war (the effects of participation, for instance). □

Let us wait and see how far the answers you give to questions of this sort differ, or remain broadly the same, after you have worked your way through this course.

References

Hardach, G. (1987) *The First World War, 1914–1918,* Allen Lane (first published in 1973).

Hause, S. C. and Kenney, A. R. (1984) *Women's Suffrage and Social Politics in the French Third Republic,* Princeton University Press.

Holton, S. S. (1986) *Feminism and Democracy: Women's Suffrage and Reform Politics in Britain, 1900–1918,* Cambridge University Press.

McMillan, J. F. (1988) 'World War I and women in France' in Marwick, A. (ed.) (1988).

Marwick, A. (1974) *War and Social Change in the Twentieth Century: A Comparative Study of Britain, France, Germany, Russia and the United States,* Macmillan.

Marwick, A. (ed.) (1988) *Total War and Social Change,* Macmillan.

Mayer, A. J. (1981) *The Persistence of the Old Regime,* Croom Helm.

Mommsen, W. J. (1988) 'The social consequences of World War I: the case of Germany' in Marwick, A. (ed.) (1988).

Reid, A. (1988) 'World War I and the working class in Britain' in Marwick, A. (ed.) (1988).

Roberts, J. M. (1989) *Europe 1880–1945,* second edition, Longman.

Roberts, R. (1971) *The Classic Slum: Salford Life in the First Quarter of the Century,* Manchester University Press.

Wright, G. (1962) *France in Modern Times, 1760 to the Present,* John Murray.

Further reading

Carr, E. H. (1964) *What is History?,* Penguin.

Hobsbawm, E. (1994) *The Age of Extremes: The Short Twentieth Century 1914–1991,* Michael Joseph.

Jenkins, K. (ed.) (1997) *The Postmodern History Reader,* Routledge.

Marwick, A. (1990) *Class: Image and Reality in Britain, France and the USA since 1930,* second edition, Macmillan.

Marwick, A. (1995) 'Two approaches to historical study: The metaphysical (including postmodernism) and the historical', *Journal of Contemporary History,* January, vol.30, no.1, pp.5–35.

Marwick, A. (1998) 'Introduction to History', units 8 and 9 and 25 and 26 of *A103: An Introduction to the Humanities,* Open University.

Marwick, A. (2001) *The Nature of History: Knowledge, Evidence, Language,* fourth edition, Macmillan.

Tosh, J. (2000) *The Pursuit of History: Aims, Methods and New Directions in the Study of Modern History,* third edition, Longman.

Unit 2 THE COMBATANTS IN 1914: SOLDIERS AND THEIR STATES

CLIVE EMSLEY

Open University students of this unit will need to refer to:

Set book: J. M. Roberts, *Europe 1880–1945*, Longman, 2000

Primary Sources 1: World War 1, eds Arthur Marwick and Wendy Simpson, Open University, 2000

Maps Booklet

INTRODUCTION

This unit begins with a discussion of the perceptions of war in 1914. It then moves on to compare and contrast the principal European countries and empires on the eve of World War I, examining, in particular, those areas usually seen as most clearly dividing one from another: the constitutional structures; the scale of economic development and performance; the extent to which each nation existed within the boundaries of a state. The overall purpose here is to prepare you for the task of assessing the impact and significance of the war on the combatant societies.

When you have completed the unit you should have a knowledge of:

- the attitudes towards war in different countries of Europe in 1914;

- the different constitutional systems in Europe in 1914, the similarities and the differences between assemblies, governments and bureaucracies;

- the scale of economic development which will enable you later to explore questions concerning: economic rivalry as a cause of war, and the economic impact of war; the perception of the 'nation' and the different kinds of 'nationalism' which will enable you to consider; nationalism as an element during the war, and the development of the concept of national self-determination during and immediately after the war.

The set book for the course, J. M. Roberts, *Europe 1880–1945*, contains important background information for sections 2, 3 and 4 of this unit and consequently each of these sections begins with preliminary reading from the book. In addition to Roberts you will also need to refer to *Primary Sources 1: World War I.*

While this course is free standing those of you who have done A221 *State, Economy and Nation in Nineteenth-Century Europe* will find the material in this unit builds on the content of that course in very obvious ways. If you have A221 in your possession then you will probably find it useful to keep it at your side and to make your own cross references as you work through this unit.

1   GOING TO WAR IN 1914

For many people the events of 1914 mark a decisive turning point after which the world was never to appear the same again; thus, for example, many history books have 1914 as a terminal date, as do many history courses. Yet turning points in history can look very different from different national perspectives. For Balkan peoples – and it was in the Balkans that events occurred which sparked the war – the conflict that began in the summer of 1914 can appear as an extension and widening of a series of wars beginning in 1912. For the Italians participation in the war did not come until May 1915. In Russia the decisive turning point is 1917 rather than 1914, and the experience of war was to continue for many Russians until 1921. Furthermore, after the end of the war against the central powers (Germany and Austria-Hungary) a few British and French troops found themselves deployed in Russia against the new Red Army.

Table 2.1   The Combatants of World War I

	1914	1915	1916	1917	1918
The Central Powers					
Austria-Hungary	July				Nov
Bulgaria		Oct			Sept
Germany	Aug				Nov
Turkey	Nov				Oct
The Entente Powers and their Allies					
France	Aug				Nov
Belgium[1]	Aug				Nov
Great Britain	Aug				Nov
Greece				June	Nov
Italy		May			Nov
Portugal			March		Nov
Japan	Aug				Nov
Montenegro[2]	July				Nov
Romania			Aug Dec		Nov
Russia	July			March	
Serbia[2]	July				Nov
USA				April	Nov

[1] Virtually the whole of Belgium was under German occupation from the autumn of 1914.

[2] Montenegro and Serbia were destroyed as independent states in the winter of 1915–16, but guerilla warfare continued and both states had governments in exile. Eventually, at the end of the war, they were amalgamated with other territories into the new state of Yugoslavia.

Besides the danger of perceiving 'key dates' or 'turning points' with a kind of national, tunnel vision, there is also the danger of perceiving such occasions with hindsight and assuming that the actors involved in events were aware of their significance and potential outcome. (Table 2.1 lists the combatants of World War I and their period of involvement.)

Exercise   Study Tables 2.2. and 2.3

1   What does the information contained in these tables suggest to you about the expectation and understanding which the soldiers and sailors of 1914 had about the physical reality of modern war?

2   When war broke out in the summer of 1914 there was talk of it being 'over by Christmas'. How might looking back over wars in the preceding half century have contributed to this? ■

Table 2.2   European wars and their duration 1853–1913[1]

War	Principal states involved	First hostilities	Armistice	Duration in months
Crimean	Great Britain France } vs Russia Turkey	23 Sept 1853	1 Feb 1856	27
Franco-Austrian	France vs Austrian Empire	29 April 1859	8 July 1859	3
Schleswig-Holstein	Prussia Austrian Empire } vs Denmark	1 Feb 1864	1 Aug 1864	4[2]
Seven Weeks[3]	Prussia Italy } vs Austrian Empire	14 June 1866	26 July 1866	2
Franco-Prussian[3]	Prussia vs France	19 July 1870	1 March 1871	9
Russo-Turkish	Russia vs Turkey	24 April 1877	31 Jan 1878	10
First Balkan	Bulgaria Serbia Greece } vs Turkey Montenegro	8 Oct 1912	22 April 1913	2
Second Balkan	Serbia Greece Montenegro } vs Bulgaria Romania Turkey	30 June 1913	21 Aug 1913	2

[1] Excluding the smaller Balkan conflicts between Bulgaria and Serbia (1885) and Greece and Turkey (1897).

[2] Truce in May and June.

[3] Smaller German states were also involved in these conflicts, notably Saxony and, indirectly, Bavaria on the side of Austria in 1866; significant numbers from the German states fought alongside Prussia in 1870–71.

Table 2.3   Other wars involving 'modern' armies 1861–1905[1]

War	Principal states involved	First hostilities	Armistice	Duration in months
American Civil	United States of America vs Confederate States	12 April 1861	9 April 1865	48
Spanish-American	United States vs Spain	21 April 1898	12 Aug 1898	5
Boer	Great Britain vs Boer Republic	9 Oct 1899	31 May 1902	32
Russo-Japanese	Russia vs Japan	8 Feb 1904	6 Sept 1905	22

[1] That is involving troops on both sides equipped with modern weapons and excluding conflicts between 'western' armies and tribal forces.

Specimen answers 1 It should be clear from Tables 2.2 and 2.3 that very few of the soldiers from the major European powers who went to war in 1914 had any experience of the reality of modern warfare against well-armed, well-trained adversaries.

2 None of the wars fought in Europe since the 1850s had lasted for more than ten months; the conflicts outside Europe had impinged little on the everyday lives of Europeans, and thus it was natural to suppose that the conflict which began in 1914 would not take much longer than its immediate, European predecessors.

Discussion Of course, some troops had experience in colonial wars outside Europe; in addition the British had fought against the Boers in South Africa and the Russians had fought the Japanese in Manchuria. Some lessons had been learned from the American Civil War about the devastating nature of modern firepower: the Prussians developed loose formation and the use of cover in response to this danger during 1870; the Russians were slower, and consequently suffered 35 per cent casualties in their initial assault on Turkish positions at Plevna in 1877. Yet the experience of battle was wanting for most troops in 1914, and the experience of moving large numbers of men in the heat and confusion of battle was wanting for most senior officers. Some generals, particularly in France, still tended to emphasize the *élan* of large-scale assaults with fixed bayonets; and certainly this was the image which inspired some popular artists and writers (and indeed which continued to inspire them when war actually came). □

Exercise Look again at Table 2.2. Do you detect a shift in the combatants and the regions of Europe where wars were fought between 1853 and 1913? ∎

Specimen answer From the late 1850s to the early 1870s the wars in Europe were between major powers and were fought in the centre and west of the continent. From then on there was no open conflict between major powers (except for the Russo-Turkish war if Turkey is considered to have been a major power) and the wars were confined to the Balkans.

Discussion The wars of the mid-1850s through to the early 1870s have a broad claim to the description of wars of liberation: out of them emerged a united Italy, under the house of Savoy, and a united Germany, under the dominance of Prussia. Note here that although Germany was united and that the king of Prussia was Kaiser (emperor) of the Reich, there were still technically twenty-five federal states in Germany (four kingdoms, six grand duchies, five duchies, seven principalities and three free cities) with varying degrees of independence and local government. The constitution of 1871 ruled that the previously separate armies formed a Reichsheer, but Prussia, Bavaria, Saxony and Württemberg retained their own military administration and – at least in peace-time – jealously guarded their independence. In times of war the Kaiser was supreme commander over the Reichsheer, and the contingent armies lost their special rights. Bavaria enjoyed the most wide-ranging special rights and is therefore often mentioned as the exception. However, Württemberg and Saxony also had military plenipotentiaries in Berlin, and the exchange of information between the provincial capitals and Berlin worked much better in the case of Karlsruhe and Dresden than it did with Munich, which was much more determined to defend its special position. The Bavarian minister of war considered himself the equal of his Prussian counterpart, though this was not the case from the point of view of the Prussians. Austria – generally referred to after 1867 as Austria-Hungary when the *Ausgleich* (compromise) acknowledged a dual monarchy in which the emperor of Austria was also the king of Hungary – had vied with Prussia for hegemony over the smaller German states. Austria had lost significantly by the wars of the 1850s and 1860s – in prestige, to Prussia, as well as lands, to Italy. The struggles in the Balkans were the result of various Slav peoples of south-east Europe seeking to break away and carve their own nation states from the last vestiges of Turkey's European empire. These conflicts had involved the great powers, obviously Russia in 1877–78. But the First and Second Balkan Wars also witnessed considerable diplomatic manoeuvring by the great powers to ensure peace and what they considered to be a proper balance in the region; this diplomacy was occasionally backed up by the threat of force, most notably in May 1913 when Austro-Hungarian troops were mobilized on the frontiers of Montenegro.

You should follow up the basic detail of great power diplomacy in the Balkans in Roberts, pp.210–13. It would be a good idea to do this now. □

The Balkans, then, were recognized as an international trouble spot when, on 28 June 1914, the heir to the Austrian and Hungarian thrones was assassinated, together with his wife, by a Bosnian Serb in Sarajevo, a town in the imperial province of Bosnia. Historians have written at length about 'the July crisis'; the term has been used as the title for books as well as chapters within books. Essentially the July crisis concerned the upper echelons of governments and their diplomats; the general publics of the great powers were largely unaware of the notes passing between monarchs, ministers and diplomats. For one thing, the assassination of royal personages was in no sense an unheard-of event in this period: the Empress of Austria had been murdered in 1898; followed by the King of Italy (1900), the King and Queen of Serbia (1903), the King of Portugal with his heir (1908) and the King of Greece (1913); several leading politicians had met a similar fate, most recently Count Stolypin in Russia in 1911. Nor had previous Balkan wars involved the powers of Europe in war against each other. Besides, in Britain and France the newspapers – and remember that people relied upon the newspaper press for their national and international news – found plenty of good copy much closer to home. For much of July 1914 French newspapers were full of the trial of Madame Caillaux; she was the wife of a former finance minister who, incensed by the campaign which *Le Figaro* had orchestrated against her husband, had shot dead that paper's editor. British newspapers were preoccupied with a worsening crisis over Ireland where Ulster Protestants were arming to oppose their inclusion in an Ireland with a Home Rule parliament in Dublin. The newspapers began to devote more and more space to the diplomatic events of the July crisis only after Austria-Hungary presented an ultimatum to Serbia on 23 July. Just over a week after the ultimatum the armies had mobilized.

There seems to be an overwhelming impression, especially in popular history books and in media representation of the beginning of World War I, of nations and populations united, and of men going cheerfully and eagerly to war throughout Europe. There is evidence of politicians declaring a new kind of national unity: for example, the president of the French Chamber of Deputies proclaimed, 'There are no more adversaries here, there are only Frenchmen'; and Kaiser Wilhelm declared, 'Henceforth I know no parties, I know only Germans'. It is understandable that internal differences would be forgotten in time of crisis, but just how deep and widespread was popular euphoria for war in the summer of 1914? What did men think about when they went to war? Why did they go?

With reference to the first of these questions, let me simply provide you with the assessment by one recent historian of Imperial Germany:

> The drama and extravagant expectations of war lent almost mystical status to the 'spirit of 1914', and not a little of this mysticism has colored subsequent historical writings on this subject. It soon became an article of faith that Germany had entered the war in euphoric unanimity. In their search for the roots of these emotions, commentators have written of a general flight from (or into) modernity, the longing to escape from the boredom of civilian life, or the venting of primitive drives. Much of the commentary is speculation; and even basic generalizations about the unanimity of enthusiasm require qualification. The evidence on which these generalizations rest is drawn largely from urban Germany. The attitudes of women and men in the countryside and small towns await the attention they deserve. Nor did the euphoria over war extend to all of urban Germany. 'There was no unified "August experience",' writes [Michael Stöcker] who has examined this phenomenon in Darmstadt, 'rather there were different August experiences'. In Darmstadt and elsewhere, anxiety was as widespread as jubilation.
>
> (R. Chickering, *Imperial Germany and the Great War*, 1998, pp.15–16)

The armies of continental Europe were made up of conscripts, and former conscripts now in the reserve. Such men really had little choice about going to war. The British Army, in contrast, was made up of volunteers and professionals. Monday, 3 August 1914 was a Bank Holiday and recruiting offices were closed, but for the rest of the week there was an average of 1600 volunteers a day. Between 4 August and 12 September 478,893 men enlisted.

Exercise   Turn to *Primary Sources 1: World War I* (Documents 1.1–1.3); read the nine explanations given in retrospect by some of these volunteers and note:

1   the reasons given for volunteering;

2   how these examples support the popular image of jingoism and eagerness for war. ■

Specimen answers   1   These extracts give a variety of reasons for volunteering: patriotism is there, but so too is the desire for adventure, and the belief that the army offered an escape from unemployment or a humdrum existence. I think it is also significant to note how young men often appear to have goaded each other on; they enlisted as groups of friends intending to share the adventure together. There also appears to have been an element of pressure from newspapers, pulpits, and then from displays on hoardings, especially that showing the famous Alfred Leese poster of Field-Marshal Lord Kitchener urging young men to join the army.

2 The extracts qualify the popular image of why men enlisted; the motives of the volunteers were complex and cannot be explained away simply with the label jingoistic. It is also interesting to note the reluctance of employers to let their men go; this reluctance is understandable, but not something which immediately springs to mind given the popular image of the beginning of war.

Discussion Of course I have only given you a few brief extracts here, and there were thousands of volunteers. Moreover these extracts are, in the main, taken from men looking back from a distance of fifty years. Recollections, of course, have to be treated with the same kinds of rigour as any other evidence. But one thing common to the British volunteers of 1914, and to the soldiers of the other powers, was an innocence about modern industrial warfare. War, and the threat of war, were still largely accepted as extensions of diplomacy and war in the popular imagination was still colourful and heroic; W. E. Henley's *Lyra Heroica*, a popular anthology of verse for boys first published in 1892, was designed, for example, 'To set forth, as only art can, the beauty and joy of living, the beauty and blessedness of death, the glory of battle and adventure, the nobility of devotion – to a cause, an ideal, a passion even – the dignity of resistance, the sacred quality of patriotism ...' (quoted in P. Parker, *The Old Lie*, 1987, p.139). Such attitudes to war were not something purely English or British. Ernst Jünger enlisted in the Hanoverian Fusiliers at the end of 1914 aged only 19; he went on to win the Iron Cross, First Class and the *Pour le Mérite*, and to become a lieutenant of the crack stormtroopers. In his autobiography of the war years he recalled:

> We had left the lecture-room, class-room, and bench behind us ... We had grown up in a material age, and in each one of us there was the yearning for great experience, such as we had never known. We had set out in a rain of flowers to seek the death of heroes. The war was our dream of greatness, power and glory. It was a man's work, a duel in the fields whose flowers would be stained with blood. There is no lovelier death in the world ... anything rather than stay at home ...
>
> (E. Jünger, *The Storm of Steel*, 1929, p.1)

For Jünger the glamour of war lingered, but for others – probably for the majority – the trenches were to be a rude awakening. The horror of the war from the soldier's point of view paradoxically may have contributed to an overemphasis on the patriotic eagerness and enthusiasm of July and August 1914. It also contributed to the more sombre reactions which greeted the outbreak of war in 1939, and again perhaps, this has distorted the sentiments and attitudes present at the beginning of World War I. □

Exercise Turn again to *Primary Sources 1: World War I* and read Document I.4. To what extent does the content of these documents also call into question the universality of an eagerness for war in 1914? ■

Specimen answer The documents show that at least two groups were either lukewarm or downright hostile to the war: socialists and some British intellectuals who were reluctant to see their country going to war against 'civilized' Germany and on the side of the Slavs.

Discussion   In the decade or so immediately before 1914 some socialists, as well as Liberals like Norman Angell (author of *The Great Illusion* which argued that no-one could profit from war), had continually taken a pacifist line; a few socialists had even adopted it as policy that a declaration of war would be taken as a signal for a general strike, the herald of socialist revolution. European governments' fears of the socialists, and of the effects of socialist and of anti-war propaganda were probably greater than the reality. At the same time it suited many of these governments to play up the extent of the perceived 'threat' to their own advantage. □

In 1914 the largest party in the German *Reichstag* was the *Sozialdemokratische Partei Deutschlands* (SPD). An avowedly Marxist party, it had, in the elections of 1912, secured 4.25 million votes, or 34.7 per cent of the total. The party's newspaper *Vorwärts* was critical of 'the frivolous provocation' of the Austro-Hungarian ultimatum to Serbia, and it urged the government of the Reich to avoid 'war-like interference'. The SPD executive directed party members to demonstrate for peace and against Austria-Hungary; in consequence there were violent clashes between the police and demonstrators. Wilhelm II contemplated arresting the SPD leadership while some of his generals contemplated more extreme measures. However, the party's leadership was not as radical as its rhetoric, and as the diplomatic crisis deepened the SPD leaders assured the Reich government that they were loyal Germans with no plans for a general strike, for sabotage or any similar action in the event of war. The decisive event in swinging SPD opinion was the news of Russian mobilization. On 4 August 1914 the SPD deputies voted unanimously for war credits and the *Burgfriede* (a domestic political truce). This unanimity concealed a division within the party since, at a caucus meeting on 3 August, fourteen members had stood out against such a vote and only sided with their seventy-eight colleagues because of the tradition of voting as a single body; the division became public, and serious, as the war continued.

French socialism was split among several factions; the largest party, the *Section Française de l'Internationale Ouvrière* (SFIO) was much smaller than the German SPD with about 90,000 members as compared with a million. The founder and leader of the SFIO was Jean Jaurès. He was a former university teacher and a man of exceptional ability; a reformist rather than a revolutionary, a brilliant orator, and a passionate opponent of militarism. On 29 July Jaurès was in Brussels meeting with other leading European socialists; that evening he appeared to address a mass, open-air meeting with his arm around a German comrade. The meeting dispersed with crowds singing the '*Internationale*' and carrying banners with the slogan *Guerre à la guerre* (War against war). Jaurès returned to Paris, only to be assassinated there on 31 July by a demented, ultra-French nationalist. In spite of Jaurès's efforts, most notably in the SFIO newspaper *L'Humanité*, and those of others (*La Bataille Syndicaliste*, for example, the organ of the French trade unions was among those demanding that the declaration of war be met with a declaration of a revolutionary general strike), less than 2 per cent of the men called to the colours in 1914 failed to respond to the call. The French government had feared that as many as 13 per cent would fail to turn up and, as a result of the actual response, it felt able to dispense with the plans for the mass arrest of militants named on the notorious blacklist, the *Carnet B*. Following President Poincaré's declaration on 4 August of *l'union sacrée* (the sacred union of all Frenchmen for the duration of the war) socialist deputies supported the war budget; and on 26 August two of them entered the government.

The issues of nationalism and the internationalism of socialism will be taken up below, but I think it fair to conclude here that, while the different European governments found their call to arms met in 1914, and while many men went to war enthusiastically, there were others with considerable reservations.

The men who went to war in 1914 did so as the soldiers and sailors of nation states and multi-national empires. If we are to assess the impact of war on societies, then we must have some knowledge of how these states and empires were organized and how they were developing before the war. It is to these issues that I want to turn now.

2   CONSTITUTIONAL SYSTEMS

Legislative structures

Exercise If we are going to explore the impact of World War I on the different states and empires of Europe then we need to have some idea of how they functioned before the war. I want you to start by reading Roberts, Chapters 5 and 6, concentrating particularly on pp.98–103; 116–18; 136–40; 146–56; 160–4; and 167–72. As you read these chapters, answer the following questions:

1 What does Roberts consider to be a convenient way of categorizing the states prior to World War I?

2 How significant do you think such a categorization might be for assessing why these states went to war in 1914?

3 Which states did not have some kind of legislative body, chosen by some kind of elective process involving a percentage of the adult male population?

4 How were the members of these legislative bodies organized within the chambers, and what did these organizations represent?

5 If the legislatures in the autocracies were powerless, why did they continue to exist? ∎

Specimen answers 1 Roberts suggests that the convenient categorization is to distinguish how
and discussion   public affairs were run and he differentiates between:

(a) the constitutional states, mainly in the west of Europe, which generally had some form of written constitution, and within which the final authority usually rested in law-making parliaments chosen by wide electorates; and

(b) the autocracies, which were to be found to the east of Europe, which were resistant to liberal and constitutional ideas, and which, coincidentally, shared a common problem of alien nationalities within their borders.

Since we have emphasized that you need to take care over the words that you use when writing essays, it is worth pointing out here that several members of the course team would take issue with Roberts's use of the word 'autocracy'. He notes (p.144) that only the Russian empire was 'formally an autocracy'. In the historical context under discussion the equivalent term is 'absolute monarchy'. Nicholas II believed fervently in absolutism, and in practice even his rule was tempered by grudging concessions to constitutionalism. Perhaps the more appropriate term for lumping together the countries of Central and Eastern Europe is 'authoritarian', so that we should speak of 'authoritarian states'.

2   Not a particularly easy question for you at this stage, and certainly not one that lends itself to an easy answer. Clearly, the combatants in World War I did not line up as constitutional versus authoritarian states; the most ramshackle of the latter, Russia, was allied with the former. My point in posing this question was simply to underline the fact that political ideology and administrative practice does not automatically lead to political alliance. While Roberts might stress this contrast between constitutional states and autocracies, other historians might employ other categorizations or empha-size similarities – Arno Mayer, for example, whose work you will meet subsequently, maintained that an old régime persisted in Europe up until World War I, in which the power and authority of the traditional autocracies remained paramount. This leads on to the similarity which was the point of my third question.

3   All of the constitutional states and authoritarian empires discussed by Roberts had some kind of elected, legislative body. These differed widely. The French Republic had a bicameral legislature with an upper house, the Senate, elected by local representatives in such a way as to ensure the dominance of rural France, and a lower house, the Chamber of Deputies, elected by universal manhood suffrage. Britain, which boasted of having the oldest such parliament, also had a bicameral legislature: the House of Lords made up of peers of the realm and bishops of the established church, and the House of Commons, elected on a limited franchise of adult males occupying land or lodgings worth at least £10 a year. It is also important to be aware that, for all its constitutional and liberal rhetoric, Britain was one of the two European countries which had *not* adopted universal manhood suffrage for elections to national assemblies in 1914 – the other was Hungary. Generally considered to be at the other extreme to the British parliament was the elected Russian *Duma*, established only in the aftermath of the 1905 Revolution, and engineered to give a dominance to landed proprietors and businessmen. Roberts's comment that, in the constitutional states, these legislative bodies possessed an ultimate authority has already been noted. In practice this meant that, whatever their faults, these elected assemblies could bring down governments, thus requiring a new election or, at least, that the head of state (monarch or president) find a new chief minister. This was not the case in the autocracies. Here the monarchs did not choose their chief ministers from elected representatives in the assemblies; rather they looked to men who were servants of the state – diplomats, administrators, even soldiers – and who had risen through the different hierarchies of the state bureaucracy.

4 The deputies were generally organized into political parties, some of these (like the Conservatives and Liberals in Britain) claimed to be national and broad-based, but others were openly sectional. There were class parties (such as the Labour Party in Britain, the SFIO in France, the SPD in Germany), national parties (the Irish nationalists in Britain, the different national groupings in the Austrian *Reichsrath*), religious parties (the Centre Party in Germany, Christian Socialists in Austria). Some parties had clear links with economic groupings, such as the Prussian Conservatives who were tied in with the agricultural interest. It is possible to make a broad differentiation between parties of the left and of the right, but this can sometimes cloud as much as it clarifies. German Liberals, for example, may have disliked and even criticized the imperial régime for its authoritarianism, until it came to dealing with Catholics, Poles, or the Marxist SPD.

5 While they did not have the power of assemblies in the constitutional states, it is, I think, clear from Roberts that the legislatures in the authoritarian ones could make life difficult for governments. Look, for example, at the crises in the Habsburg Empire described by Roberts on pp.162–4. Franz Josef and his ministers may have ruled, temporarily, by decree, but they did not wish to do this in perpetuity; even authoritarian states were beginning to perceive the need for an element of mass, popular support and an assembly was one way of achieving this. Moreover, the longer such assemblies existed, the more they became cemented in to the governmental structure. David Blackbourn, among others, has noted the growing importance of the *Reichstag* in post-Bismarckian Germany:

which can be seen in the mounting volume of ... business, especially in committee, the growing importance of major party leaders and committee experts in influencing political decision-making, and the increasing readiness of successive chancellors to take such figures into account.

(D. Blackbourn and G. Eley, *The Peculiarities of German History*, 1984, p.227)

Politics were a public pursuit and this meant that, in the gender-structured society of Europe on the eve of World War I, they were a man's business. Woman's separate sphere was the home and family. Of course, this was an idealized vision; millions of women from the working-class and the peasantry were engaged in work outside the home and in conditions similar to, often the same as, men. Some male bastions were yielding to feminist pressure – the medical profession, for example. The demands for women's franchise had met with some very limited successes in 1907. During the 1890s the local government franchise had been extended to women in Britain, and women in France won the right to vote and representation on the *Conseils des Prud'hommes*, the councils which decided on small disputes between employers and employees. But in none of the great powers of Europe did women have either the franchise or the right to stand for election to national legislatures. □

Exercise   A tangential question here which you should be able to address from your general knowledge. I have called this section 'constitutional systems' and have discussed Britain and France as constitutional nation states. What qualification ought to be made regarding this categorization? ■

*Specimen answer
and discussion* On the eve of World War I both Britain and France had vast overseas empires. In some instances the indigenous peoples had been displaced and white settlers ruled through their own elected legislatures – such was the case most notably in Australia, Canada and New Zealand. Elsewhere there were executive and legislative councils which made law, set taxes and even recruited and maintained armies. Such councils were dominated by men from the colonizing power, though by 1914 the government of British India, most notably, was fostering a limited participation of indigenous peoples. Only in rare instances, such as Algeria, where the overseas territory was incorporated into the metropolitan state, was rule direct from the imperial capital. The indigenous peoples were generally considered to be 'uncivilized' and 'primitive'; they were thought to be at an earlier, less developed stage of human progress. They were often described as 'child-like'; as such they were excluded from direct participation in imperial politics. □

Government bureaucracy

The decades before World War I witnessed most European governments introducing, and legislatures passing, more and more legislation which increasingly involved the state in the everyday lives of the population. Governments felt the need to have more information about their populations and about the national economy; they took a greater hand in the management of the economy and provided much of the necessary infrastructure – railways, roads and communications (post and telecommunications). Public inspectorates were established to check abuses in the private sector, in factories for example. Educational provision was increased; state welfare began to be provided for the old, the sick and the infirm. In return the state required the individual's loyalty and, in most instances, it required all of its young men to serve briefly as conscripts in its armed forces.

This growth of state power did not go unchallenged. At one end of the social scale there were members of the working class who co-operated with employers against factory inspectors: new safety regulations could hamper production and reduce wages, new regulations on child labour could limit the amount which children contributed to the family budget. Peasants and members of the urban working class kept their children away from school for this last reason; also girls might be kept from school to look after younger brothers or sisters. The state responded here with more legislation, and more bureaucrats – inspectors and policemen. But the challenge to the growth of the state could also be intellectual. In Britain, for example, one strand of liberalism still clung to the notion of *laissez-faire* and it had found a champion in the popular philosopher Herbert Spencer who, in 1884, published a book with the self-explanatory title *Man versus the State*. Increasingly, however, it was another strand of liberalism that was becoming dominant.

From the middle of the nineteenth century the disciples of Jeremy Bentham had urged the growth of the state to alleviate injustice and squalor on the one hand, and working-class 'idleness' and irresponsibility on the other. In the last two decades this kind of liberalism was boosted further by the publication (largely posthumous) of the work of the Oxford philosopher T. H. Green. Green argued that society only existed for the proper development of individuals and that civic and political institutions were valuable only in so far as they aided this development. In France there was also debate over the power of the state *vis-à-vis* the individual. France had the largest state bureaucracy in Europe in the mid-nineteenth century; the prefectorial system, dating back to the first Napoleon, put a state official (the prefect) in an administrative and supervisory capacity at the head of each *département*, and thus ensured a degree of central government involvement in provincial life undreamed of in Britain. Yet in the closing years of the nineteenth century the Council of State, the supreme judicial courts of administrative law, succeeded in impeding the development of welfare services and actually forbade municipalities from developing publicly owned enterprises in competition with private firms.

The growth of the state meant the growth of state bureaucracies. For much of the nineteenth century 'bureaucracy' had meant literally 'rule from the bureau' and in consequence it was sometimes contrasted with rule by representative government. Such 'bureaucracies' appeared to be most prominent to the east of Europe and it is generally acknowledged that the most efficient of the pre-war bureaucracies, in the more general sense, was that of Prussia. It was in the period before World War I that the more general meaning of bureaucracy was fostered, partly through the growth of the state but also through the work of the German sociologist Max Weber. Briefly Weber defined bureaucracy as a system of administration conducted by trained professionals according to prescribed rules. Ideally his bureaucracy had four principal attributes:

1   It was hierarchial; there was a division of labour with the different officials responsible to a superior.

2   There was continuity; bureaucratic posts were full-time, salaried occupations with a career structure.

3   It was impersonal; strict rules prescribed the officials' actions; the officials acted without arbitrariness or favour, and kept written records of their proceedings.

4   It was marked by expertise; bureaucracies were staffed by trained professionals, selected according to merit.

Exercise   As with any theoretical social model the four points drawn from Weber and noted above constitute an ideal type; such models provide a means for analysing institutions, they are not developed so that historical (or any other) data might be used to prove simply that the model is correct. Is there anything about the social structure of late nineteenth- and early twentieth-century Europe which you think must have impeded state bureaucracies from developing in this ideal form? ■

Specimen answer   It seems to me that the hierarchial structure of pre-World War I society in Europe, together with the lack of equal educational opportunities, were bound to militate against the selection and promotion of personnel according to merit.

Discussion   In parts of the bureaucratic structures of most states, generally those parts away from the centre or connected more directly with local administration, it was possible to rise through merit. A man born into the British working class could, for example, join the police as the lowest grade of constable and end his career as the head of a borough police force. A Russian peasant could rise to the rank of colonel in the Russian army and, indeed, two-fifths of the Russian officer-corps up to and including this rank originated in the peasantry or the lower middle class. But while possible in theory, it was never the case that a British working man joining the police before World War I had risen to be the chief constable of a large county police force, or of one of the principal city forces; such positions were reserved for 'gentlemen'. Similarly the Russian peasant colonel could not rise to command élite regiments or serve on the General Staff, where aristocratic birth and bearing remained crucial. Of course even at the centre of government tasks varied greatly. In some areas aristocrats clung on to their offices in the belief that their birth and education gave them special qualities. The diplomatic corps is the obvious example; even in republican France up until 1894 candidates for posts in the foreign service had to have a private income of 6,000 francs a year. Treasury departments, in contrast, were acknowledged as requiring rather different abilities and skills. □

Exercise   But what impact do you suppose the growth of state bureaucracies had on their 'openness'? ■

Specimen answer   The bigger the bureaucracies became, so the necessity emerged of offering posts to a wider variety of people. It simply was not possible for a small élite to staff the expansion even at the centre of government.

Discussion   Thus the expansion of the state can be said to have had a diluting effect on the traditional élites. Of course the new men drawn into the upper echelons of state administration were drawn from the well-educated classes; generally they were the sons of successful business and professional men. To take another example from republican France: if a young man wanted a good post in the ministries of finance or foreign affairs, it was in his interest to attend the *Ecole Libre des Sciences Politiques* which had something of a monopoly in preparing candidates for these ministries; but the *Ecole* was a fee-paying institution. However, the key question in all this is: were these new men actually 'diluting' the élites and making them more open? Or were they simply scrambling to be part of the old élite and ultimately helping the preservation of its values? □

Exercise   A final question for you to ponder in this section: the ideal bureaucracy is meant to act impartially, without arbitrariness or favour, but can you see the possibility of a different relationship between the chief state ministers and the chief state bureaucrats in the East and the West of Europe? ■

Specimen answer   There surely is a difference in that ministers in the West had some claim to being the elected representatives of the people and there was thus some separation between government and the professionals of the state bureaucracy. In the East, however, the ministers were appointed by the monarchs with no reference to the elected legislatures and the ministers had invariably risen through the ranks of the state servants, many of whom belonged to the nobility.

Discussion   Bureaucrats in both the East and West aspired to be apolitical, working in the national interest. But this division from 'politics' and perceptions of the 'national interest' varied considerably because of the constitutional systems. In the West state bureaucrats were responsible to politicians and, while they may have disapproved of certain politicians (and even been obstructive), it was these politicians who defined the current national interest. In the East, in contrast, governments claimed to be working in the 'national interest' and above the squabbles of elected party politicians in the assemblies. Arguably this state of affairs in the East helped to confirm the élites' views of elected assemblies (they feared what would happen if such irresponsible individuals ever acquired the reins of government) and confirmed the elected deputies' suspicions of governing élites as dismissive of the popular will. □

3   ECONOMY

First read Roberts, pp.11–36 on population, economy and world trade, and pp.78–89 on imperial expansion. Appendices 1 and 2 (pp.488–9) give you some useful statistical information on population and industrial development. Read these sections now.

Economic structure

Exercise   Study Tables 2.4 and 2.5 and answer the following questions.

1   What does Table 2.4 suggest about agriculture in contrast to industry in Germany before World War I?

2   What does Table 2.5 suggest about the pattern of landholding in pre-war Europe? ■

Table 2.4   Agriculture and industry in Germany

	Agriculture	*Industry*
(a) Contribution to Gross National Product in percent		
1848–54	45.2	21.6
1870–74	37.0	31.7
1895–99	30.8	38.6
1910–13	23.4	44.6
(b) Share of active employed force in percent		
1849–58	54.6	25.2
1878–79	49.1	29.1
1895–99	40.0	35.7
1910–13	35.1	37.9
(c) Absolute numbers employed (000s)		
1849	8,298	3,491
1871	8,541	5,017
1900	9,754	9,525
1913	10,701	11,720

(From Robert G. Moeller, ed., *Peasants and Lords in Modern Germany*, 1986, p.4)

Table 2.5   Landholdings before World War I

		Less than 5 hectares[1]		5 to 100 hectares		100 hectares and over	
		% of landholders	% of area	% of landholders	% of area	% of landholders	% of area
Austria	(1902)	71.8	–	27.5	–	0.7	49.5
France	(1892)[2]	85.1	27.0	12.5	30.0	2.4	43.0
Germany	(1907)	74.2	15.3	25.4	61.5	0.4	23.2
Hungary	(1895)	72.6	16.1	26.9	42.1	0.5	41.8

[1] A hectare is roughly two and a half acres.
[2] The figures for France are for less than 10 hectares, 10–100 and 100 and over.
(From Jerome Blum, *The End of the Old Order in Europe*, 1978, p.437)

Specimen answers   1   Table 2.4 suggests three things:

(a) agriculture's contribution to Germany's Gross National Product was declining, though it remained significant;

(b) agriculture and industry had roughly changed places in their contributions in the half century before the war;

(c) agriculture's share of the labour force was declining, though the numbers employed continued to rise.

2   Table 2.5 shows clearly the great discrepancies in landholding in pre-war Europe; a very large percentage of landowners held tiny parcels of land, while a very small percentage of landowners held vast estates. □

Analyses of economic development before World War I often used to ignore the importance of agriculture and the very large numbers engaged in agricultural work. Perhaps we are rather too inclined to generalize from perceptions of our own country's past, but Britain was, as in many other instances, quite exceptional in having, by the middle of the nineteenth century, a majority of its population living in urban areas and as few as one-fifth of its labour force engaged in agriculture. By the beginning of the twentieth century Germany was the only other major power with a higher percentage of its labour force engaged in industry rather than agriculture; as you can see from Table 2.4, this change had been very gradual and the preponderance of the industrial labour force was still only marginal.

There were great variations in agricultural practice between different countries and between the different regions of different countries. Britain, as in so many other ways, was the exception in European agriculture: first, it had been geared overwhelmingly to cash cropping since the eighteenth century; second, it had no peasant proprietors, indeed it had no real peasantry. In the western and southern regions of European Russia private, capitalist farming was becoming dominant with thousands of peasants working as hired labourers; in central Russia, in contrast, peasants worked more or less permanently on allotments assigned to them by their commune. In Italy it was only the four northern provinces of Piedmont, Lombardy, Veneto and Emilia-Romagna which underwent an agricultural revolution partly to meet the needs of the industrial triangle whose fixed points were Milan, Genoa and Turin. These cities, where industry boomed at the beginning of the twentieth century, helped to absorb the surplus peasant population of the northern provinces; the cities of the south offered no similar haven and peasants of the backward south migrated in their thousands to the USA and Argentina. Generally speaking it was only on the larger holdings producing cash crops where agricultural improvements and new techniques were liable to be found. In the Balkans agriculture was backward, regardless of whether the land was held principally in large estates, as in Romania, or by small peasant farmers, as in Bulgaria. It was only during the second half of the nineteenth century that the Balkan populations began moving from semi-nomadic, livestock breeding communities, to more settled communities practising arable, mainly grain, farming. This change occurred with only a very gradual introduction of natural fertilizers and hardly any mechanization. Nor were all of the developments in agriculture at the end of the nineteenth and beginning of the twentieth centuries in what might be considered as 'progressive' directions. In France, for example, there were positive efforts to revive sharecropping between 1880 and 1914. Sharecropping involved a division between the sharecropper, who provided the labour, and the landowner, who provided the land and probably also the working capital, animals, machines and fertilizers. The resulting produce was divided, generally, on a fifty-fifty basis. The reason for this revival appears to have been less for economic and more for social benefits; sharecropping was seen as a way to keep the peasantry quiescent and to maintain the authority of the existing ruling classes.

Throughout Europe the larger agricultural enterprises were hit by the depression which lasted from the mid-1870s to the mid-1890s. The depression led to a decrease in the amount of cultivated land in Europe; the expanding population benefited from the ability of American farmers to produce food which, in spite of transportation costs, was cheaper than that grown in Europe. The depression also encouraged the exodus from the countryside to the towns where wage rates were generally higher. Farmers found themselves having to pay higher wages to keep workers on the land and having to rely more and more on seasonal migrant labour. There were enormous seasonal movements of agricultural labour during the period 1890 to 1914; German farmers recruited labourers, often female, from Russian Poland and Austrian Galicia; French farmers attracted labour from Italy, Spain and Belgium. Sometimes these seasonal agricultural labourers could also be seasonal industrial workers: Frenchmen in the Limousin moved from porcelain factories to wood cutting according to season; many workers in the large textile enterprises of Moscow province shifted seasonally from factory to land and back.

In other ways the division between factory worker and rural worker was blurred. While more and more of the rural immigrants to cities were staying and becoming urbanized, it was possible to find immigrant ghettos where peasants continued to speak in their local dialect and had their eyes and thoughts firmly fixed on what the French call their *pays natal* (literally 'native country'). Many of the Italian peasants who migrated across the Atlantic sent money back to their relatives, or brought money back to buy land of their own. In the decades before World War I over 300 million *lire* came to Italy each year by this route enabling it to finance a large trade deficit and to import machinery and raw materials for its new industries. In Germany, while as a result of the depression the amount of land under cultivation declined, the number of very small landholdings actually increased. Often small parcels of land were purchased by men who lived in villages but travelled daily to work in the towns. Many of the smallholdings shown in Table 2.5 were such properties; 32.7 per cent of all landholdings in Germany in 1907 were less than half of a hectare, and such a holding could only be used to supplement a wage earned elsewhere. But rural dwellers did not have to travel into the towns to participate in small-scale industry; outwork, the system by which merchants from towns delivered raw materials to a peasant family and returned to collect finished goods and pay for them, could still be found in many parts of Europe.

In Russia, in the decades immediately before the war, more than half of the industrial plant and more than half of the labour force were to be found outside the cities. The principal reason for this seems to have been that employers found labour to be much cheaper in the countryside, and they were prepared to invest in massive complexes which combined a variety of processes under one roof (metal working with mechanical construction, for example) as well as providing machine repair shops, workers' housing, hospitals, schools, abattoirs and bakeries. Moreover, until the reforms of 1906 the institutions of the commune tended to tie the peasant to his village. The Russian peasant had been freed by the Emancipation of 1861, but in most instances land had not been transferred to the individual peasant who worked it but to the commune in which he lived. Since from time to time the commune might decide on a redistribution of land among the villagers, peasants were reluctant to break their close links with their village in case they lost out in such a redistribution. Also the commune could be reluctant to let a peasant leave, and could prevent him from doing so, as this could mean the loss of one of those responsible for sharing its financial burdens. The reforms of 1906, introduced partly to reduce peasant discontent and disorder, weakened the hold of the commune and enabled the peasant to consolidate personal holdings; a government-financed bank was also established to help peasants purchase more land, and technical assistance was offered in farming. These reforms, together with the fostering of migration to Siberia, increased the amount of Russian land under the plough, improved agricultural yields, and helped in the formation of a class of well-to-do peasants. In 1914 about 80 per cent of the population continued to derive their livelihood from the land.

Table 2.6   Industrial establishments in France

	Percentage of total number	
	1896	*1906*
Less than 10 employees	62	59
11–100 employees	17	16
Over 100 employees	21	25

(From Roger Price, *An Economic History of Modern France 1730–1914*, 1981, p.233)

Table 2.7   Percentage of employees by trade and size of establishment in France 1906

	1–10	*11–100*	*Over 100*
	Number of employees		
Food	62	25	13
Wood	58.5	32	9.9
Building and public works	47	40	13
Quarries	28	46	26
Printing and allied trades	18	45	37
Metal processing	27	27	47
Glass	14	30	56
Chemicals	11	36	53
Paper	7	34	59
Textiles	9	22	69

(Based on information in François Caron, *An Economic History of Modern France*, 1979, pp.164–5)

Exercise   What do Tables 2.6 and 2.7 indicate about the balance of large and small firms in France before 1914? ■

Specimen answer   Table 2.6 points to a gradual increase in the number of large enterprises in France, though it also shows that a high percentage of small firms remained. The figures in Table 2.7 indicate, predictably perhaps, that different kinds of establishments had different sizes of workforce, and that what might be considered as the establishments benefiting from machine production and industrial development had larger numbers of people within the same plant.

Discussion   Developments of this sort were common throughout Europe, though the actual figures for different countries vary considerably. Generally speaking the largest concerns involved heavy industry and combined the mining of coal and iron with steelmaking, processing and machine construction; several giant concerns of this kind were to be found dotted throughout Europe, notably the works of Krupp at Essen in the Ruhr and those of Skoda in Bohemia.

But it would be wrong to think of this stage of European industrialization simply witnessing more and more people working in bigger and bigger factories. Industry required services, which meant, for example, more transport work, more dock labour; the latter was generally casual work often with men from the poorer areas of seaports and cities hired by the day. Furthermore many industrial concerns required skilled labour and not simply machine minders. The new motor vehicle industry offers a good example. The motor car was initially seen literally as a 'horseless carriage', a luxury vehicle for the well-to-do crafted by skilled artisans. France had become Europe's premier car and lorry maker by 1914, yet there was no mechanized production line and each worker built, on average, a mere 1.6 cars a year. However car makers like Louis Renault in France and Giovanni Agnelli of Fiat in Italy were looking to Henry Ford's developing production system in the United States. While modern, mass car production remained a long way off, by 1914 Fiat in particular was on the point of producing cheaper cars in much greater numbers. □

The patterns of economic development

It is easy to make the assumption that because Britain experienced the first industrial revolution in the late eighteenth and early nineteenth centuries, it provided the model of industrialization which other countries had to follow. However, the more that economic historians probe the processes of industrialization, the clearer it becomes that there are a variety of routes which can be taken. You ought to be clear, from your reading of Roberts and from the previous section, that there were considerable variations in the extent of industrialization in the European states in 1914: some of these states can be termed 'advanced' while others were 'backward'; and even within the states there were major differences. Some German historians have written of the *Gefälle* or gradient in various aspects of Europe's economic and social life. Industrialization had begun, and by 1914 had its strongest grip in the north-west of Europe: Britain, the Ruhr, the north-east of France and Belgium; the further east and south that you travelled, the more sparse the pockets of industrialization became. In the Balkans industrialization could scarcely be found at all; here small-scale handicraft industry was the norm, but agriculture dominated the national economies.

In many respects the Austro-Hungarian Empire demonstrates the *Gefälle* in miniature. Cisleithania (that is the German dominated western half of the empire, generally known as Austria) had been on a level with Germany as an industrial power until the latter's rapid spurt ahead in the last third of the nineteenth century. The Czech lands were the most industrialized area of Cisleithania; by 1900 they were more heavily industrialized than France, and in 1914 the area around Prague and Brno and along the northern frontier with Germany was one of the most advanced industrial regions of Europe. In contrast the Hungarian-dominated half of the empire (Transleithania), together with the northern and southern extremities, remained overwhelmingly agricultural. The two economies became interdependent: Hungary, like its Balkan neighbours, switched from stockbreeding to grain production, most of which went to Austria, and it imported a high percentage of its manufactured goods from Austria. Arguably this relationship gave Hungary a higher income than it would have enjoyed on its own but, at the same time, it checked its industrial development. Such industrialization as there was in Hungary in 1914 was primarily the result of Austrian investment seeking an area where labour was cheaper.

Investment is crucial to industrial development; but investment cannot generate industrialization on its own – entrepreneurs, competent managers, a pool of relatively mobile labour to work new processes in new centres, and markets for the new products, are all also required. In the early instances of industrialization from the late eighteenth to the early nineteenth centuries, these elements were, to some degree, all present within those few societies which began an industrialization process. Alexander Gerschenkron, one of the dominant figures in economic history in the late twentieth century, argued that economically 'backward' societies had to find substitutes for these elements in their own processes of industrialization. Gerschenkron's work concentrated principally, but by no means exclusively, on Russia, which experienced a massive spurt in economic development during the 1890s. He argued that:

1   The state provided investment for industry 'substituting' for the lack of investment from private entrepreneurs and banks. The money for this investment was raised by foreign loans and by heavy taxes (to pay off the loans) imposed on the peasantry. This taxation was largely indirect on cloth, sugar, tallow, tea, vodka and yeast, but it had the additional, money-raising attribute of forcing the peasantry to sell more grain which could then be exported; the money raised from grain exports was used to pay for valuable imports.

2   The state imposed prohibitive tariffs on foreign manufactured goods and, where there was no internal market for Russian products the state itself 'substituted' as a buyer, particularly through its programme of railway building – hence the concentration of Russian industry on iron, steel and machinery.

3   The most modern manufacturing equipment was purchased (principally from Germany) and this 'substituted' for the shortage of skilled labour.

4   The very large industrial plants which were a prominent feature of Russian industrialization 'substituted' for the lack of managerial and entrepreneurial talent in the empire; massive plants enabled the small amount of such talent as was available to be spread to supervise industry.

Exercise   1   What growing national institution figures prominently in the substitution process as described above?

2   In the light of the previous discussion, try to generalize about the role of this institution in the industrialization process, and particularly in the industrial catching-up processes of backward economies at the end of the nineteenth and beginning of the twentieth centuries. ∎

Specimen answers   1   The state.

2   In Gerschenkron's model the state plays a significant role in the catching-up process, and a much larger role than in the first industrial nations. But we have already noted the increasing power of the state in the decades before World War I and its greater involvement in the lives and behaviour of its people. Gerschenkron's insistence on the importance of the state in forcing backward economies to catch up is probably right, but even in advanced economies the state was expanding its involvement. ☐

During the early and middle years of the nineteenth century the dominant ideology of leading merchants and industrialists had been free trade. Since most of these merchants and industrialists were British, and since Britain's industrial superiority enabled them to undercut their competitors, it might be argued that free trade was in their own, and consequently in Britain's own, interest. But free trade was also the aspiration of many European liberals, particularly where, for example in early nineteenth-century Germany, they saw internal customs barriers inhibiting trade. However the industrialization of powers other than Britain meant competition and this, together with depression (notably that during the 1870s), brought strident demands for protection. In his study of technological and economic development across this period, David Landes described the emergence of a kind of Darwinian perception:

> The shift from monopoly to competition was probably the most important single factor in setting the mood for European industrial and commercial enterprise. Economic growth was now also economic struggle – struggle that served to separate the strong from the weak, to discourage some and toughen others, to favour the new, hungry nations at the expense of the old. Optimism about a future of indefinite progress gave way to uncertainty and a sense of agony, in the classical meaning of the word.
>
> (D. S. Landes, *The Unbound Prometheus*, 1969, pp.240–1)

Within nations, and sometimes across national frontiers, industrialists organized cartels to protect prices and to control output. These were notable in the chemicals, coal and iron industries, and particularly successful in Germany where the cartels could enforce their contracts in the courts. The Rhenish-Westphalian Coal Syndicate, established in 1893, became the model for many; the German Steel Producers Association set up eleven years later involved eighty-nine firms and controlled virtually all of Germany's basic steel production. Yet even before the development of these cartels the states of Europe had begun taking action to protect and foster their native industries; most of the leading states made significant moves towards the rebuilding of high tariff walls during the 1870s.

I have said little about the British economy so far in this section. From being the 'workshop of the world' for much of the nineteenth century, Britain was, by the closing decades, lagging behind several of its economic competitors. It could no longer depend on industrial superiority to undercut and outsell competitors, and rivals were aware of Britain's vulnerability to their own, in many instances, technically superior industries. During the mid-1890s there was a particularly pained outcry in Britain against 'unfair' German trading in markets like Australia, South America and China, which the British had tended to regard as a private preserve; even the United Kingdom itself was being infiltrated by a variety of cheap German goods – the government had actually purchased Bavarian pencils! Yet the British economy was continuing to expand and, while dropping behind competitors in some industries, Britain was strengthening its position as a service centre for the international economy. It enjoyed massive invisible earnings from insurance, from shipping – its merchant fleet was the largest in the world – from overseas investments, and from banking. Britain had gone on the gold standard, by which the monetary unit of a country is kept at the value of a fixed weight of gold, in 1821. France, Germany and the United States had followed suit during the 1870s, and from the mid-1890s the gold standard was an international system involving most of the world's great trading nations and establishing an international medium of exchange and unit of account. The London money market, with its long experience of the gold standard, became the focal point of international finance and exchange.

Economic rivalry, investment and imperialism

The idea that economic rivalries fed into the tensions which culminated in World War I has a long pedigree. Among Europeans before the war and immediately afterwards the popularity of Darwinian perspectives fostered the notion of economic growth as economic struggle in which the strong would survive and prosper while the weakest went to the wall. One of the problems with this perspective, however, is that it tends to slot economic development into traditional national boxes, and while governments had economic policies trade and investment were, very largely, the work of private economic actors whose main concern was profit and who did not necessarily put national self-interest or national borders into their equations when it came to investment.

Table 2.8   Geographical distribution of foreign investments, 1914 (in millions of dollars to the nearest $50 million)

	From: UK	France	Germany	USA	Others	Total
To: Europe	1,050 (9%)	4,700 (39%)	2,550 (21%)	700 (6%)	3,000 (25%)	12,000 (100%)
Latin America	3,700 (42%)	1,600 (18%)	900 (10%)	1,650 (18%)	1,050 (12%)	8,900 (100%)
Oceania	2,200 (96%)	100 (4%)	–	–	–	2,300 (100%)
Asia	3,550 (50%)	1,250 (18%)	700 (10%)	250 (3%)	1,350 (19%)	7,100 (100%)
Africa	2,450 (60%)	900 (22%)	500 (12%)	–	200 (6%)	4,050 (100%)
North America	7,050 (63%)	500 (4%)	1,150 (10%)	900 (8%)	1,500 (15%)	11,100 (100%)
Total	19,950	9,050	5,800	3,500	7,100	

(Adapted from William Woodruff, 'The emergence of an international economy 1700–1914', in Carlo M. Cipolla, ed. *The Fontana Economic History of Europe: The Emergence of Industrial Societies* – 2, 1973, pp.710–11)

Exercise   Look at Table 2.8 which gives the amount and distribution of foreign investment on the eve of World War I, and answer the following questions:

1   Who was the principal creditor nation in 1914?

2   Where were the principle investments of the European powers in 1914?

3   Does anything surprise you about this pattern of investment? ■

Specimen Answers   1   Britain. I made this point in the preceding section, but the figures here flesh the matter out.

2   Most investment was in Europe and North America.

3   Perhaps there is nothing surprising about the pattern of investment shown here. Money was being put into economies which were growing and from which good returns might be expected. □

From your reading of Roberts you will recall the imperial expansion at the end of the nineteenth and beginning of the twentieth centuries. The 'grab for Africa' and the acquisition of other colonies by European powers has often been seen as having economic motives with colonial conquest driven by the demands of capitalist imperialism. This may have been the case (though there is considerable debate over the matter), but, as the table makes clear, for all its size there was remarkably little investment in Africa by Europeans. Some imperialists and colonisers may have seen the new territories as sources of raw materials and potential markets. Some businessmen were sympathetic to imperial aspirations. A group of powerful German industrialists, for example, were involved in attempts to acquire a Central African Empire, and when these aspirations appeared thwarted in the two years before 1914, the notion of a German-dominated *Mitteleuropa* became popular, though there was no single perception of what *Mitteleuropa* might be – something more than a customs union certainly – or how far it might stretch – to the Balkans? To Bagdad? Yet these were essentially political ideas with the economics scarcely thought through, and the fact of the matter was that such profits as came from newly acquired African colonies were tiny. When it came down to it, the serious incidents which arose out of imperial rivalries, from the Franco-British confrontation at Fashoda in 1898 through to the two Moroccan crises involving Germany in the decade before World War I, had their origins in national pride and imperial aspirations rather than economic rivalry.

A whole series of points might be developed about the patterns of European investment on the eve of war:

1   Overseas investment followed a variety of different routes. While much British export capital was invested in infrastructure (railways, ports and harbours, and other public utilities), French investors generally favoured fixed interest government securities. The French invested heavily in Russia. Between 1899 and 1914 never less than one quarter of the total French overseas investment was held in Russian Bonds and just over a quarter of the Tsarist government's debt was owed to French investors. German money played a significant role in Italian industrialization. The Banca Commerciale and the Credito Italiano were both established in the 1890s with German and Swiss money and German management; they supplied both long-term credit and much of the entrepreneurship behind northern Italy's industrial spurt.

2   At times governments became concerned about such investment. In the decade before the war the French foreign office began leaning on French banks to ensure that loans to overseas governments were tied to purchases from French manufacturers. Concerned for the demands of the domestic economy, the German government sought to discourage German investment for a time. Moreover, when German capital did go abroad it was often tied closely to German exports and native industry as, for example, in the case of Siemens electrical and tramway companies in Austria, Italy and Latin America. Yet, in the end, national governments could not dictate to bankers and investors about where they should put their money.

3   Industrial cartels were much more prominent and successful in Germany than they were in Britain and France, and, as you can see from Table 2.8, it was Britain and France which were the largest exporters of capital. In contrast, though not shown in the table, Italy and Russian were major *importers* of capital.

Exercise   Look again to Table 2.8. The principal investor was Britain, but where was the bulk of her investment? And in what ways did she differ from her nearest rivals in this respect? ■

Specimen answer   The bulk of British investment was in North America. The bulk of French and German investment was in Europe. □

Discussion   In the period immediately before the war France and Germany were increasingly looking for investment opportunities outside Europe. But you need to be aware of the inter-relationship between Britain's investments and her main imports before World War I since there was a significant strategic pay-off during the war.

Since the eighteenth century Britain had been an overall importer of grain. On the eve of war grain accounted for over 17 per cent of the weight of cargoes landed in Britain, and the shipping of grain was a major task of the British merchant marine. The shipbuilding industry owed much of its prosperity to the trade in grain; and so too did much of the profit from the British investments in overseas infrastructures. In *The First World War: An Agrarian Interpretation* (1989), Avner Offer argues that, in the years before the war, 'Britain's large food deficit acted as a pump for the world's commerce' (p.85) since her overseas' investments not only created the capacity for moving staple exports but also required that Britain buy these staples for the investments to pay off. Offer argues further that in the decade before the war British planners, aware of their vulnerability as an import economy, developed a strategy of 'Atlantic Orientation' based on the power of the English speaking-world to ensure the country's wartime food supply from Canada, the United States and Australia. Germany was becoming similarly dependent on food imports and, between 1900 and 1914, there was a vast increase in such from primary producers in South America. But Germany had neither the merchant nor war fleet capability to maintain such imports during the war, nor the ethnic and investment links upon which Britain was able to build. □

4   NATIONALISM

First read Roberts, pp.8–11, on the complexity of nationality, and pp.49–51 on nationalism and racism.

Contemporary beliefs

Nationalism, the nation and the nation state were all concepts current in Europe in 1914, and concepts of considerable weight in political perceptions and discourse. Nationalism had been a liberal aspiration during the first half of the nineteenth century in Europe as many young, intellectual romantics, loosely allied with business and professional men, sought the unification of their countries under progressive governments and with assemblies elected, generally, on a property-based franchise. The high point of this romantic nationalism had been the revolutions of 1848, often referred to as the 'springtime of peoples'; ultimately reaction triumphed over the revolution, yet the nationalist aspirations of 'forty-eighters' in Germany and Italy were, at least to some extent, achieved by unification later in the century. Towards the end of the nineteenth century much of the liberalism in nationalist ideals was giving way to notions drawing on Darwin's theory of natural selection: nation states were engaged in a struggle for national survival and the weakest would go to the wall. In the previous section I quoted David Landes on how economic growth was being perceived, increasingly, in terms of struggle with the weakest going under. In 1898 Lord Salisbury, the British Prime Minister, could tell a meeting of the Primrose League:

> You may roughly divide the nations of all the world as the living and the dying ... the living nations will gradually encroach on the territory of the dying and the seeds and causes of conflict among civilized nations will gradually appear.
>
> (Quoted in Z. S. Steiner, *Britain and the Origins of the First World War,* 1977, p.16)

For General Friedrich von Bernhardi such causes were well apparent when he published *Deutschland und der nächste Krieg* in 1912 declaring: 'Strong, healthy, and flourishing nations increase in numbers. From a given moment they require a continual *expansion* of their frontiers, they require new territory for the accommodation of their surplus population.' Furthermore when a state renounced the extension of its power and recoiled from a war necessary for expansion, then it was doomed. In Russia, General A. A. Kireyev argued similarly: 'Of course we, like any powerful nation, strive to expand our territory, our "legitimate" moral, economic and political influence. This is the order of things.'

   If successful nations were to fight in order to expand and survive, then much depended on the manhood of the nation. Again Darwin's ideas were of significance in the way that many contemporaries thought about the issue. Some believed that they could pinpoint the perfect race; the poet, philosopher and musician Houston Stewart Chamberlain, for example, published two volumes of mumbo-jumbo in 1899 called *Foundations of the Nineteenth Century* in which he pointed to the Teutons as the master race. Other work was more serious if, to modern eyes, equally wrong-headed. Many contemporary observers, notably in Britain, France and Germany, were concerned about preserving their nation/ race (and the two were often intertwined) from what they perceived as an alarming, degeneration. In France such observers looked anxiously at the declining birth rate; the disaster of 1870 seemed to have been the herald of an overall national decline. Adopting medical metaphors, and drawing on contemporary medical research and theories, they feared that their nation was grievously ill; alcohol, pornography and prostitution were both symptoms of, and contributory elements to, the disease. Some of the more extreme commentators on the situation went so far as to link feminist demands for equality and emancipation with it. According to Henri Thulié, writing in 1885,

> [Emancipation] will mark the beginning of the woman without breasts, for ... it will not be long before these organs begin to disappear ... Soon, [women] will no longer want to be mothers; this will mean the organization of abortion, and, for the prudent, the triumph of lesbianism. Once sterility has been organised and *les politiciennes* [i.e. female politicians] refuse to offer their wombs for maternity, we will be obliged to have women whose special function is reproduction so as to prevent the race from being extinguished while *les citoyennes* [i.e. female citizens] engage in politics and homosexuality.
>
> (Quoted in A.-L. Shapiro, *Breaking the Codes. Female Criminality in Fin-de-Siècle Paris*, 1996, p.197)

The remedy was seen to be re-emphasis on women's role in the domestic sphere and the promotion of masculine health and vigour through sporting organizations, many of which were established in the years immediately before 1914.

Similar British fears about the decline of the national stock had originated in the concern over the squalor of the urban slums and the 'residuum' which inhabited them. The poor level of fitness among recruits during the Boer War aggravated these concerns. Proposals were made to segregate the residuum who were accused of benefiting unduly from welfare provision; 'the survival of the most fertile' was, according to one eugenicist, in danger of replacing 'the survival of the fittest'. The decade before 1914 saw a campaign organized by some concerned gentlemen, politicians and military officers for the regeneration of British 'national efficiency'. Again, as in France, demands that women be allowed to participate fully in public life were seen as contributing to the problem. 'Women', declared Hargrave Adam in 1914,

> have continued, and do still continue, to drift farther and farther from the important and responsible duties of maternity, to embark on the, to her, demoralising activities of the prominent and sordid affairs of the world. As a result she is becoming, either directly or indirectly, more and more concerned in crime.
>
> (Quoted in L. Zedner, *Women, Crime, and Custody in Victorian England*, 1991, pp.70–1)

From about 1900 there was concern in Germany about a gradual decline in the birth rate, though it was as yet less marked than in Britain and far less marked than in France. The concern was stimulated by Germany's rapid industrialization and urbanization; and, as elsewhere, pornography, prostitution and what were seen as varieties of abnormal sexuality, were seen as both contributing to, and as manifestations of, national degeneracy. The issue exploded in a series of homosexual scandals involving a number of the Kaiser's entourage in the first decade of the twentieth century. Concerns about degeneracy led the state to clamp down on the traffic in erotic materials and to co-operate with purity crusaders. German feminist leaders dropped their support for abortion and added to their list of reasons for women having the vote the fact that they bore and bred the nation's soldiers. Professor J. D. Steakley, among others, has suggested that the homosexual scandals led the Kaiser, his entourage, and many military officers to adopt aggressive public postures of military manliness, though for obvious reasons precise evidence of a causal connection is difficult to prove in such instances.

Two cartoons from the period of the Eulenburg scandal: (a) from Jugend *(published in Munich, 28 October 1907) portrays Philipp, Prince zu Eulenburg-Hertenfeld (the central figure in the affair) on the left, and General Kuno, Count von Moltke, the military commander of Berlin, on the right. The caption is 'New Prussian coat-of-arms (Liebenberg design)' and the banner reads 'My soul, my little old man, my one and only cuddly-bear' (Photo: Bildarchiv Preussischer Kulturbesitz); (b) from* Der wahre Jacob *(published in Stuttgart, 26 November 1907) portrays the commander of the élite Garde du Corps, Lieutenant General Wilhelm, Count von Hohenau, about to inspect his regiment. Von Hohenau, a relative of the Kaiser, had recently been charged with homosexual behaviour. The title of the cartoon is 'Military innovations', and the caption reads: 'Since when is an about-turn order given for inspections?''At your service, Captain. Beg to report that the division is being inspected today by Count Hohenau.' (Photo: Professor J. D. Steakley, University of Wisconsin-Madison).*

(a)

Nationalism and the European states

When discussing nationalism and the state in Europe before 1914 it is possible to differentiate broadly between three different kinds of state:

- those, like Britain and France, which were long established and had long recognized an identity between nation and state;

- those, like Germany and Italy, which were newly created on the basis of such an identity; and

- the multinational empires, Austria-Hungary, Russia and, on the south-eastern fringe of Europe, Turkey.

As ever, of course, this division requires qualification and, furthermore, it must be remembered that as well as minority nations existing within these nation states and empires, there were also the Pan-German and Pan-Slav movements which claimed to speak respectively for two racial types and transcended the boundaries of the states.

In Britain and France the unity of the nation and the state was perceived as going back hundreds of years. Welsh independence had disappeared at the close of the middle ages. The Scottish crown had been united with that of England in 1603; the parliaments were united in 1707. English occupation and plantation had a long history in Ireland; the parliaments were united in 1801. Both Scotland and Wales had relatively homogeneous cultures akin to that of England, but while Scottish authors (writing in English) found a ready market within their own country (as well as England), and while the use of the Welsh language was both vigorous and expanding, Scots and Welsh nationalists made little headway during the nineteenth century. Furthermore the pluralistic 'British' political culture had strong roots in Scotland and Wales as well as in the dominant England. Ireland, however, was another matter. Here there were two cultures: that of the Ascendancy, and that of the native Irish. Throughout the nineteenth century Irish nationalists had created problems for governments at Westminster; and proposals for Home Rule created problems with both Ulstermen and English members of parliament. The British government's Home Rule proposal of 1914 created a situation in which civil war threatened in Ireland, with some British army officers threatening mutiny, and the Conservative Party, in opposition, publicly sympathizing with recalcitrant Ulstermen and mutinous soldiers.

In a book published at Quimper in Brittany in 1914, Camille Le Mercier d'Erm made a comparison of vanquished nations: alongside Bohemians, Irish, Finns and Poles he placed the central 'nation' of his book – the Bretons. The gradual moulding of Auvergnats, Bretons, Gascons and others into Frenchmen between 1870 and 1914 is the theme of Eugen Weber's influential *Peasants into Frenchmen*. Weber argues that this transformation was effected through new roads and railways, which aided migration and the spread of 'national' news, through schooling, and through conscription. Critics have challenged the extent of peasant separateness and urged that Weber puts too much emphasis on the south and west of France, where primitive peasant farming had remained strong and where French was often the second, rarely spoken, language. Yet Weber marshals considerable evidence to support his case. One issue which he does not raise, yet which adds weight to his conclusions about a general lack of French sentiment among peasants in 1870, is the relatively small number of natives of Alsace and Lorraine who opted to move to France when their provinces became part of the German Empire following the Franco-Prussian war – but then again, it could be argued that moving is scarcely an option for peasants. These provinces became the focus for the aggressive rhetoric of French nationalists, yet only 12.5 per cent of the population decided to keep their French nationality when the provinces were transferred to German control, and these were overwhelmingly from the urbanized middle class, probably the most 'French' of the population. About one and half million people remained under German control, and in 1914 Imperial Germany got nearly its full quota of reservists from Alsace Lorraine.

Of course, as far as the rulers of Germany were concerned the provinces won in 1870–71 were German anyway; the peasant population spoke a variant of German, and the German Empire was a federation of twenty-five other 'states'. The united, Prussian-dominated Germany emerged out of customs unions and war; it was not the result of a mass, nationalist movement, but essentially of Prussian power. Italy, the other 'new nation', was similarly not brought into being by a mass, national movement; the military intervention of the state of Piedmont had been crucial. It was only after unification that Kaiser Wilhelm I and Bismarck, and Victor Emmanuel II and Cavour became, respectively, German and Italian national heroes.

The problem of transforming peasants into Italians was even greater than that portrayed by Weber for France. The difficulty was especially great in the south, or *mezzogiorno*, where farming was primitive, landholding was often semi-feudal, and banditry was rife. A strong military presence had to be maintained in the south to 'civilize' as well as contribute to the Italianization of the peasantry.

The situation in Italy was further complicated by the relations between the unified state and the Catholic Church. The last military action in the unification process had been the storming of Rome by the Italian army in 1870. This left the Pope, self-styled as 'the prisoner in the Vatican', confined to a tiny enclave within the capital city. The Pope refused to have any dealings with the new state, and instructed all Catholics to abstain from Italian politics. Such Catholic political groupings as were established were closely watched by the Italian police. Governments elsewhere in Europe were also suspicious of the supra-national authority of the Catholic Church. Bismarck waged a campaign against it in Prussia during the 1870s. In France the vertical divisions of society between Catholic and republican was often more apparent than any horizontal division between classes.

In the years before the outbreak of World War I both Italy and Germany had politicians and publicists who argued that expansion and colonial possessions were imperative to demonstrate their status as great powers. Both participated in the scramble for Africa, and this brought them into conflict with other powers. The Italian seizure of Tripolitania (part of present-day Libya) involved war against Turkey and confrontation with Austria-Hungary. Wilhelm II's adventures in Morocco brought confrontation with Britain and France. The question is, however, was there something about the 'newness' of the two new nation states which, in itself, prompted a heightened or more aggressive nationalism, or was this 'newness' simply an opportunity for politicians to play to the gallery (possibly to divert popular attention from internal difficulties) and to urge that their nation had as much right to empire as any of their longer established rivals? In Germany such political arguments interacted with an intellectual tradition extolling the superiority of the state as, in the words of the philosopher Hegel, 'the realized ethical idea', and, in the words of the historian Treitschke, 'the highest conception in the wider community of man'.

The identification of state and nation was rather more difficult in the empires to the east and south of Europe. (Given that the bulk of its remaining imperial possessions were outside Europe I shall not look at Turkey in any detail. However, it is important to be aware that the disintegration of Turkey's empire in Europe had resulted in the formation of the Balkan states and of different Habsburg protectorates.)

Exercise   Study Tables 2.9, 2.10 and 2.11 and look at map 2 in the *Maps Booklet.* Then answer the following questions:

1   Which, statistically, were the identifiable national majorities within the two empires?

2   Comparing the ethnic compositions in the two empires, which 'nationality' do you find listed as existing in Russia but, curiously, not in Austria-Hungary? ■

Table 2.9   National composition of the Romanov Empire

'Russia' (1897)

Nationality	Population (in millions)	% of total
Russian	55.7	44.3
Ukrainian	22.4	17.8
Polish	7.9	6.3
Belorussian	5.9	4.7
Jewish	5.1	4.0
German	1.8	1.4
Lithuanian	1.7	1.3
Latvian	1.4	1.2
Mordvin	1.0	0.9
Estonian	1.0	0.9
Other Finno-Ugrian	1.5	1.5
Others (mostly Asiatic)	16.4	15.9
Total	122.7	99.9

The Grand Duchy of Finland (1890)

Nationality	Population	% of total
Finnish	2,048,500	86.1
Swedish	322,500	13.5
Russian & Germans	9,000	0.4
Total	2,380,000	100.0

(From Raymond Pearson, *National Minorities in Eastern Europe, 1848–1945,* 1983, p.69)

Table 2.10   National composition of Austria-Hungary in 1910

Nationality	Population (in millions)	% of total
Germans	12.0	23.9
Magyars	10.0	20.2
Czechs	6.5	12.6
Poles	5.0	10.0
Ruthenes	4.0	7.9
Rumanians	3.25	6.4
Croats	2.5	5.3
Slovaks	2.0	3.8
Serbs	2.0	3.8
Slovenes	1.25	2.6
Others	2.9	3.5
Total	51.4	100.0

(From Pearson, *National Minorities*, 1983, p.46)

Table 2.11   Religious affiliation in Austria-Hungary in 1910

Religion	Population (in millions)	% of total
Roman Catholic (including Uniate i.e. those employing Orthodox liturgy under Papal Licence)	39.0	77.2
Protestant	4.5	8.9
Orthodox	4.5	8.9
Jewish	2.1	3.9
Muslim	0.5	1.1
Total	50.6	99.8

(From Pearson, *National Minorities*, 1983, p.46)

Specimen answers

1 In the Russian part of the Romanov Empire the largest national group (though not an absolute majority) were the Russians; there was an overwhelming majority of Finns in the Grand Duchy of Finland. In Austria-Hungary the two largest national groups, Germans and Magyars, almost made up the same percentage as Russians in Russia, but taking the empire as a whole there was no single dominant nationality.

2 Jews appeared as a nationality in the Romanov Empire; they appeared as religious group in the Habsburg Empire. □

Discussion   Eastern European censuses taken at the end of the nineteenth and beginning of the twentieth centuries, need to be treated with caution, though the 1897 Tsarist census has a high reputation among demographers. Given the ethnic complexities of these empires the census was fraught with political problems. It is probable that local bureaucrats in the Romanov Empire falsified their returns to curry favour with their political superiors; they knew what the government wanted to see. Moreover this problem was exacerbated by the fact that the criterion employed by the census was language, not 'nationality' as such. Russian was the language of the empire and it was spoken by many educated non-Russians. It is possible that the number of Russians was, in the end, over-estimated by as much as 5 per cent. In Hungary, where the dominant Magyars were eager to boost their numbers, there was official pressure to this end and here Jews, not unwillingly, were often registered as Magyars. Religious affiliation was often central to national identity: the Poles clung to their Catholicism, and the Catholic hierarchy saw in this the opportunity of extending its influence among the Polish people; the Finns clung to their Lutheran Church as another way of maintaining their separate identity from Orthodox Russians; in Bohemia the Czechs focused on their national Hussite Church to maintain their distance from the Catholic Germans; the Slovaks remained loyally Catholic to distance themselves from Protestant Magyars. Bosnian nationalists increasingly looked to Islam.

The rulers of Russia did not perceive their state as a multinational empire and the census of 1897 appears to have given them something of a shock. The result of the census was to boost the policy of 'Russification'. This policy was not an all-out attack on every national minority, nor was it conducted with the same degree of intensity against every ethnic group. The worst sufferers were the Jews, who, by legislation, were generally confined to particular geographical areas in the west (in Poland). They were commonly made scapegoats for local or national problems; some pogroms were spontaneous, but the Tsarist government also sought to cash in on popular antisemitism. Yet in spite of the violence directed against them, and the financial incentives to convert, the Jewish communities within the Russian Empire clung steadfastly to their religion and their cultural heritage; and while thousands emigrated, notably to the United States, many more remained.

The Finns, who had enjoyed a considerable degree of autonomy, were subjected to a vigorous Russification policy and to tighter control by the Tsarist government in St Petersburg. Moves among Finnish activists for a Greater Finland comprising Estonians and other Baltic peoples were the cause of this action; the Tsarist government feared such moves could lead to a call for independence. The Polish lands of the empire had been cowed, militarily, following the abortive rising of 1863. Russification was not enforced with any great rigour in the years before 1914 and the campaigns for a modicum of Polish autonomy were very low key.

The groups that were most consistently 'Russified' were the Russians' fellow Slavs – the Belorussians and the Ukrainians. Russification was accompanied by the suppression of the Uniate Church, which had many adherents in the Ukraine. By 1914 the Belorussians were almost entirely integrated. The Russification of the Ukrainians was rather less successful; the Ukrainian language was kept alive by the peasantry and, in intellectual circles, almost single-handedly, by the nationalist poet Taras Shevchenko. In 1914 political nationalism was non-existent in the Ukraine itself, but it could be found among the Ruthenes, a Ukrainian sub-group, in the Galician province of Austria.

The *Ausgleich* had divided power between the two largest national groups in the Austro-Hungarian Empire. The Magyars dominated governmental, administrative and teaching posts in Transleithania. While they had been liberal in the early years of the division of power, they became more and more oppressive towards their subject nationalities: the Slovaks had their centre of cultural nationalism closed in 1875 for 'promoting Pan-Slavism'; the Croats had their degree of autonomy revoked in the 1880s. Yet the Magyars had the more difficult national elements in Transleithania, and their problems were aggravated by the progressive disintegration of the Turkish Empire in the Balkans with the consequent creation of independent states whose respective majority ethnic groups were minorities under Magyar rule.

After the Germans the largest ethnic group in Cisleithania was the Czechs. They enjoyed a strong cultural revival in the second half of the nineteenth century; the performance of Smetana's *Ma Vlast* (My Country) in Prague in 1882 became a great patriotic rally. But it can be argued that Czech nationalism was disarmed politically by prosperity; the Czechs' economic development outstripped the rest of the empire and few could see much point in agitating for autonomy, let alone independence, with the possibility of losing the considerable benefits that they were enjoying. Similarly the Polish gentry in Galicia, while always conscious of their nationality, were quiescent and content with a degree of autonomy and economic prosperity. Yet all was by no means peaceful in Cisleithania. In parts of Bohemia ethnic antagonism gave rise to two independent workers' parties, one Czech, one German, and both calling themselves 'national socialist'.

Minorities in the east and south-east of Europe engendered suspicion and fear; they also gave governments the opportunity to foster difficulties for their neighbours. There was friction between Italy and Austria-Hungary over the petty persecution of the Italian minority remaining within the empire; German and Italian students came to blows at the University of Innsbruck in 1902. The government in Vienna supported anti-Italian Slavs on the Adriatic littoral. The government in Rome encouraged outposts of Italian culture and influence in Trieste and the Southern Tyrol (or the Alto-Adige as the Italians called it). The government in Vienna allowed Ukrainian nationalists to organize in Galicia; at the same time it was alarmed by Pan-Slavism which appeared to be a Russian conspiracy to threaten the internal security of the empire – Slavs, after all, constituted over 40 per cent of the Habsburg's ethnic groups. □

In all of the states of Europe before 1914 there were political parties which played the nationalist card. Some of these parties were explicitly nationalist in their names; though none of these so-called 'nationalist' parties was ever significant enough to dominate the government of any particular state. Probably the most extreme of these parties was the Union of Russian People, established in 1905 and determined to preserve all things Russian – notably the God-given autocracy of the Tsar – from the encroachments of liberalism, capitalist industry and other such 'selfish' interests which had originated in the West. Initially the URP drew support from all classes, though its increasingly populist stance lost it support from many of the more well-to-do. It became involved in street violence, economic boycotts, strike breaking and political assassination; paramilitary gangs were organized. Historians in both the USA and USSR have referred to it as Europe's first 'fascist' party.

Besides the nationalist parties there were also nationalist pressure groups like the German Navy League (*Flottenverein*) and Colonial Association (*Kolonial-gesellschaft*) and the British Navy League and its more extreme offshoot, the Imperial Maritime League. Like the nationalist parties, such organizations were small but exceedingly vocal. In the same kind of category were the Pan-Germans and the Pan-Slavs. The *Alldeutscher Verband* (Pan-German League) never had more than 18,000 members and its monthly magazine, at its peak, had a circulation of only 5,000. Its members had high, and varied, hopes: the unification of all members of the German 'race', a German-dominated Europe, the expansion of the German people into living-space (*Lebensraum*). Such ideas slotted in conveniently with the dream of the German-dominated *Mitteleuropa*. The League encompassed the aspirations of many German liberals in 1848, but the aggressive, expansionist aims of many of its members spread in a more sinister direction. Pan-Slavs had similar aspirations; their focal point was Russia which was seen as becoming the liberator and protector of southern Slavs from Muslim Turkey, and the guardian of all Slavs against contamination and/or domination by the peoples of the west. The Pan-Slavs looked forward eagerly to what they perceived as the imminent, and permanent, disintegration of the Turkish and the Habsburg empires. By 1914, however, Pan-Slavism was losing out to the nationalism of the new Balkan states, and the Bulgarians certainly did not perceive Russia as a protector. At the same time many of the south Slavs of the Austro-Hungarian monarchy were inspired by the idea of a large, united Slav state – Yugoslavia.

But if these pressure groups and nationalist parties remained small, nationalist ideas permeated much of the press and many popular books. In Britain the emerging popular press was influential in the 'We want eight and we won't wait' campaign for dreadnoughts; the proprietor of the *Daily Mail*, Alfred Harmsworth, allegedly claimed that the average Briton liked 'a good hate', and his paper offered the opportunity. Children's books carried patriotic messages (see the title page of *Jeanne d'Arc*) and so, very often, did lessons in school. Such books and lessons were not necessarily directed against other nations or people; more commonly authors and teachers appear to have been eager to inculcate a love of the motherland. Two questions arise here:

1   To what extent was this inculcation of patriotic and nationalist sentiment deliberate policy on the part of governments to undermine internationalism (particularly socialist internationalism) and to ensure loyal soldiers in the event of war?

2   To what extent was this inculcation (whether deliberate or not) successful?

Both of these questions are enormous and all I can do here is to offer a few fundamental observations. Certainly, in all the powers of Europe before World War I there were men in positions of power and influence who were worried about the internal stability of their country. The idea of thwarting socialist parties, which threatened revolution, by inculcating a love of country appealed to such men. There were also fears of external threats and war between nations,

JEANNE D'ARC

PAR

M. BOUTET DE MONVEL

E. PLON, NOURRIT & Cⁱᵉ, IMPRIMEURS-ÉDITEURS, 10, RUE GARANCIÈRE, PARIS

GRAVURE DF DUCOURTIOUX ET HUILLARD   ENCRES DE LA MAISON CH. LORILLEUX ET Cⁱᵉ

Title page of M. Boutet de Monvel's Jeanne d'Arc *(1893) (Pierpoint Morgan Library, New York)*

which underlined the different governments' needs for large, loyal armies. But it is a considerable jump to argue that because some men in positions of power perceived such needs, that they were able to mount successful campaigns of nationalist indoctrination to satisfy them. In those countries where teachers were civil servants, teachers could be instructed to teach love of the motherland. In France, for example, teachers were expected to teach 'not just for the love of art or science ... but for the love of France'. History and geography were central here; Ernest Lavisse's *La Première Année d'Histoire de France* was published in 1884 as a school textbook, and the children reading it were told that through it 'you will learn what you owe your Fathers, and why your first duty is to love above all else your homeland (*la patrie*) – that is the land of your Fathers'. In Germany, the army, dissatisfied with the products of schools and concerned about socialist propaganda, set about educating conscripts with lectures designed 'to create and reinforce a sense of national identity'. The question, of course, is how many individuals were converted by such education? Clearly some young Germans went into the army from socialist party (SPD) families, experienced this indoctrination while with the colours, returned to their SPD homes, voted SPD in elections and supported their 'country' (like the bulk of the SPD) when war came. It is naïve to believe that nationalist or patriotic propaganda in schools, in the army and through the media, had nothing upon which to build. I have already noted the 'nationalist socialist' workers' parties in Bohemia. When national frontiers have divided peoples, the image that one group of workers has had of their counterparts in another country has not often been noted for its generosity. Nationalism (and nineteenth-century imperialism) received multi-class support, and it has therefore been tempting for some of those who believe that the working class should have combined and acted in its own interest, rather than in the so-called 'national' interest, to argue that the working class was misled and/or manipulated. This was the line taken by Lenin in his study of imperialism.

> The receipt of high monopoly profits by the capitalists in one of the numerous branches of industry, in one of the numerous countries, etc., makes it economically possible for them to bribe certain sections of the workers, and for a time a fairly considerable minority of them, and win them to the side of the bourgeoisie of a given industry or given nation against all the others. The intensification of antagonisms between imperialist nations for the division of the world increases this urge.
>
> (Lenin, *Imperialism*, 1964 edn, p.301)

The difficulty with such an argument is that by identifying the problem (why didn't the working class oppose imperialism and/or war-mongering and the outbreak of World War I? And why didn't it act in its own interest?) it is suggesting that there is such a thing as objective class interest; it also provides an answer to the initial problem (manipulation) which absolves the unfortunate, misguided working class and blames the unscrupulous ruling class.

This leads to a final problem: naturally governments, the leaders of certain pressure groups and parties, and some press barons, hoped that the masses would respond to particular issues in particular ways. Yet it would be very difficult to show a conspiracy among these disparate groups within one nation to manipulate the majority of that nation. In some countries, and Germany seems the obvious example, the ruling élite commonly adopted an aggressive nationalist stance, yet their policies did not follow wholeheartedly the demands of the different nationalist pressure groups or the aspirations of the Pan-Germans. Politicians were much more commonly pragmatists, who would play the nationalist card when it suited them but who might also be wary of extremist nationalist groupings. Politicians could also be sharply divided among themselves on issues regarding the 'nation', and this was not always simply a division between socialist parties and others as is revealed by the division over Irish Home Rule in the British Parliament in 1914.

5   SUMMING UP AND LOOKING AHEAD

This unit has been largely introductory and has ranged widely over a variety of issues. Of course, you cannot expect to remember everything that has been discussed, so let me finish by picking up on some of the topics and outlining some of the questions that you ought to be thinking about as the course progresses.

(a) I have discussed the expansion of the state in Europe in the period before World War I; by 'state' I mean that collectivity of institutions which act on behalf of, and which include, government and central administration, but which can also carry on regardless of government. The state in 1914 was in many ways far more powerful and better organized than it had been a hundred, even fifty years before. How far did this enable better mobilization for war – not just in the summer of 1914 but throughout the conflict? And how far did war foster even more powerful and better organized states?

(b) Roberts points to a convenient categorization of the European states in 1914 under the headings constitutional and autocratic (though 'authoritarian states' might be better in the latter case). Did the constitutional or authoritarian structure of a state (or empire) have an influence on how it performed in the conflict? Did the pressures of war mean that the constitutional states became more authoritarian? Was there also a move in the other direction?

(c) There were divisions in all of the states and empires on the eve of World War I, but how far did the war ameliorate or exacerbate these? Why did people see themselves as German (or British, or French, subjects of the Habsburg Empire, etc.) before seeing themselves as working class (or as Catholic, or Jewish, or Czech, Irish, Polish, etc.)? And at what point for some did alternative identities become more important?

(d) The war broke out in the summer of 1914, just before the harvest. The schoolmaster of Lalley, in the *département* of the Isère in south-west France, reported that:

... the appearance of our village changed. Out of a population of less than 400 inhabitants, 53 young men, the young, the strong, those who shouldered the weight of the work in the fields had gone. A grim calm, a sense of the void descended. Haymaking had not yet finished; the harvest beckoned imperiously, with a south wind drying the corn and turning the oats yellow. And so, people came to each other's aid. There were signs of remarkable dedication: young lads aged 15 to 20, young girls taking off their aprons and putting aside the needlework they had begun, resolutely took up their sickles and lent a hand to the women left alone with their young children.

(Quoted in Jean-Jacques Becker, *The Great War and the French People*, 1985, pp.15–16)

The mutual assistance and dedication which struck the schoolmaster of Lalley has become part of national mythologies of twentieth-century total war, but it was not something apparent to every commentator. The shortage of labour brought about by the conflict gave new economic muscle to those who remained at home and within days of the outbreak of the war there were complaints of French farm labourers demanding double or triple the usual daily wage. Similar complaints were made by industrial employers across Europe as the war dragged on. Were such demands by peasants and workers an example of selfishness, or the result of new wartime pressures? Or, perhaps both? And as for the women now taking over men's work – a feature of all the societies engaged in the war – was this really a step in the direction of liberation? Or did the war help to re-emphasize the separate spheres of men and women? War, after all, was a political and public activity. Fighting was reserved for men, and while men were away at the front fulfilling their public role, women's place could be re-emphasized as the private one of carer for the wounded, 'angel of the hearth', and producer and nurturer of future warriors.

References

Becker, Jean-Jacques (1985) *The Great War and the French People*, Berg.

Blackbourn, D. and Eley, G. (1984) *The Peculiarities of German History*, Oxford.

Blum, J. (1978) *The End of the Old Order in Europe*, Princeton University Press.

Caron, F. (1979) *An Economic History of Modern France*, Methuen.

Chickering, R. (1998) *Imperial Germany and the Great War*, Cambridge University Press.

Jünger, E. (1929) *The Storm of Steel*, Chatto and Windus.

Landes, D. S. (1969) *The Unbound Prometheus: Technological Change and Industrial Development in Western Europe from 1750 to the Present*, Cambridge University Press.

Moeller, R. G. (ed.) (1986) *Peasants and Lords in Modern Germany*, Allen and Unwin.

Offer, A. (1989) *The First World War: An Agrarian Interpretation*, Clarendon Press.

Parker, P. (1987) *The Old Lie: The Great War and the Public School Ethos*, Constable.

Pearson, R. (1983) *National Minorities in Eastern Europe, 1848–1945*, Macmillan.

Price, R. (1981) *An Economic History of Modern France 1730–1914*, Macmillan.

Shapiro, A.-L. (1996) *Breaking the Codes. Female Criminality in Fin-de-Siècle Paris*, Stanford University Press.

Steiner, Z. S. (1977) *Britain and the Origins of the First World War*, Macmillan.

Woodruff, W. (1973) 'The emergence of an international economy, 1700–1914' in Carlo Cipolla, ed. *The Fontana Economic History of Europe. The Emergence of Industrial Societies – 2*, Collins/Fontana.

Zedner, L. (1991) *Women, Crime, and Custody in Victorian England*, Clarendon Press.

Unit 3 GENDER, CLASS AND CULTURE

ARTHUR MARWICK

Open University students of this unit will need to refer to:

Set book: J.M. Roberts, *Europe 1880–1945*, Longman, 2000

Primary Sources 1: World War I, eds Arthur Marwick and Wendy Simpson, Open University, 2000

Course Reader: *Total War and Historical Change: Europe 1914–1955*, eds Clive Emsley, Arthur Marwick and Wendy Simpson, Open University Press, 2000

Secondary Sources: Jane Rendall, ' "Uneven developments": women's history, feminist history and gender history in Great Britain'.

AIMS

1   To help you towards an understanding of the way in which the words 'gender', 'class', and 'culture' are used, and to help you towards an appreciation that the very way in which these words are used can affect the answers given to questions about the nature of social and cultural change and the relationship of war to it.

2   To develop further the comparison and contrast between the different European countries on the eve of war by examining two phenomena which are intrinsically international in character, that is to say, social structure (or 'class') and culture ('high' and 'popular') with the overall purpose of further clearing the ground for our discussion of how far, if at all, World War I brought social and cultural change.

1   GENDER AND CLASS

Non-metaphysical source-based history and 'women's history, feminist history and gender history'

'Non-metaphysical, source-based history' is what, perhaps with a few occasional exceptions, we, in common with most universities, teach in our programme of history courses. In a moment, I shall be asking you to read the article in your *Secondary Sources*, ' "Uneven developments": women's history, feminist history and gender history in Great Britain' by Jane Rendall. Professor Rendall is rather critical of 'conservative historians', writers, presumably, of non-metaphysical history and of whom, in her view, I am no doubt one. In *my* view, conservative historians are most obviously distinguished by a reluctance to think about what history is, and how and why one does it, and to set out systematically its basic principles: in their view, you learn about history simply by doing it, and you do it in the amateurish way which used to be typical of the posh universities. I have been arguing for a more systematic, a more reflexive, approach to history since the late 1960s. It has taken me forty years, but I reckon that I now have pretty clear and coherent ideas about how one should study history and what 'learning outcomes' (to use the current jargon) one can expect from studying history. Recalling what I said in Unit 1 with reference to aim 5(b), I want to add a few more words on these matters here. From them you will realize when you come to read Rendall's excellent article, that there are parts of it with which I am not in agreement. But I shall simply be using the article as a source of important information and shall not engage in any critical analysis of it.

Because sources, and historians, are fallible, because history engages with matters of value and emotion, because historians are affected by career aspirations and human vanity, completely objective history is an impossibility. But there is a crucial difference between history which strives to be objective, and history which makes no such effort. Historians, as citizens, are fully entitled to their political views, but, as historians, they should do everything they possibly can to suppress them. As in the natural sciences, historians learn from the work of their predecessors and colleagues. History is a co-operative enterprise in which the most recent work is likely to be an advance on earlier work. But there is a difference between work which has been reflected on and argued over by historians, qualified and corrected, and work which is mainly the product of the latest fashion. There is a difference between work based on sources which have been carefully analysed and evaluated, and work which is simply based on metaphysical speculation, or drawn from the theories of such alleged authorities as Marx or Foucault. There is a difference between work which is very precise in its use of language, and work which depends upon rhetoric, metaphor, playing games with language.

It is good that we have the Rendall article among our *Secondary Sources*, and I want you now to read it carefully.

Some issues to think about

In my young days lecturers could always raise a laugh with some such remark as: 'I am now going to discuss the population of Edinburgh, broken down by age and sex'. 'Sex' was the word used in government statistics when distinguishing between males and females. 'Gender', originally a purely grammatical term, as Rendall points out, came into use after feminists and post-structuralists (remember Aim 5 of Unit 1) in the 1970s began to argue that differences between men and women were as much 'culturally constructed' ('gender') as biologically determined ('sex'). 'Gender studies' have become very fashionable and, as Rendall remarks, involve discussion of the 'construction' of 'masculinity' as well as that of 'femininity'. Obviously such studies do have relevance to our course in that, in all the countries we are studying waging war was thought to be a 'masculine' activity.

If you have been following a course of studies in history, you will have had many warnings about how important words often have two or more meanings. This is now the case with 'gender'. Because 'sex' now usually signifies 'sexual intercourse' even the British government (since 1995) has begun to use the word 'gender' in its statistical tables. There is thus now a potential ambiguity every time the word 'gender' is used. Does it refer to biologically determined differences, which no one can contest, or does it refer to 'culturally constructed' differences – an extremely contentious matter?

Even when gender is firmly defined as relating to biologically determined differences, the evidence is, I would argue, that, for the period we are studying, and the issues we are concerned with, such differences were of less importance than differences of class. I am convinced that, with regard to the major issues of total war and social change, the differences in the circumstances of working-class men and working-class women, are less significant than those between working-class women and middle-class women. That is an opinion you are fully entitled to disagree with (of course, in war, men of all classes always suffer higher death rates than women of all classes).

Of course, the question of the effects of war (if any) on, as I put it, 'the role and status of women' – already touched on in Unit 1 – is an exceedingly important one, and figures prominently in this course (I return to it in Unit 4) as it did in the predecessor course, A318. I remain attached to the view that the constantly expanding methods of the historian[1] are perfectly adequate, and unpersuaded of the need for a 'new history' which focuses on rhetoric and discourse and insists on the 'cultural construction of reality'. Who, I always ask, does the 'constructing'? As explained in Unit 1, I do regard ideological circumstances, along with structural and institutional ones, as crucial in determining what change is possible. As always, you are free to disagree with me (and the Rendall article is there to provide you with ammunition if you want to use it). BUT, since this is a course in history (not cultural theory, not literary studies) you must first show that you have mastered the historical methodology which our history courses exemplify. A history course provides a training in writing essays based on evidence; we want to discourage you from writing essays based on metaphysical speculation. We want you, in your own reading, to be able to distinguish between books and articles based on careful analysis of the sources (primary and secondary) and ones which simply rely on unsupported assertions.

Rendall gives a very lucid account of the emergence of 'gender history' (and, I would be the first to recognize, does stress the importance of studying the widest possible range of primary source materials). She also lists the many other important areas into which history has expanded over the past 30 years or so: demography, history of the family, literacy and education, witchcraft, deviance and criminality. One cannot but welcome the way history continues to take in new topics and address new problems; but one must always be on the lookout for historians (affected, as I have said, by career aspirations) making exaggerated claims for their own particular new specialism. One must recognize that debates over 'votes for women', to which I introduced you in Unit 1, have rather disappeared from recent books and articles; so too have debates over class[2]. But even if historians have got bored with these topics, that does not necessarily mean that they are no longer of central importance; it certainly does not mean that they should be kept from you, studying this course on twentieth-century European history. Gender certainly is a very fashionable topic at the moment, in part because of the accelerating numbers of women coming into the historical profession.

Let me repeat that this course gives a great deal of attention to the question of the changing role and status of women (in fact you could probably get about one fifth of your marks by answering questions related to that topic). But I remain very sceptical about the notion of 'gender history', and most certainly about 'gender studies'. My reasons are:

1   The ambiguity of the term 'gender' – in fact as the Rendall article indicates, those who talk about 'gender history' automatically *assume* that gender is culturally constructed;

[1] As explained in 'The Introduction to History' from the Level One course *The Humanities: An Introduction* and in our Level Two courses A220, *Princes and Peoples: France and the British Isles 1620–1714* and A221, *State, Economy and Nation in Nineteenth-Century Europe*.

[2] Discussed in focus point 8 of AA303, *Understanding Comparative History: Britain and America From 1760*.

2   This assumption, as the Rendall article also makes clear, is also bound up with political belief, in socialism and feminism and/or acceptance of Marxist and Foucauldian theory;

3   In fact, theories about gender and sexuality must be tested against the latest scientific work in sociobiology and genetic psychology, an aspect totally ignored by the gender theorists, and one which we, as historians, do not have the time to get into;

4   This course of ours would become quite hopelessly overloaded if we did not keep to the main topics which have already been outlined in Unit 1 – however interesting in themselves gender issues may be, they can easily become distractions: my own view is that the subordination of women throughout the period we are studying is obvious enough, and does not require reiteration, and that what is really interesting is how women by 1955 had managed to break out of many of the restrictions which caged them in 1914.

However, it is right that I should mention some recent works relating to gender which, perhaps at summer school, you might wish to have a look at for yourself. Women's history, gender history, whatever we call it, has done invaluable service in drawing attention to the roles and achievements of women in the past, previously obscured (though never totally neglected, as Rendall points out). Particularly important to record, in my view, is the managerial role within the family occupied by women (but then that, most gender theorists would say, is just women conforming to a male-imposed stereotype). Also very important is the attention that has been focused on previously neglected work by women writers, artists, etc. So let me mention Catherine O'Brien's 1996 article 'Beyond the can[n]on; French women's response to the First World War'. In this course we direct your attention to only one French novel of the First World War, *Under Fire* by Henri Barbusse; and the only poem we study is by a British male, Wilfred Owen. I don't think it is wrong that one should give some priority to men who fought in this most horrific of wars, but, undoubtedly, the O'Brien article is of great interest in telling us of some of the French women who were writing novels and poems at the time: if you are interested in war and the arts you may well want to read this article some time. (Though I would recommend that you avoid puns and plays on words like that in the title: precision and explicitness should be a characteristic of historical discourse.)

Rendall, absolutely correctly, refers to important work on the previously neglected Lancashire female cotton workers. More recently, the American scholar Kathleen Canning has done a massive study of female textile workers in Germany. I have enormous admiration for the vast amount of primary research undertaken, and some sympathy with some of the ideas being expressed, but I cannot commend her way of writing to you as a model to be followed in your own TMAs. At the end of the book Canning claims that 'inherent in' the distinction between men at work and women in the home

were particular perceptions of the female body. Depicting the expansion of female factory employment as a 'temporary pathological symptom of the social body', the narratives of social reform implicated the female body centrally in the making of the social and identified the 'female organism' as a key site of intervention for both the regulatory and tutelary regimes of state social policy.

> (K. Canning, *Languages of Labor and Gender: Female Factory Work in Germany 1850–1914*, 1996, p.326)

For those of you unfamiliar with this type of postmodernist discourse, I could translate for you, though I feel bound to point out that there seems to me no sound evidence for believing in such metaphysical categories as 'narratives of social reform' or 'key sites of intervention'. I hope you will write your TMAs in such a way that no translations are needed.

In June of 1984 the entire issue of the *American Historical Review* was devoted to 'women's history'. This venture was repeated in vol. 95, no. 4 of October 1990. There were two articles of apparent relevance to our concerns in this course: Susan Pedersen, 'Gender, welfare, and citizenship in Britain during the Great War', and Seth Koven and Sonya Mitchel, 'Womanly duties: maternalist politics and the origins of welfare states in France, Germany, Great Britain, and the United States, 1880–1920'. First thing to say about these two articles is that they flatly contradict each other: this is perfectly appropriate to academic work, but does suggest some caution in believing that there is a coherent discipline of gender history which will bring us all great enlightenment. They are full of valuable new detail, which is the function of the traditional learned article, and they are full of the fashionable, but I would say specious claims, that by focusing on 'gender' they are doing something strikingly new.

Pedersen writes: 'By 1917, the pressures of war had led the state to accept the introduction of benefits for soldiers' wives on an unprecedented scale' (p. 1000). I couldn't have put it better myself. Pedersen sees this development as underpinning the 'economic and sexual rights over wives and children' of the husband. In the sense that it was in keeping with the prevailing ideology of the time I would certainly agree. However, Pedersen decrees that this represents a 'shift toward a gender-based model of welfare provision'. This is nonsense in that there certainly wasn't a non-gender-based model in existence before the war. She then complains that this alleged 'shift' was

> unwittingly aided by the responses of feminists and Labour women, who misunderstood the administrative logic underlying the allowance system but welcomed its practical effects ...

> (Ibid., p.1000)

Later Pedersen adds that feminists during and after World War I, 'allowed a dangerous analogy between the national obligations of the soldier and those of fertile women ...' (p.1004). Pedersen is against the emphasis on women's fertility and on the funding of maternalism.

Koven and Mitchel take an exactly opposite view, singling out maternalism as the central issue which both enabled women to play a part in shaping welfare states, and which brought concrete benefits to women:

> Without maternalist politics, welfare states would surely have been less responsible to the needs of women and children, for maternalists raised issues – or highlighted them in specific ways – that seldom occurred to male politicians.

> (S. Koven and S. Mitchel, 'Womanly duties', 1990, p.1107)

Earlier Koven and Mitchel write: 'Maternalism was perhaps the most significant thread tying together the disparate women's movements in Germany from the 1880s till the 1920s' (ibid., p.1089).

Again the detail is fascinating and invaluable, but one really cannot say that this aspect of developing welfare states, and women's role in it, has been utterly neglected in the past. And the fact is, that having made big claims for women's role, the authors have to keep qualifying these claims. They admit that where women's movements were strongest, for example in the USA, the legislative effects were least. One sentence perhaps gives away more than is realized:

> The Paris branch of the Maternité Mutuelle, like so many other maternal and child welfare agencies in France, was established by a man but relied on a large corps of well-to-do patronesses to implement its directives.
>
> (Ibid., p.1100)

Still, this is a well-balanced and illuminating article – if scarcely a revolutionary one – neatly comparative:

> Once established, the German and French state welfare systems, through direct programs and indirect subsidies, offered more and better resources than did those of the United States and Britain. However, French and German women generally had much less control than did their British and American counterparts over the formulation and administration of policy.
>
> (Ibid., p.1106)

I commend both articles to you, but in all honesty do not feel that they compel me to alter what I want to say in Book 2 about the war and welfare reform.

Another book with the kind of tricksy title that I strongly caution you against is *Behind the Lines: Gender and the Two World Wars* (1987), edited by M. Higgonet, with Jane Jensen, Sonya Mitchel and Margaret Collins-Weitz where there is a pun on 'lines' as both lines of writing and military front lines. This book has an introductory chapter which simply *asserts* that relationships between the male and female are permanently in the form of the intertwined strands of the double helix, with the female in the subordinate position. This is history by metaphor, which I must advise against. Metaphor may illustrate something, it never explains it. Explanation, if I dare say it again, must be based on evidence. There is, let me be clear about this, much to be learned from writing on women's history and on gender: you can always look out for the propagandist elements, if they are there, and discount them. But it simply cannot be denied – and, indeed, this is recognized by Rendall – that much writing in that area is bound up with postmodernist assumptions.

With reference to our course, Susan Kingsley Kent, *Making Peace: The Reconstruction of Gender in Interwar Britain* sounds promising. How promising, I will leave you to decide when you have read this paragraph from the end of the opening chapter:

> It will be evident that I am drawing on poststructuralist theories of language in my analysis of war, gender, sexuality, and feminism. Such an approach starts with the assumption that every language act produces meanings that exceed the author's intention; that all texts create multiple meanings; that these meanings may contradict one another; and that interpretation of the text does not recover a 'true' or original meaning but is itself a part of the play

of signification that produces textuality. I do not wish to imply that the meanings I have attributed to the texts, particularly the literary ones, quoted throughout this book, are the only ones, but rather to argue that the texts produce at least the meanings I identify. For the purposes of my analysis, the more complex work of textuality has been left unaddressed.

(Susan Kingsley Kent, *Making Peace: The Reconstruction of Gender in Interwar Britain*, 1993, p.11)

Let me just say, with regard to your training towards the learning outcomes we specify, that I believe the two main contentions here are, at least with respect to the study of history, false. If you are very careful and precise in your use of language you will say exactly what you mean, no more, no less: you will not 'exceed' your 'intention'. When you analyse a text, or a primary source, as we prefer to say, you will, provided you have a precise topic in mind, and provided you follow the techniques we are inducting you into, be able to extract firmly definable information relevant to that topic.

I do not think you should get diverted into studies presenting the argument that we would not have wars if it were not for culturally-constructed masculinity. However, if you are interested there are three titles in the 'Further reading' section.

2   SOCIAL STRUCTURE AND SOCIAL GROUPS

The language of class

Students, we know from experience, are not particularly keen on discussion of the different possible meanings of such words as 'class'. Why can't we just settle for one set of simple definitions and get on with it? There are a number of reasons which I shall list here.

1   Historians, whose books and articles you will be reading, do in fact use the word 'class' in different ways, and it is important that you should look out for this and be aware of the implications of the different usages.

2   Some writers slide from one meaning to another without seeming to notice: it is impossible to develop a logical argument if the words one uses keep changing in meaning.

3   Each country, and we are studying several in this course, has its own language of class: we have to be very careful that in using an English translation we don't in fact distort the original meaning. For example, in Germany people sometimes speak of the *Mittelstand*, which literally means 'middle estate', where in ordinary English usage we would probably say middle class, or perhaps lower-middle class (we'd have to go back to the eighteenth or early nineteenth century to find such a phrase as 'middling estate'). Does this matter? Well, I think we do have to look at the issue quite closely before deciding that it does or that it doesn't. In France, ordinary people quite readily use the term 'bourgeoisie', though in a variety of ways and with a variety of qualifying adjectives; in Germany there is the

analogous word *Bürgertum*, a more general word than *Mittelstand*, and one which is sometimes rendered in English as 'middle class' and sometimes as 'bourgeoisie'. The British – academic sociologists and historians and political propagandists apart – do not normally use the word 'bourgeoisie'. When discussing France and Britain, should we use 'middle class' throughout, or 'bourgeoisie' throughout, or should we conclude that while we have a middle class, France has a bourgeoisie? But if so, what is the difference? These are all matters which have to be looked at, particularly if we are going to make comparative evaluations as to whether World War I had a greater or lesser effect on the class structure of France or Germany than it had on that of Britain.

4   The particular language used will usually relate to a specific theory about the nature of class. How one thinks about class may affect the answers one gives to particular historical questions relating to class. In this course, we have a special concern with establishing how, if at all, European societies were changed by World War I. Very important questions to answer are: Were class structures changed? Did the working class become more powerful or, say, more unified? What happened to the upper class? What happened to the middle class? As you can see immediately, how we define these terms, or whether we accept their legitimacy in the first place, will shape our answers to such questions.

As I don't want to continue to deal in abstractions, I am going now to give you a very striking concrete example. The major work by a German historian, Jürgen Kocka, concerning the effects of World War I on Germany is (to give the title of the English translation) *Facing Total War*. In discussing 'the situation in 1914' Kocka spends a good deal of time establishing the position, status and outlook of the white-collar workers, craftsmen and small shop keepers, all regarded in the Germany of the time as belonging to the 'new *Mittelstand*'. Kocka concludes his long discussion thus ('dichotomous' means 'divided into two'):

> ... their objective class position was not the defining condition for the life-styles, expectations, organisation and political behaviour of either white-collar employees or of *Handwerker* [craftsmen] and *Kleinhändler* [small shopkeepers]. Both groups organised themselves predominantly against those whose class position they shared. Together they formed a significant factor by which Wilhelmine society was distinguished from a clearly marked, dichotomous class society.

(Jürgen Kocka, *Facing Total War*, 1984, p.84)

He then continues with a sentence which in effect sums up one of his major points about the effects of the war on German society:

> Encouraged by the State, they acted as a sort of padding, which somewhat muffled the growing class conflict. During the War, this padding was ripped apart.

(Ibid.)

Now I hope that you, without necessarily at this moment grasping the full implications of what Kocka is saying, can see how the manner in which he chooses to discuss class sets the framework for the answers he is going to give about the effects of the war, thus colouring, if not determining, the nature of these answers.

Exercise   What approach to class is Kocka taking? If possible, single out at least one phrase (I think there are certainly three, and perhaps four) that clearly indicates the approach being followed by Kocka. ■

Specimen answer   The key phrase, I think, is 'their objective class position'. The 'objective class
and discussion   positions' Kocka refers to are those of, on the one hand, the owners of capital who employ others, and, on the other, those who are employed and have no possession but their labour, the working class. I imagine that, if you answered that one at all, you said 'Marxist'. If you are at all puzzled you should refer back to Unit 1. (Kocka is also strongly influenced by Weber; in Unit 1 I suggested that Marx and Weber shared a common 'conflict model' of society.) But the main point for now is that you should see that being aware of the different usages of class *does* matter.

The same point is involved in the phrase 'those whose class position they shared'. 'Dichotomous class society' means society divided into two classes – again the capitalist class on one side, the working class on the other. Kocka seems to be suggesting that Germany was rather peculiar in departing from this model, but that the war helped to bring matters back to the true Marxist state of affairs. 'Class conflict' is, of course, central to the Marxist notion of how historical change takes place. □

The quotation I gave you from Kocka was rather brief and, standing on its own, perhaps not too easy to grasp. What he is saying is that the white-collar employees really ought to occupy one 'objective class position', whereas, in fact, both groups find themselves organizing against the other occupants of their own 'objective class position'.

There is one main view of class which starts from a theoretical position; and there is another approach which looks at the complexities that actually exist and draws its picture of class structure to conform as closely as is possible with these complexities without necessarily postulating 'class conflict' between 'objective classes'. I believe that Kocka exaggerates the distinction between the German *Mittelstand* and analogous groups in Britain, France and America. I believe that in all three countries something which can legitimately be called a new middle class or a lower middle class had come into being. However, do note again that the Germans themselves do not speak of a class here but, to repeat, of a middle estate. They speak of a working *class* because they perceive the workers as organizing themselves in support of their own interests in accordance with the Marxist model, whereas they see the *Mittelstand* as too heterogeneous and disunited to be called a class in the Marxist sense. Personally, belonging to the non-Marxist persuasion, I think the word 'class' is perfectly appropriate in the sense of designating a broad group which is distinguished by its particular position in the social hierarchy. But I leave you to decide where you stand. For the important thing is to understand the nature of the different approaches. Again, you could seek guidance from the Further reading section.

Social structure in 1914: did the aristocracy still govern?

In the previous section I was concerned mainly with illuminating the distinction between Marxist and non-Marxist approaches to class, but I wanted you also to learn a little about the nature of the *Mittelstand*. In this section I shall mainly be concerned with discussing the major question of who dominated Europe in the pre-war years, particularly with reference to Arno J. Mayer's contention that the old aristocracy still governed, a clarifying of this whole issue being essential if we are subsequently to be able to decide if, and how, World War I changed the distribution of power and wealth within societies. But it will be necessary to continue to be very self-conscious about the terms in which social structure is described and the meaning that is given to class.

If you are not already sufficiently familiar with them, I want you to read the opening pages of Arno Mayer's *The Persistence of the Old Regime* reprinted in the Course Reader (Chaper 2). But then, for the purposes of this next exercise, I want you to concentrate on, and read very carefully, the part of the Introduction beginning, 'In any case ...', and ending '... this towering hegemonic edifice'.

Exercise   Before reading carefully the passage from Mayer just identified, read the following questions, and then write down your answers once you have finished your reading.

1   What explanations, in this passage, does Mayer give for what he sees as the continuing predominance of the old aristocracy?

2   What phrases indicate that Mayer shares with Kocka Marxist views about 'history' and about 'classes'?

3   (This is the difficult one.) Taking it that the information communicated by Mayer is broadly accurate, can you see a different way, using the same information, of pinning down who formed the dominant class or classes in the Europe of 1914? ■

Specimen answers   1   The explanations Mayer gives are that:
and discussion

(a) Helped by the central position still maintained by the monarchy (except in France) the aristocratic, landed class continued to control the main organs of government, profiting from the money made by the bourgeoisie, but keeping the latter firmly in their place.

(b) It adapted and renewed itself by recruiting from below.

(c) Without abandoning their aristocratic ways, they adopted capitalist money-making methods.

(d) The bourgeoisie contributed substantially by itself accepting a subordinate place and seeking obsequiously to gain aristocratic honours and titles.

(e) The bourgeoisie 'denied themselves' and instead bolstered the existing aristocratic cultural and educational system.

2   The phrases I noted were:

'the *grande bourgeoisie* kept denying themselves by imitating and appro-priating the ways of the nobility in the hope of climbing into it'. This implies that the bourgeoisie *ought* to have done something else, that is to say, to fulfil their 'historical mission' of actually overthrowing the aristocracy.

'by disavowing themselves in order to court membership in the old establishment, the aristocratizing bourgeoisie impaired their own class formation and class consciousness and accepted and prolonged their subordinate place'. Again we have this implication that the bourgeoisie *ought* to act class consciously on behalf of their own bourgeois class, that they are somehow 'wrong' to aristocratize themselves, disavow their bourgeois nature, and impair the development of their class consciousness which *ought*, of course, to be directed to *overthrowing* the aristocracy.

'The bourgeois allowed themselves to be ensnared ... the self-abnegating bourgeois'. Again there is this implication of the bourgeoisie failing to do what they *ought* to do.

3   Mayer's formulation is that, partly because the aristocracy exploited its own assets and cunning, and partly because the bourgeoisie deferred to it, the aristocracy continued to be the dominant class.

There are at least two other formulations one could give entirely consistent with the information Mayer presents:

1   The more successful members of the bourgeoisie saw absolutely no point in trying to overthrow the aristocracy. It was much pleasanter, and much more fun, to actually join the aristocracy and enjoy all the delights of aristocratic life. Thus the dominant class in 1914 was in effect an amalgam of the older aristocracy and the most successful bourgeois elements. This would be my own preferred explanation – though of course we will have to recognize that the exact situation (the exact extent to which successful bourgeois families had penetrated the aristocracy) differed from country to country.

2   Alternatively, one could argue that, *while remaining a separate class*, the bourgeoisie were *sharing* power with the aristocracy. Some historians (including Roberts) would feel that Mayer exaggerates the power of the aristocracy, and underestimates that of the bourgeoisie. □

However, I want you to consider very seriously Mayer's main contention that an older aristocracy, linked in most cases with the monarchy, continued to be of predominating importance in the Europe of 1914. It should be said that the argument is not nearly as novel as Mayer claims. As early as 1963, Michael Thompson, in his *English Landed Aristocracy in the Nineteenth-Century*, pointed out that the landed aristocracy in Britain preserved their dominant position throughout the nineteenth century. So let us look at the writings of some other top historians, to see how far they confirm and how far they conflict with Mayer's basic contention.

I'll start with Norman Stone on Russia.

Exercise   Bearing the following three questions in mind, read the passage which follows from Norman Stone's *The Eastern Front*, and then write down answers.

1   Summarize briefly what Stone is saying and decide whether that conforms or not to Mayer's thesis of continuing aristocratic domination, or to one or other of the two alternative formulations given above.

2   Norman Stone is very definitely a non-Marxist historian and might well be described as a 'conservative' historian (though, as I have already remarked, I do not necessarily think that a historian's political views need affect his or her

writing of history). Norman Stone is also renowned for his cutting wit. Can you spot an example of this as well as examples of his non-Marxist, 'conservative' outlook?

3   Does 'gentry' mean the same thing as 'aristocracy?'

Tsarist Russia was not so uncomplicatedly a 'gentry-bourgeois State' as has sometimes been suggested. On the contrary, gentry figures provided much of the active opposition. Their economic basis had been weakened by emancipation of the serfs, and loss of two-thirds of their lands. Some found a way forward in the bureaucracy, or the *zemstva* [local assemblies]; some stayed on their lands, and tried without much success, to make a go of them; some went into active opposition to the State now, seemingly, leaving them little place. A large number of liberals and revolutionaries came from their ranks – a tradition promoted by the Decembrists [a radical political group] in 1825, and continued, in one form or another into the ranks of the Bolsheviks, of whose leaders at least Lenin and Chicherin could lay some claim to patrician status. It was useful to the State, in the circumstances, to recruit peasants whom it could then release against their masters; and such ex-peasants were frequently encountered in the army and the police, as Count Tolstoy discovered when the police raided his house, on suspicion that literacy was practised there.

(Norman Stone, *The Eastern Front, 1914–17*, 1975, p.21) ■

Specimen answers and discussion

1   Stone is denying that the landed gentry in co-operation with the bourgeoisie dominated the Russian state. The gentry had been economically weakened; many of them were leaders of the opposition to the state. For its part the state made use of peasants.

This view would certainly be in conflict with Mayer's view about the continuing dominance of the landed class and, though there is no detail on the bourgeoisie in this passage, it also seems to be opposing the notion of the landed class and the bourgeoisie coming together to form one dominant class. There is not really enough to go on here, but Stone's views could be compatible with the notion that the landed class and the bourgeoisie both, separately, were important classes. It might be noted that if the gentry still do have a considerable influence on the running of the state (Stone does not really go into this here), *and* they provide the leadership for the opposition, this would tend to suggest that they are pretty important.

2   The wit is in the last phrase, 'on suspicion that literacy was practised there'. Stone resists the Marxist notion of one dominant class controlling the state; in fact, he says, members of the gentry were leaders of the opposition to the state. He is clearly not overly sympathetic towards the peasants who were recruited into the service of the state and, indeed, his joke is in some measure directed against them.

3   Stone seems to be using 'gentry' as a synonym for 'landed class'. However, it is very important to bear in mind that in most countries the landed class divided into rich and powerful landowners who were strongly placed to

exploit the challenge of industrialization, and lesser men, who may well have been 'aristocrats' rather then mere 'gentry' but who were much more likely to suffer from industrialization. □

Let us note that just because some members of the landed class lead the opposition that does not mean that, as a class, they are not powerful – indeed it suggests their importance in different aspects of Russian life. Likewise the fact that *some* peasants serve the state by no means implies that as a class the peasants have power; the true nature of their condition is explained by another Russian expert, Hans Rogger:

> Redemption dues and taxes were a heavy burden. Together with over-population, a low level of agricultural techniques, an exhausted soil, inadequate rainfall, frequent crop failures, a slump in grain prices and a steep rise in land values, they were the classic ingredients of what had become a deep-seated depression of most of peasant farming.
>
> (Hans Rogger, *Russia in the Age of Modernization and Revolution 1881–1917*, 1983, p.77)

But for the moment I want to continue our exploration of what class, or classes, dominated the different European societies on the eve of war. I am now going to give you a series of extracts from standard secondary authorities on each of the countries we are concerned with. I want you to keep in mind Mayer's contention about the continued dominance of the traditional landed class, together with the two alternative formulations which I have offered.

Exercise   Read each of the following extracts, (a) to (d), and at the end of each extract note down what is being said about the nature of the dominant class, and how this relates to Mayer's version. You will find that one of the extracts presents a view of a merging of the aristocracy and bourgeoisie similar to the one I favoured in my alternative formulation, and also offers some elements similar to Stone's analysis; try to spot which extract this is. Finally, I hope you will note that the account given of Italy in extract (d) differs in one significant aspect from all of the others; see if you can also spot what this is.

Extract (a) (Germany)

For the shrewd and dynamic merchant or entrepreneur there was a great deal of money to be made. Despite repeated fluctuations, there was a general upward trend in income from investments. In the commercial centres like Frankfurt, Hamburg or Cologne, wealth had been accumulated over a longer period and was, perhaps, also less conspicuous. But new wealth was being generated very fast in places like Berlin, the capital of the German Empire and a major industrial and commercial centre. It was also acquired in the Rhineland in heavy industry, in Saxony and Silesia, or in Mannheim and Stuttgart with their growing engineering industries. Munich and Leipzig are other examples of cities which saw a good deal of affluence. In 1896, the Prussian Inland Revenue counted 9,265 taxpayers with an income of 30,500–100,000 marks and 1,699 with an income of over 100,000 marks per annum. By 1912 these figures had risen to 20,999 and 4,456 an increase of 126 per cent and 162 per cent respectively. And the *nouveaux riches* of the Industrial Revolution enjoyed showing off this wealth. In the late 1870s, the Krupps

built their famous Villa Hügel in French chateau style on the southern fringes
of Essen, overlooking the Ruhr valley and surrounded by quasi-royal
splendour. Gerson Bleichröder, Bismarck's banker, was also doing quite well,
as Benjamin Disraeli, a visitor from a not exactly underdeveloped country,
had occasion to witness: 'The banqueting hall, very vast and very lofty, and
indeed the whole mansion, is built of every species of rare marble, and where
it is not marble it is gold. There was a gallery for the musicians who played
Wagner, and Wagner only, which I was very glad of, as I have rarely had an
opportunity of hearing that master. After dinner we were promenaded
through the splendid salons – and picture galleries, and a ballroom fit for a
fairy-tale, and sitting alone on a sofa was a very mean-looking little woman,
covered with pearls and diamonds, who was Madame Bleichröder and whom
he had married very early in life when he was penniless. She was unlike her
husband, and by no means equal to her wondrous fortune.'

Indeed Bleichröder's was a very different story from that of the Prussian
Junker [landowner] who saw their economic position disintegrate while
trying to maintain the life-style to which they were accustomed. As one of
them, Elard von Oldenburg-Januschau exclaimed in 1904: 'Being poor is no
misfortune, but lapsing into poverty is one!' Meanwhile, in 1895, Udo Count
Stolbert-Wernigerode, son of an old Prussian landowning family, was forced
to sell his town-house in Berlin because he was unable to afford the rates.
This social humiliation provides a telling contrast with Bleichröder's affluence
and illustrates what the Industrial Revolution was doing to the agrarian upper
class on the one hand and the well-to-do bourgeoisie on the other ...

The point to bear in mind ... is that pre-war Germany was a clearly stratified
society in which upward mobility beyond the class boundary was difficult.
With the process of rapid industrialisation and urbanisation creating so much
disruption at the grass-roots of society, the upper strata reacted all the more
strongly against what they perceived as dangerous 'levelling' tendencies. The
reaction was to maintain social barriers and to deny social recognition to
those who had succeeded in acquiring the material pre-requisites of entry
into the higher class. Thus a Berlin businessman who had amassed enough
wealth to buy himself an estate north-east of the capital would more often
than not fail to gain social recognition by the local Prussian nobility and
squirearchy.

(Volker Berghahn, *Modern Germany*, 1982, pp.7 and 12)

Extract (b) (Austria-Hungary)

As these economic developments occurred, the pattern of Austria's social and
political forces had, up to a point, adapted itself to them, although the effects
had inevitably lagged behind the causes which produced them. The most
immediate and obvious of them were those deriving from the growth in
numbers, wealth, and in the influence which it was able to exert through such
channels as the Press, of the upper strata of the German-Austrian bourgeoisie
of the German and Bohemian lands. This class, as we have seen, supplied the
Ministers and their supporters from 1861 to 1878, and the legislation enacted
by the Reichsrats [Imperial councils] of those years was, in the main, dictated
by their interests and their *Weltanschauung* [general view of the world]. Even

after the government slipped from their hands as from 1878, their wishes and interests remained something which no government was able to, or tried to ignore.

The advance of the bourgeoisie was naturally accompanied by retreats on the part of its chief opponents, the aristocracy and the Catholic Church. By 1890 the direct power of the aristocracy was a shadow of what it had been in 1848, not to speak of 1748 ...

One must, however, be careful not to exaggerate the extent to which the bourgeoisie had triumphed over its rivals. The losses of those two factors were not mortal, and those of the Church, hardly even crippling ...

Nor were the great landowners at all a negligible force, even in 1890 ... Aristocrats still filled a large proportion of the highest administrative posts: in 1905–7 twenty-one of the thirty-four officials in the Ministry of the Interior of the grade of Ministerialat [ministerial adviser] and upwards were Counts or Barons, eight out of nineteen in the Ministry of Agriculture, and nine out of twenty-four Heads of Departments in that of the Railways. Only aristocrats were heads of *Stathaltereien* [provinces]: one Prince, seven Counts, five Barons, and one Ritter [knight]. And this position, too, was still backed by great wealth. The landed magnates had had their share of the difficulties that had overtaken all Austrian agriculture after 1849, when it had had to face the full competition of Hungarian wheat, livestock and wine, to which, after the mid-1870s, had been added the competition (which threatened Hungary also) of overseas wheat and cattle. But ... most of the big men had survived this. With the compensation which they had received under the land reform, and the credit which they had been able to obtain after it, relatively easily and cheaply ... they had been able to modernize and rationalize their production, cutting their labour costs by mechanization and extensive employment of seasonal labour, and to go over largely to the production of industrial crops, among which an enormous part was played by the production of sugar beet. The cultivation of this crop, after its small beginnings in the 1830s, had made extraordinary progress after 1850: in 1892, 175,800 hectares were under it in Bohemia and 73,500 in Moravia (it was almost confined to these two Lands). Most of this was grown on the big estates, and where it was grown by peasants, they took it to the local magnate's refinery. Thus in 1886, eighty out of the hundred and twenty refineries in Bohemia belonged to magnates, as did five hundred of the nine hundred breweries and three hundred of the four hundred distilleries. Another source of wealth was timber and its products. Many of the forests had, indeed, been bought by the big new industrial companies, but the magnates still had a share in the ownership of the forests and the exploitation of their products, including paper. In Bohemia, in 1886, they had in their service 72,000 workers, 300,000 day labourers, 15,500 foresters and gamekeepers and 40,000 carters.

It is true that appearance was often rosier than the reality, for many of the great estates were heavily mortgaged, and when Prince X figured as owner of a sawmill or refinery, he might well be only a very minor participant in its profits. Nevertheless, the big landowners had been able not only to retain the nominal ownership of most of their estates, but to extend them ...

(C.A. Macartney, *The Habsburg Empire 1790–1918*, 1969, pp.620–3)

Extract (c) (France)

By the early years of the Third Republic [i.e. after 1870], one can speak of a single 'traditional governing class' fighting to preserve its power. The term 'notables' is perhaps the commonest among historians today, and is certainly more satisfactory than 'bourgeoisie', for the challengers too were bourgeois, and the line between conservatives and liberals ran through the middle class. In his book *La Grande Bourgeoisie au pouvoir* (1960), Jean Lhomme argues that it was the 'grande bourgeosie' who held economic, social and political power between 1830, when the aristocracy finally bowed out, and 1880, when it yielded power in its turn to the 'classes moyennes'. This perhaps underestimates the extent to which the aristocracy retained its social influence and remained part of the 'notables'. In the 1870s, the distinction between Legitimism [followers of the Bourbon dynasty] and Orleanism [followers of the Orleanist branch of the dynasty] still existed, and was based on the traditional class loyalties of the families concerned, but as the years passed it faded, and the conservative upper class came to think alike.

One element in it which was prominent at the time of the National Assembly was the provincial landed gentry, a class still thick on the ground in certain regions, which maintained a very distinctive set of values well into the twentieth century. They were Catholic, had a strong sense of patriotism and public service (generally frustrated by their reluctance to serve the Republic), and were inclined to see themselves as the last upholders of decency and tradition in a vulgar, materialist society. The romantic hopelessness of the Legitimist cause, especially after 1883, well expressed their social alienation. Some of them were small squires (*hobereaux*), but others were rich, and all retained some influence through their position as landlords. Land-ownership carried with it influence over tenants and other dependants, and a traditional position in the local community, at least in the many areas where there survived 'a conception of daily life and social organization founded on respect for the principle of property and for the hierarchy of ownership'.

The richer Legitimist nobles, however, were absentee landlords who lived in the larger provincial towns or in Paris (traditionally in the Faubourg Saint-Germain) and visited their estates only during the shooting season. At this level, it is difficult to see much difference between the older families and the Orleanist ones, whose wealth came originally from banking or industry but who had also become great landed proprietors. Conversely the nobility did not shun business activities. The agricultural depression beginning in the 1870s stimulated their movement into the boardrooms of industrial and commercial companies (and their willingness to marry bourgeois heiresses), but the phenomenon was not a new one: nobles had pioneered the development of coalmines, glassworks and ironworks on their estates since the eighteenth century, and in the nineteenth their local influence helped them become railway directors (30 per cent of whom were noble in 1902). That their role was not purely decorative was proved by aristocrats like the Marquis de Dion, who extended his class's sporting proclivities in a new direction by founding the Automobile Club and becoming a leading motor manufacturer. It seems true to say that by around 1900 landed and industrial wealth were integrated with each other, and that the topmost strata of French society formed a cohesive and powerful social group.

(Robert Anderson, *France 1870–1914*, 1977, p.33)

Extract (d) (Italy)

Steelworks and railways were not built solely, or even mainly, for economic reasons; and the 'economy' affected every aspect of social life, as is clear from the peasants' living conditions. Above all, the rulers of Italy were not essentially concerned with economic growth or prosperity. In 1881 ... there were about 200,000 'independent' landowners, rentiers and entrepreneurs, and about another 100,000 'professional' men – doctors, lawyers, engineers and the like. Often there was no real distinction between these two groups. Landowners and rentiers did not usually inherit until they were in their forties; until then, it was proper to follow a gentlemanly profession, like the law or the army ... But sometimes the distinction was real enough, particularly after 1876 when the 'professional' classes enjoyed more political power, and when income from land began to decline. In any case, the two groups together formed the élite, who dominated Italian society, and about whom we know far too little. These 'independent' classes were, of course, outnumbered by their less prosperous 'petty-bourgeois' fellows: smaller landowners, shopkeepers and the 'dependent' middle classes, e.g. clerical workers. There were 100,000 Italians holding respectable white-collar jobs in the private sector, and there were also 250,000 in non-manual public employment, including around 75,000 teachers. A government post was the next best thing to unearned income, and the number of clerical employees on the railways never failed to surprise foreign observers.

Only in Northern Italy were there significant numbers of commercially-minded businessmen, mostly engaged in activities linked to agriculture, or in banking and insurance. Even in these sectors professional managers often had to be imported from successful growth economies like Britain ... Italy lacked an entrepreneurial middle class, nor could the deficiency be supplied from below. Her skilled artisans were being squeezed by international competition, and in any case lacked the finance, contacts and literacy essential for founding successful businesses. On the other hand, she was over-endowed with a host of officials and clerks, squabbling among themselves for the spoils of office; and the holders of economic power were still mainly a landowning 'gentry' class, living off the peasants. Over most of Italy the upper and middle classes were not 'modern', not educated or travelled or enlightened. Many of them disliked and feared industry. They prized unearned income above earned, relied on rents or governments for their prosperity, and clung firmly to 'traditional' values. They even preferred to settle their quarrels by duel, to great public acclaim. In short, they were not 'middle class' at all, but aristocrats *manqués*.

And the real aristocrats were still numerous. Sicily alone could boast of 208 princes, 123 dukes, 244 marquises, and 104 counts; and the mainland South (the old Kingdom of Naples) did even better, with 172 princes, 318 dukes, 366 marquises and 81 counts. There were 321 patrician families in Rome, 28 of them with the title of prince. The other regions, especially Tuscany and

Piedmont, were also well stocked with noble blood. Throughout Italy there were 7,387 noble families, plus 318 '*signori*' in Piedmont and 46 hereditary '*cavalieri*' in Lombardy and Veneto.

What role did these aristocrats play in society? The Prefect of Naples, when asked this question by Carpi, gave an uncompromising answer: 'The ancient and modern nobility is powerless, uneducated, generally poor and with little influence ... incapable of any initiative whatsoever, not at all diligent, and consists of a large number of needy families, a few moderately well-off ones, and a rare wealthy one.' This seems fair comment for Naples, but the Italian aristocracy was by no means a spent force elsewhere, especially in the countryside. The princes and noblemen may not have enjoyed the social prestige or political power of their Russian, Prussian or English counterparts, but they still owned vast tracts of land, especially in Sicily and the *Agro Romano* [Roman territories] near Rome: ten families owned 17 per cent of all Latium [i.e. Lazio]. The acquisition of Church lands enabled some of them to *extend* their landholdings in the 1860s and 1870s; this was true even of the Papal aristocrats in Rome, including those closest to the Vatican.

Moreover, as cities grew larger, there were plenty of opportunities for aristocratic landowners to benefit from property ownership. This was particularly the case in Rome, where the building boom was most intense. Via Veneto, for example, was built on the site of the Villa Boncompagni Ludovisi, which Henry James had thought the finest park in Europe. Aristocrats were welcome on the boards of the banks that financed those operations. Then there were forests to be sold off for railway sleepers, and rich heiresses to be married. In hard times, too, there were certain Court posts, in diplomacy or the army, where outdoor relief was available for the upper class; at least one-third of the diplomats in the foreign service were noblemen. Even politically some aristocrats survived ... In short, aristocratic landowners retained much of their wealth, and formed an important, if often underestimated, part of the social élite.

(Martin Clark, *Modern Italy 1871–1982*, 1984, pp.28–30) ■

Specimen answers 1 Berghahn first of all shows the way in which many members of the
and discussion   bourgeoisie were gaining enormously in wealth, while, in contrast, some landed families were doing extremely badly. However, he then goes on to point out how rigid German society was and how difficult it was for the bourgeoisie to penetrate or replace the aristocracy. This, then, is a very finely balanced picture in which the strengths of both bourgeoisie and aristocracy are brought out. Overall, it coincides quite closely with the picture given by Mayer – the landed class are tenaciously maintaining their position (despite often adverse economic circumstances).

2 A rather similarly balanced position is given by Macartney: advances by the bourgeoisie, but the aristocrats holding on to positions of power, in some cases through themselves engaging in the commercial and industrial exploitation of their holdings. Here again we have considerable support for the Mayer thesis.

3 Anderson definitely differs from Mayer. He does not see the bourgeoisie deferring to the aristocracy but, as in my formulation, sees bourgeois and aristocrat merging, with the bourgeois buying land and the aristocrat involving himself in commerce and business. The element that is reminiscent of Stone is the way in which he points out that a class can be split politically between government and opposition, between conservatives and liberals.

4 You will have noticed (perhaps with some anguish!) that none of these accounts by first-class historians is simple. Unfortunately the realities of social structure and of the distribution of wealth and power do not conform to concise summaries, let alone political slogans. The special point which Clark brings out is that, apart from a few areas in the North (and even here there was a marked absence of entrepreneurial talent), Italy, unlike the other three countries (we shall have to look at Russia again), did not have a genuine rising bourgeoisie. On the other hand, he does point out that in many areas the landed aristocrats and the professional classes were really all one class. Clark paints a picture of opposition to industrial growth and suggests that the middle interests were not truly middle class but really failed aristocrats. Finally, he stresses the continuing importance of the major aristocrats. In one sense, then, Italy would seem to be a prime example in support of Mayer's thesis of the persistence of the old regime and of the landed aristocracy; at the same time the detail of the Italian situation as presented by Clark is rather different from that generalized about by Mayer. The existence of a large number of petty bureaucrats is important, and may be compared with Kocka's comments on Germany. □

Class and stratification

My concern in this section is to establish a picture, or map, of the social composition of the various countries which went to war in 1914. Then we can compare these pictures or maps with how the countries looked after the war, with a view to trying to determine if the war itself had any effects. I shall be talking about 'classes', but since I do not endow 'class' with the central explanatory power of Marxist analysis, and since I do not follow Weber in making a distinction between 'class' and 'status', many sociologists would maintain that what I am really talking about is 'social structure', or to use a more pompous phrase, *social stratification*. I am not interested in getting entangled here in argument over whether what I call 'class' and 'classes' should really be called, respectively, 'social stratification' and 'status groups'. The basic point is that, as an overwhelming mass of evidence shows, all of the societies we are concerned with did, in 1914, break down into distinctive social aggregates, distinguished from each other by, for example, different levels of wealth, power, freedom of various sorts, and by different patterns of living conditions and cultural behaviour. Whether we call these classes or not is for each individual to settle: *but be sure you know what you have settled*!

However, it is vital that I remind you of three distinctive features of the Marxist approach, partly because, as already explained, you should be aware of them when you encounter them in the various secondary authorities, and more particularly because they are central to some of the primary documents relating to European socialism which you will be studying.

Marx made a distinction between a class 'in itself' and 'for itself'. A class was only fully mature when it recognized its own interests, which were in conflict with those of other classes, and acted 'for itself' in support of these interests. You will find writers talking of a social aggregate 'acting as a class'; the implication is that an aggregate is not really a class unless it recognizes its own interests and acts in accordance with them. (I, on the contrary, would argue that you can have a distinctive social aggregate, recognizable as a class, in which, however, different individuals may act politically in very different ways.) Marxists speak of individuals or groups being 'class conscious', by which is meant actively aware of their (as seen by Marxists) class interests. (I believe that individuals can be aware of belonging to a class, without actually being conscious of it in the technical Marxist sense, and therefore I sometimes use the phrase 'class aware'.)

It was very much part of Marx's original political philosophy that the future lay with the working class, or 'proletariat', and that this class had a special destiny in the creation of the classless society.

Lastly, there is the Marxist belief in revolution. Mayer, we saw, chides the bourgeoisie for not fulfilling *its* destiny in carrying through revolution against the aristocracy: this leaves out of account the possibility, strongly urged by a whole school of French sociologists, that what actually happens in the development of human societies is not that one class overthrows another, but that the more powerful elements of one class join with the superior class, thus steadily transforming its character. This, to come back round to where we were, is to me a more plausible explanation of what was happening in the upper reaches of society in 1914 – the successful members of the bourgeoisie were joining the aristocracy (itself, of course, suffering from some aspects of economic change), thus creating a new upper class with many of the characteristics of the old aristocracy, but much of its wealth coming from bourgeois activities. The process had reached different stages, and had particular peculiarities of its own, in the different countries.

The whole issue of class and social structure, then, is quite a difficult one. Yet, we simply cannot enter into questions about the effects of war if we are not able first of all to pin down the nature of social structure and class relationships in the various societies we are studying. Historians today are very conscious that social distinctions are a matter of attitude, language and custom, as well as a simple economic 'relationship to the dominant mode of production'.

Can we then now move towards getting some overall idea of the social structure, or better, social structures, of the European countries in 1914? How many classes were there? Already from what you have read in this unit, and in previous units, you should be able to provide such a list.

Exercise   Starting with the wealthiest and most powerful at the top, and going down to the poorest and least powerful at the bottom, give a list of the main classes in the various European countries in 1914. Where, from what you have already read in this unit, there is some argument about the nature of a particular social group, add that as a comment. ■

Specimen answer   Well so far (with variations of name) we have encountered the following:

List	Comment
Aristocracy or landed class Bourgeoisie Gentry	But there are arguments over whether the bourgeoisie had already supplanted the aristocracy (traditional Marxist view; also the view of Roberts, a non-Marxist, who, on p.45, says bourgeoisie are taking over and have fundamentally different assumptions from aristocracy), or whether the most successful elements in the bourgeoisie have joined the aristocracy transforming it into a new upper class, with variations in the different countries (my own view). Some landed families are undoubtedly going down in the world, generally the smaller landholders.
Mittelstand, middle class, or lower middle class	There are Kocka's arguments that part of the *Mittelstand* really belong to the bourgeoisie, and part to the working class. Other questions which you may not have thought of are: where do doctors, teachers, lawyers, successful small businessmen figure? Are they members of the bourgeoisie, or what? Is there an 'upper middle class', or maybe a 'professional middle class'?
Peasants	Do these include farmers, independent smallholders, landless labourers, and so on, or should each be fitted into different classes (e.g. farmers into the middle class, landless labourers into the working class)?
Working class	Are they 'above' the peasantry, 'below', or level with, them? Are they bottom of the heap, or are there yet more unfortunate people below?
Riff-raff, 'under class', or residuum	This aggregate has not appeared in our discussion so far. Mayer talks of the persistence of the old regime exclusively from the point of view of, as he sees it, the continuing dominance of the aristocracy in that regime. But the old regime had its cohorts of jobless, landless, beggars, and unfortunates. Such groups still existed in the societies of 1914, together with a whole range of other dispossessed and unfortunates created by growing industrialization (we shall later encounter arguments that such groups often benefited from the changed circumstances of war). □

A really big question hangs over what is so often, and so loosely, referred to in Britain, and in British writing, as 'the middle class'. Quite evidently the sort of people Kocka was talking about are very different from the great bourgeois figures that Mayer says were avid for the titles and trappings of the nobility: the small shopkeeper who owns his shop, the skilled artisan who owns his workshop, certainly the minor civil servant tied to his desk, and even the small-town businessman employing, say, a couple of dozen, all of these are very different from the owner of the iron foundry which dominates the employment in a town of 50,000, or a banker with an interest in several major financial institutions.

These matters are sorted out for us with magisterial succinctness by one of the leading authorities on late nineteenth-century France, Professor Jean-Marie Mayeur.[3] But here again, I fear, we run into the dreaded problem of foreign languages. Students have been telling me, ever since I taught at Edinburgh University over thirty years ago, that to require a knowledge of languages from history students is a cruel and unnatural punishment, that an understanding of languages (or at least the few elementary points we are providing you with) is a badge of the privileged rich; on the contrary, language is an essential tool of the professional historian.

The excellent English version of Mayeur's major work, translated as 'The beginnings of the Third Republic 1871–1898', addresses this question of the different groups contained within what is sometimes loosely called the middle class:

> ... at the top of the social ladder reigned the upper middle class. The aristocracy still had a prestige in 'society' which should not be underestimated, but it retained social power only to the extent that it had merged with the upper middle class. Matrimonial alliances and the acceptance of directorships made this merger possible.
>
> (Jean-Marie Mayeur, 'The beginnings of the Third Republic 1871–1898', 1984, pp.65–6)

My first comment must be that this view postulates members of the aristocracy merging with the bourgeoisie, rather than successful members of the bourgeoisie merging with the aristocracy. That is an interesting way of rephrasing the position which I have myself enunciated; it, of course, differs significantly from Mayer's position. But what I have to draw your attention to is the original French, where both times in the English translation 'upper middle class' is a rendering of, in the French, *la haute bourgeoisie*, the 'high bourgeoisie'. Perhaps there is no great problem there. Let us continue. A little further on in the English version:

> It is relatively easy to trace the frontier which separated the upper middle class from the ordinary middle class. The scale of incomes establishes a primary distinction.

In the original French 'upper middle class', of course, is 'high bourgeoisie'. 'Ordinary middle class' is a translation of *la bonne bourgeoisie*, the 'good bourgeoisie', or the 'sound bourgeoisie'. Let us continue:

> ... between this 'ordinary bourgeoisie' and the people came the immense 'bourgeoisie in embryo' of the lower middle classes.

Though the French phrase remains '*bonne bourgeoisie*', the English translator, obviously having doubts, has switched from 'ordinary middle class' to 'ordinary bourgeoisie'. The translator's problem becomes clearer when we realize that 'the lower middle classes' in the English translation is, in French, simply 'the middle classes' (*les classes moyennes*). The French, you see, recognize both a bourgeoisie (in various sections) *and* the middle classes (plural) below. Bear this careful French usage in mind every time you are tempted to speak of one monolithic middle class (or, for that matter, bourgeoisie) unless you do really

---

[3] Note that in this course we refer to A.J.Mayer, J.-M. Mayeur and C. Maier. Confusing!

mean the very powerful group at the top. Below 'the middle classes' are the people who, as Mayeur reveals elsewhere, comprise the 'agricultural' or 'peasant' classes, and the 'working class'. Mayeur discusses 'the middle classes' as follows (the translation here is mine made directly from Mayeur's original French):

> They are characterized by their wish to be bourgeois, but, whether because of an insufficient income, or because of a lack of culture and proximity to popular origins, they are on the fringes of the bourgeoisie. It is the absence of manual work which distinguishes them from, in the sharpest sense of the term, the popular strata.

Social structures of France, Italy, Austria, Germany, Russia and Britain in 1914

So far what I have been saying about class and social structure has consisted of a number of general statements and some extracts from various distinguished secondary authorities. I'd like now to discuss a range of primary sources (as I did in the previous version of this course). But I mustn't impose too heavy a burden on you, and we mustn't linger too long on the pre-1914 period. So here, actually, is another secondary source.

Exercise   Read the following extract from Robert Anderson, *France 1870–1914*, then answer the following questions:

1 In what ways does Anderson, while critical of Marx, show that he has absorbed certain Marxist ideas?

2 Do the French peasantry form a class?

3 Are any other classes mentioned by Anderson in this discussion?

> The largest group of all, the peasants, do not fit into any horizontal scheme of social stratification. In a well-known passage, Marx explained how the peasants 'form a vast mass, the members of which live in similar conditions but without entering into manifold relations with one another ... the great mass of the French nation is formed by simple addition of homologous magnitudes, much as potatoes in a sack form a sack of potatoes'.
>
> Marx was correct in showing why the peasants did not act as a class, but misleading in his implication that they were an undifferentiated mass. The true picture is complex, and demands some preliminary definitions. The term 'peasant' was commonly applied to all who worked on the land, and even to rural artisans and the inhabitants of the countryside generally. 'Peasant farming' in the more limited sense of a system of family holdings worked with little outside labour was characteristic of France, but by no means all the 'peasants' were 'peasant farmers' – there was a substantial force of landless or near landless labourers. Moreover, the peasant farmer was not necessarily a peasant proprietor: much land was rented, and peasant farming could co-exist with large-scale landownership ...
>
> The statistics for 1892 show that 75 per cent of all farms were farmed directly by their owners; but because many of these holdings were small, they accounted for only 53 per cent of the land area. The remaining 47 per cent was owned by landlords, who let it out either for a cash rent (*fermage*, 36 per

cent) or on a crop-sharing basis (*métayage*, 11 per cent). Many of these landlords were bourgeois with one or two farms, or squires with an estate confined to one commune, but there were also rich landowners with an accumulation of estates which made them leading figures in their departments, although the British style of landed magnate holding sway over a vast tract of territory was unknown in France.

(R. Anderson, *France 1870–1914*, 1977, pp.39–40 ■

Specimen answers and discussion 1 He uses the phrase 'act as a class'.

2 Anderson brings out the great variety of types within the peasant aggregate – here he is in disagreement with Marx. But this very variety reinforces, he feels, Marx's view that the peasantry do not form a class. You will recall Clive Emsley's arguments (Unit 2, p.73) that many peasant families had little sense of belonging to a French nation (let alone to a national peasant class). None the less I would maintain that the bulk of the (smallholding) peasantry was 'class-aware', conscious that their rewards and their style of life were different from those of landowners, clergy, lawyers, shopkeepers, artisans, and that in this sense they did form a 'class', or certainly a distinctive social group, while the landless labourers are analogous to the town-based riff-raff. You are fully entitled to disagree.

3 Other classes mentioned are: the landholding class, and the small 'bourgeois' landholders; in my terms, the landed sectors of, respectively, the upper class, and the upper middle class. Although other factors come in (such as ethnic compositions), class structure is closely related to the nature of the economy. In trying to pin down the distinctive features of the class structures of the different countries in 1914, you will find it useful to raise the points made about the different economies (and about nationality) in the previous unit. France, remember, had a much smaller working class and a less fully developed industrial bourgeoisie than Britain, and a much larger agricultural class (more than half of the population). ☐

You have already received a picture, from Martin Clark (extract (d)) and from Clive Emsley in the previous unit, of Italy as a relatively 'underdeveloped' society: small working class, very large peasantry, and a lot of bureaucrats desperately conscious of their status.

Exercise   In *Primary Sources 1: World War I* (I.5), which is an extract from a legal textbook summarizing the Italian social legislation of the time, there seems to be a pretty clear conception of the existence of a working class. How, in the exact words of the document, is that working class defined? ■

Specimen answer   'Italian citizens of both sexes who render service of work by the day or who in general do work which is predominantly manual for third parties or also on their own account, provided that, in this latter case, they do not pay, in whatever form, taxes to the State higher than 30 lire a year.'

Discussion   The key points of the definition are that the work is manual, and that the earnings are limited. When we discuss class structure we must remember that classes are constantly changing. Since the period discussed by Clark, more land workers have moved to the towns, thus a larger working class, more typical of developed industrial countries, is in the process of *formation*; the working class is being *recruited* from the country areas. These notions of class formation and class recruitment are important ones. Classes are not some permanent abstraction detached from the main processes of demographic, economic and social change. □

Austria-Hungary was an even more variegated state than Italy (again with more than half the population deriving a living from the land).

In Unit 2, Clive Emsley told you that Germany was the only country apart from Britain with less than half the population deriving their living from the land. Germany's working class, therefore, is next in size to that of Britain – but don't neglect the German peasantry, who play a more significant role than British farmers or British agricultural workers. We've already learned a little about Russian society. However, important as the qualifications made by Stone are, I think we would be wrong not to seize upon the fundamental facts that great landowners of Mayer's old regime type still, under the autocracy of the Tsar, possessed great powers, and that, despite apparent gains, the lot of the peasants as a whole, a few lucky exceptions apart (those who became elders or scribes, or government officials), was extremely bad, and in some ways getting worse.

Britain at this time had the most developed industrial working class of any nation in the world, quite simply because industrialization had come to it first. Because of the development of financial and administrative institutions, Britain also had a very developed lower middle class (similar to the German *Mittelstand*).

The significance of class

From Mayer, whether his precise account of the processes taking place is correct or not (I think not), we can see that in all countries the main positions of economic and political power are held by a relatively small number of families grouped at the top of society. Class, or social structure if you prefer, is very important to the way wealth and income are distributed. Berghahn, Kocka and Mayeur give us some of the more subtle, but very important, influences of class: the way people lived, the resentments they felt, the forms of organization they adopted, were very strongly influenced by their place in the social structure.

Of course, people are grouped together in other ways than just by social group or class.

Exercise   Name the other kinds of associations or affiliations or groups that people can have which might affect their outlook, behaviour and life chances. ■

Specimen answer   Religion, nationality, town, village, other local community. Possibly also sex or 'gender'.

Discussion   Clearly in Austria-Hungary the question of nationality is of great importance, probably more important than that of class, with religious denomination (Catholic, Orthodox, Protestant, Jewish, Muslim, often being closely bound up with ethnic community). Berghahn steers a nice position in regard to Germany, and his analysis would apply in greater or lesser degree to the other developed continental European countries. As the most advanced industrial society Britain probably was more affected by class than by the other distinctions. Here is another extract from Berghahn:

... there were two currents which tended to cut across the stratification of Wilhelmine society in terms of a specific class culture. These cross-currents complicated the overall picture because they did not act to reinforce existing divisions along class and infra-class status lines, and they were: regionalism and [religious] denomination.

The importance of regionalism and local consciousness cannot be emphasised too strongly ... Local uniformity of a particular accent has occasionally been taken as proof that regionalism was a stronger bond than class. Wilhelmine Germany was deemed to be less class-ridden than Edwardian England where the accent immediately betrayed a person's social background. It may be that a Bavarian felt particularly Bavarian in Berlin or Cologne; but this did not mean that he or she had lost the capacity or propensity to place other Bavarians within the Empire's overall social structure. He might be pleased to meet a fellow-businessman from Munich in Prussia. Yet he was as unlikely to befriend a Bavarian factory worker outside Bavaria as he was to have social intercourse with him back home.

Religious belief was the second factor which cut across class and status barriers ...

(V. Berghahn, *Modern Germany*, 1982, pp.10–11) □

Class is related to political belief and activity, though not always in a completely direct way. The growth of the working class in Austria was giving rise to a socialist movement; there were similar movements in other countries. But, inevitably when you think about it, the active members of these movements were a rather small minority of the working class as a whole. Just where the other classes, and indeed the working class itself, stood in relation to conservatism and liberalism is something best explored in the next unit.

3   HIGH CULTURE AND POPULAR CULTURE

Historical study of culture

Class was bad enough, you may think, but culture! Like Goering you may well want to reach for your gun. It has always been a fundamental characteristic of history teaching at the Open University that we believe that history embraces all the activities of human societies in the past – political, economic, social and cultural. But for those of you who like your history to be about political parties, trade unions, international treaties, and rates of inflation, let me develop this point.

The question of the effects of war on the arts is a very central one in any comprehensive discussion of war and social change. To get a feel for the nature, and limits, of the debate, I want you now to read the fourth paragraph of 'The birth of the modern: 1885–1914' by G. D. Josipovici, reprinted in the Course Reader (Chapter 3). Please do make a point of reading this now since in the space of a few lines it sets up a very important issue.

Now, if you can put your hand on your heart and swear to have read that extract, read the following paragraph, which is from an essay entitled 'The First World War and the Literary Consciousness' by R. Gibson:

It would clearly be wrong to attribute the modern humanists' malaise exclusively to the impact of the First World War. The traditional bases of humanism were in any event being gravely eroded by the effects of spectacular advances in science and technology, by the challenging new ideas of anthropologists and sociologists, and, most particularly, by the revolutionary theories of Freud. At the same time, the effect of the war should not be underestimated either. It provided its own irresistible impulse to forces which were already dynamic, brutally stripping away illusions and confronting Man with the frailty of his body and the fragility of his beliefs. Man has, ever since, been left to come to terms with the daunting conclusion that the principal cause, as well as the principal victim, of war is Man himself.

(John Cruickshank (ed.) *French Literature and its Background:*
6 The Twentieth Century, 1970, p.70)

One cannot understand the twentieth-century if one does not have an understanding of its most important cultural movement, modernism. The twentieth-century historian who does not know something of Proust, Joyce, Picasso, Klee, Schönberg and Stravinsky, is missing much which is central to the age. What I am speaking of here is, of course, 'high culture', and I am for the moment making a case for the necessity for studying high culture.

Purely on this limited issue of high culture, Mayer makes another less general, more traditionally historical, argument for the study of high culture in *The Persistence of the Old Regime* (in the section entitled 'Official high cultures and the avant-garde' to the end, reprinted in the Course Reader).

In a moment I am going to ask you to read that section, but first I want you to read the whole of the Josipovici chapter. As you may find this quite heavy going (though personally I find it a brilliant exposition of a difficult topic), I will indicate the main points you should get from the essay.

As a preliminary, let me stress that our concern here is with the condition of modernism on the eve of World War I in order to provide a basis upon which we can subsequently assess the effects, if any, of that war on the further development of modernism. Josipovici has to delve far back into the nineteenth century, but our concern is purely with the artists still practising in 1914, and above all with ones who went on working over the World War I period. We are not at this stage concerned with those who only came to the fore after World War I (T. S. Eliot, for instance). Let me therefore list the artists (in addition to the six already mentioned, the novelists Proust and Joyce, the painters Picasso and Klee, and the composers Schönberg and Stravinsky) who are relevant to our studies: Braque (painter), Kafka (novelist), Jarry (playwright), Debussy (composer), Diaghilev (ballet director). The other names mentioned by Josipovici are important simply in explaining the early development of modernism. There are one or two other names that I wish to bring in, such as Thomas Mann, the German novelist, Anton Chekhov, the Russian playwright, and Richard Strauss, the German composer.

The key points about the nature of modernism made by Josipovici are:

1   Modernism is a reaction to decadent, self-indulgent Romanticism. (In making this point, it should be noted, Josipovici is grossly unfair to the opera composer Wagner, stressing the weaknesses of his self-indulgence

and 'magic' but, of course, passing over the immense strengths of this creator of great music drama.)

2   Modernism recognizes the limitations upon art and the clear differences between the various forms of art: painting is brush strokes, poetry is groupings of words; and so on.

3   Modern art seeks to make the viewer or reader work hard by showing him/her the familiar in a new light and by drawing him/her into the actual processes through which the work of art is produced.

4   While modernism may have begun as a reaction against Romanticism it is in reality nothing less than a complete break with centuries of tradition in art. There are three main aspects of this which I shall number points (a), (b) and (c).

(a)   Modernism recognizes that the traditional Western way of looking at things is only one way among many (here direct historical influences are important, the discovery of Japanese art, African sculpture, and so on).

(b)   Traditionally, the artist was concerned with either, or both, expressing himself and imitating external reality. The modern artist, instead of seeing his work as an expression of himself, deliberately separates himself from his work. This can be seen, for instance, in the long series of novels produced by Proust (of great interest to us, since the first one was published just before the war, the second just at the end of the war, and the remainder in the post-war years), *À la recherche du temps perdu* (conventionally translated as *Remembrance of Things Past*), which, in one of its aspects, is not a traditional novel, but is a discussion of how the central character, Marcel, might write a novel.

(c)   Modernism also breaks sharply with the idea of imitating the external world: it breaks 'with four centuries of mimesis' ('mimesis' simply being an elegant way of saying 'imitation'). Modern artists are aware that they produce according to particular conventions, particular rules of the game; they are not presenting a slice of external reality. Proust is a good example again in that he breaks sharply from the nineteenth-century tradition of presenting rounded characters whose every action is consistent with the character carefully delineated by the author. Proust seeks to show that we never really know what other people are like, or indeed what we ourselves are like, and that in fact we all act in all sorts of inconsistent ways, there being no definite, clearly perceived, 'external' character. Proust also shares with modernist writers a preoccupation with the conventions of art: what art is, the nature and purposes and possible achievements of art, these are questions which run through Proust as also through much of the work of Thomas Mann.

Exercise   I want you to read the piece by Josipovici, and then the section by Mayer already indicated. As you read through Josipovici make sure, for your own studies, that you note where the main points I have made occur in his text.

1 Note down what Josipovici says about actual geographical centres of modernism.

After you have read both Josipovici and Mayer, note down answers to the following:

2   Remember that earlier I said Mayer offered a reason for historians to study high culture. What is it?

3   Write a sentence or two pinning down the ways in which Josipovici and Mayer agree and disagree in their views of the significance of modernism. ∎

Specimen answers   1   Josipovici says that 'the modern movement ... was an urban movement ... to be found in all the great cosmopolitan centres of Europe: Vienna, Munich, Prague, and especially Paris'.

2   Mayer says that the dominant class which he is writing about uses high culture, on the one hand, to exalt its regime and validate its moral claims, and on the other hand to display its wealth, taste and status. (This, then, becomes the fourth argument for historians giving attention to the study of culture, or in this case, high culture.)

3   Both writers seem to agree in their belief in modernism, that it is, as it were, 'a good thing'. Perhaps because he is not basically concerned with the historical and social aspects, Josipovici rather gives a picture of the steady advance and triumphs of modernism, whereas Mayer is arguing that this old regime which he believes is still dominant preserves the older pre-modern or 'historicist' as he calls it, culture, and that the avant-garde, the proponents of modernism, are, before 1914, largely unsuccessful.

Discussion   This is a very important issue. It is on the whole true that most modernist art appealed only to a minority of a minority, and that much (though by no means all) was scoffed at even by the educated audiences at which it was aimed. It is relevant to the point made at the end of the Josipovici piece that while the Post-impressionists gained wide acceptance in artistic and intellectual circles in Paris, they did not do so in London, Proust was deeply respected within his own intellectual coterie, but he could not find a commercial publisher for his first volume, and had to have it published privately. □

Excellent as the Josipovici essay is, it has at least one omission. Josipovici leaves out developments in science and technology, which apart from their important effects on material life and the nature of warfare, also affect high culture and modernism. Critically important are the undermining of the notion of a stable physical world associated with Newtonian physics, through the discoveries of Heisenberg, Schrödinger, and Einstein, and of the stable human personality through Freud's claims to have discovered the deeper, sub-conscious human drives. For these points, and a good explanation of the differences in the ways in which new ideas affect élites (the proponents of high culture) and more popular audiences, read Chapter 7 of Roberts's *Europe 1880–1945*, to the middle of page 183.

Culture as historical evidence

A fifth reason for studying cultural artefacts is, of course, that, like everything else created by the age the historian is studying, they can prove to be valuable sources.

It has often been argued that certain works of art and literature, some within the realm of high culture, some perhaps more properly belonging to popular culture, reveal that there was 'a will to war' in European society before 1914. The phrase is both metaphysical and question-begging, but there simply can be no question that many works aiming at a limited, intellectual audience, as well as many aiming at a much wider audience, expressed attitudes of jingoism, national rivalry, and a happy expectation of war.

One very striking example is the French poet and essayist Charles Péguy, who was born in 1873 and came from a poor rural family. He was both a socialist and a supporter of traditional French rural life. But well before 1914 he had turned towards the exaltation of heroism, patriotism and military glory. In 1913, in his poem 'Prayer for we others', he wrote:

> Happy are those who have died for the charnel earth,
> But provided that this was in a just war,
> Happy those who have died for four corners of earth,
> Happy those who have died a solemn death ...

In a series of novels about military life in North Africa, Ernest Psichari expressed a viewpoint which can be summed up in this short quotation from *The Call to Arms* of 1913: 'Guns are the most real of realities, the only realities of the modern world.'

Péguy, despite his humble origins, perhaps belongs in the world of high culture; Psichari is a more popular writer appealing to all who are literate. *Primary Sources 1* (I.6 and I.7) are both extracts from popular writings, one German, and one British, which demonstrate expectancy of war.

Militarism, glorification of violence, expectation, and even anticipation of war, are very marked characteristics of the pre-war movement in the visual arts known as Futurism, and also in the British offshoot known as Vorticism. These movements are illustrated in the art pack and its associated audio-cassette, where I shall try to identify the influences of war on culture. Here my basic objective is simply to establish that modernism was already in full flow well before 1914. I also want to demonstrate that sound historical methods can be applied to cultural artefacts. There is no need for 'cultural theory'.

Religion and popular culture

Changes in the nature of religious belief as it operated in the realm of high culture can be traced in Roberts, pp. 53–9. Roberts also touches on religious practice and belief as an important part of popular culture. In general, his is a picture of decline in religious practice and belief. It is true that in industrial areas religion had never meant much to the under class. Read the section on 'Religion' in Roberts now; however, bear in mind these points which, in my view, Roberts does not stress sufficiently:

- In rural areas, however poverty-stricken, traditional religious practice and belief continued to be a fundamental element in everyday life.

- Among many working-class families in all countries religious observance was certainly one element in everyday life (active socialists, particularly in Germany, as Roberts says, were usually exceptions; however, in Britain, many socialists continued to be practising Christians).

- Even where there were strong anti-clerical movements, as in France, and, towards the end of the period, in Italy, opposition to what was thought of as clerical dictatorship did not necessarily mean abandonment of an acceptance of the tenets of Catholicism.

Traditional religious belief was under attack well before 1914, but across Europe as a whole religious belief was still very much a part of everyday life. We have to be clear about this before we can, in the next book, assess the effects of World War I on religion.

Other aspects of popular culture

Popular novels such as we have already mentioned come within the realm of popular culture. So also do popular newspapers, popular songs, trade-union banners, brass bands, folk dancing and spectator sports, such as football. (If you doubt the existence of classes, just reflect on the leisure activities of the upper class. Neither the working class nor the middle class had country estates for 'huntin' an' shootin', nor did they appear at the Henley Regatta, nor at such exclusive clubs as the *Tir au Pigeons* (in France)). Spectator sports are a product of the later nineteenth century; popular newspapers of a sort have a longer history, though the modern mass-circulation daily newspaper is really only a product of the very end of the century. Just, however, as high culture in the twentieth century was to be strongly characterized by modernism, so popular culture in the first half of the twentieth century was characterized by one strikingly new cultural medium.

Exercise   What is this new popular medium? ■

Specimen answer   The specific new medium is the cinematographic film, actually an invention of the 1890s and, of course, still silent in the period we are studying. □

Later developments in the technologically based mass media are sound radio, talking film, colour film, and, eventually, television. It will be another task of our course to discuss how far, if at all, war affected the development of these mass media; and also to discuss the use of these media in wartime.

The question of how far film had already developed *before* 1914 is one which must be treated with some care. It would be fairly widely agreed that it was in the period 1908–14 that film in the more advanced European countries became an important field for commercial investment, and that it was in the same period that film moved from being a small component of music hall or fairground shows to providing a complete evening's entertainment in 'picture palaces', either converted theatres, skating rinks, and so on, or, increasingly, specially built, with fancy trimmings designed to attract wealthy middle-class patrons in addition to the working-class ones who were the mainstay of cinema audiences.

Programmes were still often made up of a large number of short items, but already the American industry was beginning to provide real feature films, with sufficient prestige to attract top European, as well as top American, theatrical performers – for example, the Italian opera star Lina Cavalieri. All the elements, then, of commercial silent cinema seem to be there. However, cinemas had not really spread far outside the main urban centres; audiences remained overwhelmingly working class; much of what was shown was of rather simple interest, and rudimentary in quality, feature films which developed a proper story still being pretty rare; and many commercial speculators felt that film was merely a passing fad out of which money should be made as quickly as possible.

References

Anderson, R. (1977) *France 1870–1914: Politics and Society*, Routledge and Kegan Paul.

Berghahn, V. (1982) *Modern Germany: Society, Economy and Politics in the Twentieth Century*, Cambridge University Press (second edition 1987).

Canning, Kathleen (1996) *Languages of Labor and Gender: Female Factory Work in Germany 1850–1914*, Cornell University Press.

Clark, M. (1984) *Modern Italy 1871–1982*, Longman (second edition 1996).

Cruickshank, J. (ed.) (1968–70) *French Literature and its Background*, Oxford University Press.

Kingsley Kent, Susan, (1993) *Making Peace: The Reconstruction of Gender in Interwar Britain*, Princeton University Press.

Kocka, J. (1984) *Facing Total War*, Berg.

Koven, Seth and Mitchel, Sonya, 'Womanly duties: maternalist politics and the origins of welfare states in France, Germany, Great Britain, and the United States, 1880–1920', *American Historical Review*, vol.95, no.4, October, pp. 1076–108.

Macartney, C.A. (1969) *The Habsburg Empire 1790–1918*, Weidenfeld and Nicolson.

Mayeur, J-M. (1984) 'The beginnings of the Third Republic 1871–1898' in Mayeur, J-M. and Rebérioux, M., *The Third Republic from its Origins to the Great War, 1871–1914*, Cambridge University Press.

O'Brien, Catherine (1996) 'Beyond the can[n]on; French women's response to the First World War', *French Cultural Studies*, vol.7, no.2, pp.201–14.

Pedersen, Susan, (1990) 'Gender, welfare, and citizenship in Britain during the Great War', *American Historical Review*, vol.95, no.4, October, pp. 983–1006.

Rogger, H. (1983) *Russia in the Age of Modernization and Revolution 1881–1917*, Longman.
Stone, N. (1975) *The Eastern Front, 1914–1917*, Hodder and Stoughton.
F.M.L. Thompson, (1963) *English Landed Aristocracy in the Nineteenth-Century*, Routledge & Kegan Paul.

Further reading

Cannadine, D. (1998) *Class in Britain*, Yale University Press.

Goldthorpe, John H. and Marshall, Gordon (1992) 'The promising future of class analysis: a response to recent critiques', *Sociology*, vol.26, no.3, August.

Hunter, Anne E. (ed.) (1991) *On Peace, War, Gender: A Challenge to Genetic Explanations*, Feminist Press New York.

Kuhlman, Erica A. (1997) *Petticoats and White Feathers: Gender Conformity, Race, the Progressive Peace Movement, and the Debate over War, 1885–1919*, Westport Conn., Greenwood Press.

Marwick, A (1965, 1990), *The Deluge: British Society and the First World War*, Macmillan.

Marwick, A. (1974) *Women at War*, Imperial War Museum.

Marwick, A. (1980) *Class: Image and Reality in Britain, France and the United* States, Macmillan (second edition 1990).

Melman, Billie (ed.) (1998) *Borderlines: Genders and Identities in War and Peace, 1870–1930*, Routledge.

Unit 4 THE PROCESSES OF CHANGE

ARTHUR MARWICK

Open University students of this unit will need to refer to:
Set book: J.M. Roberts, *Europe 1880–1945*, Longman, 2000
Primary Sources 1: World War I, eds., Arthur Marwick and Wendy Simpson,
Open University, 2000

AIM

To establish a firm basis for your subsequent analysis of the exact place of World War I in the major social changes which took place in twentieth-century Europe, by establishing what changes were *already* taking place *before* war broke out.

1   HOW CHANGE COMES ABOUT

Structural, ideological and institutional circumstances

I introduced these distinctions in Unit 1. The main structural circumstances are demographic (relating to population), economic and technological. A country where everyone has just about enough to eat, where the population is not declining rapidly, where the economy is sound and there is steady technological advance is more likely to be subject to change, than one where the opposite is the case. Also important to change are new ideas, new philosophies, new ways of looking at things (*ideology*). Ancient *institutions* are likely to be a drag on change, newly created ones *can* encourage change.

These circumstances establish the broad possibilities for, and the limitations upon, change. It is within these possibilities and limitations that 'high politics', the deliberate actions of prime ministers, emperors, etc., operate, producing what I call 'guided' (or 'political' change) – as distinct from 'unguided' change brought about by broad forces or circumstances.

Marxism and 'modernization'

There are totally different ways of handling this issue. Marxism, as you know, has an all-embracing theory of how change comes about, that is through the development of new modes of production and through the conflict that engenders between the existing dominant class and the rising new class. Marxism, in effect, is an example of an approach which stresses the centrality of structural factors to the exclusion of almost everything else. Other approaches stressing structural elements have been developed through Max Weber and more recent sociologists and political scientists. One such approach involves the concept of 'modernization'.

> ... modernization is the process of change towards those types of social, economic, and political systems that have developed in Western Europe and North America from the seventeenth century to the nineteenth, and have then spread to other European countries and in the nineteenth and twentieth centuries to the South American, Asian, and African continents.
>
> (S.N.Eisenstadt, *Modernization: Protest and Change*, 1966, p.1)

The importance of all this is that if we are to have a serious discussion of whether the two world wars have brought change we have to have a clear idea in our minds of how change does come about. You will remember from my quotations from Kocka at the beginning of the previous unit that Kocka's Marxist philosophy contributed to his answers about the effects of World War I on the *Mittelstand* in Germany: he was arguing that the processes of change which

Marxists see as 'normal' had become distorted in pre-war Germany and that the war, in some sense, restored these processes to their 'proper' functioning. Those who conceive of change as essentially caused by structural factors will tend to dismiss the effects of wars as being of minor account compared with longer term structural forces. One simple formulation which is sometimes put forward is that the effect of modern wars is to 'accelerate modernization'. We shall wish in this course to scrutinize such bland statements. 'Accelerate' is a metaphor borrowed from the physical sciences. Beware of all metaphors: they, at best, describe; they do not explain.

2   THE AREAS OF SOCIAL CHANGE WITH WHICH THIS COURSE IS CONCERNED

What kinds of change are we talking about? This is really rather crucial if we are to make any progress with our analysis, though it is a rather regrettable fact that even quite distinguished historians sometimes write books concerning historical change without ever defining precisely which areas they are dealing with, or what exactly they mean by 'change'. In this course it is very simple: we have to look at (a) the international and geopolitical consequences of war, and (b) the implications of war for social developments *within* the countries we are studying.

Here now is a list of the areas of concern in this course:

(a)   International, geopolitical and strategic

It is a commonplace that wars affect the drawing of boundaries between states – victorious powers annex territory, defeated ones lose it. More than this, even where political frontiers remain unchanged, the power relationships between countries may be changed significantly. (In terms of actual territory, America did not increase at the end of World War II, though Russia did; both countries, as is well known, emerged as 'super-powers'. It could also be argued that Australia's position in the world altered – from being broadly still within a British sphere of influence in the 1930s, it was now very much in an American sphere of influence.) Such geopolitical matters may seem at the furthest extreme from social and cultural ones; but in fact geopolitical changes have ramifications throughout society.

(b)   Social

Here again is the list I introduced in Unit 1:

1   Social geography

This includes population (clearly very directly affected by the destruction of war), urbanization, distribution of agriculture and industry.

In wars people are killed, family life is disrupted, disease and famine spread. Some contemporary historians consider population change to be the most basic structural factor in historical developments.

2   Economic performance and theory

This includes activities and structures, the nature of work, exploitation of science and technology. A central question (particularly in the study of war) concerns the extent to which governments themselves should directly intervene in the economy.

Wise in our generation, we know that all other questions, whether expenditure on welfare services or opera, depend upon economic performance.

3   Social structure

We know that there have been changes in social structure over the twentieth century. But the exact nature of these, and the role played in them by the two wars, are matters for precise analysis.

4   National cohesion

Some nations, for example Britain and France, were relatively nationally homogeneous compared with others such as Russia and Austria-Hungary. It is a commonplace that modern wars are likely to offer opportunities for national minorities to assert themselves.

5   Social reform and welfare policies

Although there were important antecedents before 1900, this is very much a twentieth-century phenomenon. Has the experience of war played a part?

6   Material conditions

It is another commonplace that living standards generally have risen through the twentieth century: could war, that most destructive of all human activities, possibly have played a part?

7   Customs and behaviour

This is a difficult heading, which overlaps with aspects of the next three headings (particularly with respect to popular culture and family life), yet one that serves as a useful focus for some of the items of potential change which stand out most strongly in popular memory, but are often neglected by historians, including costume and dress, eating and drinking habits, hours of work and recreation, the role of authority structures such as church and family. Do wars disrupt traditional patterns of behaviour, and bring in new customs? Are the disruptions greater in less developed, more agrarian societies, than in the more industrialized ones?

8   Role and status of women

You have already had several examples of the debates over whether or not the First World War effected real changes in the position of women. It may be noted that the great French feminist writer Simone de Beauvoir, writing in 1949, declared that women in Britain got the vote in 1918 because of their war work (*The Second Sex*, p. 155).

9   High and popular culture

In introducing (in Unit 3) the Josipovici article in the Course Reader, I indicated the nature of the major debate over war's relationship to modernism. With regard to popular culture, questions arise as to how far films, broadcasting, popular newspapers, and so on, took their basic impetus from the experience of war.

10   Values and institutions

First, I want to stress the great importance of religious belief in the Europe of 1914. Read this extract from Hugh McLeod, *Religion and the People of Western Europe 1789–1970*:

> In the polarised societies of the nineteenth century and the first half of the twentieth, sectarianism provided for large numbers of people the strongest basis for their social identity ... three types of religious movement ... flourished in this period of widespread revolt against the *ancien régime* and the state churches. Two of these – the Protestant sect and the religion of humanity – can be seen as varying forms of emancipation from the old order. The third, Ultramontane Catholicism, was the most effective of the means devised by the older churches to broaden their popular appeal and strengthen their defences against these hostile forces. All of these movements made absolute claims for themselves; they combined aggressive evangelism with the attempt to mark out sharp and clear boundaries between their own community and the world beyond. This was the age of the self-built ideological ghettos – Catholic, Protestant, liberal, socialist. These ideological communities, sometimes a nineteenth-century creation, sometimes built upon older foundations, were often able to maintain over several generations a network of institutions, and a body of collective memories, sacred rites, battle songs, devotion to legendary heroes. As the religious unity of west-European societies broke down, each of the movements which challenged the authority of the state churches tried to impose within its own sphere of influence the totalitarian controls that the state churches had once exercised, and aspired ultimately to provide bonds of unity for whole societies.
>
> (Hugh McLeod, *Religion and the People of Western Europe 1789–1970*, 1997, pp. 36)

As the story of the twentieth century and the total war unfolds, be ready to refer back to this as a base-line against which you can measure both the continuing power, and the decline of religion. Turning to another institution, you would expect the upheavals of war to disrupt the institution of the family – did they?

More generally, you already know that the European countries in 1914 varied greatly with respect to the rights enjoyed by their citizens, whether they had autocratic or representative institutions, and whether their political values were broadly liberal or authoritarian, religious or secular. Did it need war to dethrone the autocracies or, on the contrary, is war a fundamentally undemocratic activity?

3   HOW DO WE MEASURE CHANGE?

The list above is of the ten main areas within which, in the aftermath of war, we shall be hoping to identify social change or the lack of it. How, indeed, do we measure whether or not change has taken place in these areas?

Exercise   It was suggested in Unit 1 that there are two broad ways in which change can be measured. What are they? Add a sentence or two explaining the two different approaches. ■

Specimen answer   The two ways are quantitative and qualitative. When measuring economic
and discussion   performance, material conditions, demographic changes, who actually has the vote, and so on, precise statistics are indispensable. Indeed, we should always seek to quantify. However, when we are dealing with questions of political or moral values, quality of life, culture, and so on, clearly we shall be making *qualitative* judgements, relying on the more traditional type of discursive written document. □

4   STRUCTURAL CIRCUMSTANCES EXAMINED

Let us distinguish between two broad types of structural factor: (a) demographic; (b) industrial, economic and technological.

Exercise   Turn to Roberts p.11 and read from the beginning of the paragraph 'This political framework ...' to the end of the section on p.17, keeping the following questions in mind.

1   As structural forces for change, do demographic factors operate on the short term or on the long term?

2   Given that birth rates were now falling, why was population in general still rising?

3   What major long-term consequence of the main demographic changes does Roberts identify with respect to social conditions, quality of life, and so on?

4   With regard to population growth Europe splits into two halves. What are these?

5   What is the relationship between population growth and great power status? Which country was most adversely affected by this relationship?

6   Within countries, what was the most noticeable shift in population?

7   Does Roberts make any suggestions about possible effects of war on demographic trends? Can *you* think of any possible effects? ■

Specimen answers   1   Long term. The reason for asking this question is to bring out that it may
and discussion   be that demographic trends operate on a totally different timescale from any possible effects of war which, obviously, one would expect to be apparent within the war and post-war periods themselves. However, also consider the response to question 5.

2   The population was still rising because of falling death rates, *above all among infants in the first twelve months of their lives.*

3   Human beings began to expect, and demand, more in the way of better living conditions, amenities of life and so on (p.15). I posed this question because it is sometimes argued that wars raise expectations; we shall have to consider that argument within the long-term context which Roberts is setting.

4   Higher population growths in the poorer southern and eastern countries; lower ones in the richer northern and western ones.

5   A large and growing population is necessary for sustaining the military power upon which great power status ultimately rests. France, with a practically negligible rate of population growth, was increasingly in a serious position (which helps to explain some of her phobias in respect to her powerful neighbour, Germany).

6   A shift from the country areas to the towns – though note Roberts's very careful words on the subject.

7   Although Roberts discusses demography throughout practically the whole period of this course, he does not refer to the two world wars. However, one might predict that the large destruction of life in wartime, and in particular the destruction of potential fathers, and also the separation of husbands from wives, might have adverse effects on population growth. On the other hand, Roberts does cite medical advances and rises in living standards as important factors behind population growth (the decline, in central and (north) western Europe at least, in rates of perinatal maternal mortality in the *c.*1900–1930 period is important). It may be (this has yet to be determined) that wars encourage such improvements and thus, paradoxically, enhance population growth. ☐

Because Roberts is writing a comprehensive work of history endeavouring to bring out the complex interrelationship between historical forces as they actually operate, he is not able to separate out the different 'areas of change' and 'the three circumstances governing change' in the way in which, in order to simplify and clarify, I have done. However, the section from p.17–32 broadly sets out the main structural circumstances, other than the demographic ones which we have just discussed. Remember that our main purpose is to try to determine how far the main structural circumstances which have shaped Europe in the twentieth century were already clearly in operation before 1914, and how far we have to seek their critical origins in the period after 1914, the period of the two world wars. Roberts writes with clarity and lucidity but the purpose of his book (to provide a general history of modern Europe) is, of course slightly different from that of this course (to illuminate the interrelationship between war and society). Rather than set a series of questions on this passage from Roberts, I shall simply offer a series of headings which, I hope, will help to drive home the relevance to our studies of the points Roberts is making, with just the occasional question to highlight particularly relevant issues.

Exercise   With this summary beside you, read through the section in Roberts headed 'The economy before 1914', noting answers to the questions I ask as you go along.

The first three paragraphs summarize what Roberts in the fourth paragraph refers to as 'the foundations of Europe's wealth' – basically in fact geographical factors.

In the next three paragraphs he introduces the question of the basic economic system, capitalist, large-scale, and involving specialization. He notes that with population growth European countries more and more had to import food; but he also discusses the different types of improvement in domestic food production happening in the different countries.

Roberts then (on p.21) moves on to the growth of industry, the fundamental dynamic factor in shaping European society. Very quickly he makes two contrasting points, one suggesting that pre-1914 Europe is still rather different from the Europe of the later twentieth century, and one suggesting that in essence it is the same.

1   What are these points? Write them down now.

     Roberts's discussion of the basic economic system continues with an identification of the traditional bases of industrial production, and their uneven distribution and of the resumption (after the so-called 'depression') of industrial expansion in the 1890s.

2   What does Roberts say about growth rates in Russia?

3   On p.25 Roberts goes on to discuss 'new industries'. He mentions three. What are these?

     Then we have a passage running from p.27, 'The relations of ...', to p.29, '... and a capital-importer', comparing industrial advance in the different European countries. Germany is in some ways surpassing Britain, France is remaining behind.

     Note the three classes into which Roberts divides the European economies (p.29).

     Roberts then goes on to a very important discussion (running to the end of the section) of the way in which the European economies are both closely interrelated with each other and with the wider world economy. Again Roberts seems to be saying on the one hand that here we have basic economic structures which were to dominate the rest of the twentieth century, and on the other he seems to be saying that the conditions existing before 1914 were to be seriously changed after 1914.

4   Pick out two phrases used by Roberts which suggest that conditions obtaining in 1914 were to be changed after 1914. ■

Specimen answers   1   On the one hand he says that it is important to remember how much of
and discussion   an older economic world was still interlocked with the new industrial world, while on the other he claims that 'the industrial Europe of 1940 can be seen in that of 1880'.

                     2   Russian rate of growth was very high (p.24) (though of course Russia was still very 'backward' in the sense that total output was still small). We have to bear all of this in mind when considering the effects of war and revolution on Russia.

                     3   Chemicals, electricity, internal combustion engine (the latter two very obviously technology-based).

4   Roberts refers to a 'golden age' of intricate international integration (p.29) – the implication being that the golden age did not exist after 1914. He also, on pp.30–31, refers to economic life being 'more completely self-regulating' (before 1914) than *since*. □

5 IDEOLOGICAL CIRCUMSTANCES AND THEIR RELATIONSHIP TO 'GUIDED' CHANGE

Across the Europe of 1914 quite a range of political and social ideas were held, and sometimes vigorously advocated, by different individuals and groups.

Once again, I'm afraid, we are in an area where (as with class) the happy tossing around of labels is no substitute for careful historical exposition. The same label (for example, 'liberalism' or 'socialism') can mean different things in different countries, or in different periods, or indeed to different people in the same country at the same period. The names taken by political parties do not necessarily represent a total, or even partial, commitment to any particular set of political ideas (the majority party in French parliaments throughout most of the period we are studying called itself the Radical Socialists, though it was certainly not socialist, and it is a moot point how far it was radical). In this section I want to explore the relationships between the major political philosophies and the actual policies of rulers, political parties, trade unions, and the many associations and pressure groups which play a part in social change. Politicians and parties, even the most purely opportunistic, operate within their own framework of ideas and values, reacting of course to particular events, crises, and necessities: out of these reactions spring what I have termed guided change.

At this point, I shall suggest a list of the main political and social philosophies current in the Europe of 1914, with notes on their complexities and on their relationship to actual politics.

Conservatism

Across the countries of continental Europe this term implied support for the principles and institutions of what Mayer calls the old regime, and resistance to change. It involved support for monarchy, aristocracy, and whatever church establishment these two upheld. The most celebrated conservative in late nineteenth-century Europe was Bismarck (see Roberts pp.170–3); Bismarck, like some, though by no means all, other conservatives was prepared to concede social reforms in order to maintain the unity of the nation and contain opposition. The party label 'conservative' was not widely used on continental Europe, though there was a 'Conservative' party in Germany from 1876–1918. The monarchist groups in France were extremely conservative; the Centre Party in Germany was a Catholic party, and therefore in some areas very conservative. The most successful Conservative Party was that of Great Britain and the British party was, ironically, a good deal less conservative than its European counterparts - it shared most of the dominant values of British society of the day, including representative government and moderate social reform. We sometimes describe conservative reform within the maintenance of the existing social order as 'paternalist'.

Liberalism

This word does sometimes figure in party labels, though often with a qualifying adjective (as in the German 'National Liberals'), but it covers a range of meanings at least as wide as that of conservatism. Some European 'liberals' were more conservative than British Conservatives, their sole distinguishing feature being their anti-clericalism. In its broadest sense liberalism is the philosophy of those who oppose the old regime, support representative government, and uphold the ideas of individualism and private enterprise. By 1914 most genuinely liberal parties (in this sense), whatever their exact label, accepted that the establishment of elementary rights for the poorest sections of the population did necessitate some social reform, but in essence liberalism maintained that government intervention in social and economic matters would be likely to curtail individualism. Essentially the Radical Socialists, or Radicals as they are usually termed, in France were a liberal party, committed to republicanism, representative government, private enterprise and anti-clericalism.

Nationalism[1]

This is a particularly tricky one. Sometimes 'nationalism' is spoken of as a 'force' in history – this is nationalism conceived of as a 'natural', and perhaps scarcely conscious, wish to associate oneself with one's own community and nation, and repulse attempts of alien communities to rule over one. Here, on the contrary, I am speaking of a conscious political and social philosophy. Nationalism as a political movement was often associated with liberalism - both believed in representation, self-determination, and the rights of the individual. For subject nationalities, such as the Czechs before 1918 or the Ruthenes, nationalism, on the whole, continued to have this association. But in countries where the nation was already practically synonymous with the state, such as France and Britain[2], nationalism could as often be allied with a kind of jingoistic conservatism. Liberals in Britain supported subject nationalities abroad, but on the whole favoured internationalism rather than a belligerent assertion of British claims. In discussing popular culture in the previous unit, I pointed out the way in which an aggressive nationalism was assuming an important place in French life in the years before 1914. In Germany an aggressive nationalism, deeply subservient to existing autocratic and militaristic institutions, was dominating German liberalism by the beginning of the century. On this point, let me quote here the leading authority:

> ... nationalism had always been an important part of liberalism's historical development in Germany. Liberals had been instrumental in defining national issues and in making them a central element in German political life. By

[1] A topic very fully explored in A221, State, Economy and Nation in Nineteenth-Century Europe.

[2] Again discussions in A221 are very relevant.

setting the search for national unity within a broader ideological context, liberals had given political meaning to the concept of nationality; by mobilizing popular support for the cause of national unity, liberals had provided nationalism with an institutional base. Both ideologically and institutionally, therefore, liberalism was the means through which cultural nationalism and traditional patriotism were transformed into a political commitment to national unification. Throughout the first two-thirds of the nineteenth century, liberals disagreed among themselves about the character and relative importance of this commitment. Most liberals assumed, however, that the freedom of the German *Volk* at home was inseparable from the freedom of the German *Volk* to define itself as a nation. The struggles for nationhood and for political reform seemed to be against the same enemies and for the same goals.

After 1866, the relationship between liberalism and nationalism was fundamentally altered. The first and most obvious reason for this was the way in which the Bismarckian 'revolution from above' had severed the link between foreign political success and domestic political progress. Even though some liberals tried to maintain that there was an inevitable connection between unity and freedom, the lesson taught by Bismarck's triumphs became increasingly apparent: nationalism was not an inherently liberal concept and national goals need not be part of a progressive political ideology. On a number of levels and in a variety of ways, national issues were separated from a commitment to domestic reform. In school books and public rituals, periodicals and popular literature, the nation was presented as an autonomous source of values, a pre-eminent focus of loyalties, a political end in itself. As early as 1871 Treitschke had begun to argue that nationalism should be the primary source of cohesion in German life. 'Immature youth,' he wrote, 'is inclined to think of parties with the idealistic enthusiasm which a grown man reserves for his country.' Nationalism, not liberalism; the army, not the parliament; war, not domestic politics – these were to be the formative values, institutions, and experiences through which social solidarity and political stability could be maintained.

(James J. Sheehan, *German Liberalism in the Nineteenth Century*, 1978, p. 274)

But, to repeat, in many parts of Europe, particularly those ruled by Russia and Austria-Hungary, nationalism as a political creed was closely intertwined with liberalism, democracy and, often, socialism. Roberts, who – though not a Marxist – clearly sees a close association between the evolution of liberal ideas and values, the development of capitalism and the rise of the bourgeoisie, suggests repeatedly that the greater the acceptance of liberal values the greater the stability and potential for orderly development in a given society. His point is that it is not enough for a few politicians to put forward, or pay lip-service to, liberal ideas; these have to be deeply embedded in society. I shall shortly ask you to identify particular phrases used by Roberts in making this point.

Socialism

Socialism is a word to be found in European writing well before the publications of Karl Marx, and thus independent socialist traditions developed quite early in both France and Britain. In its essence, socialism takes the community rather than the individual as its basic unit, and calls for the community to organize all aspects of social and economic life on behalf of the community as a whole; this, of course, conflicts sharply with the faith in private enterprise and *laissez-faire* fundamental to nineteenth-century liberals, and increasingly upheld by conservatives. Marx brought to socialism the ideas we have already discussed, particularly those of class conflict, of the inherent contradictions within capitalism leading inevitably to its supersession, and of the need to achieve that supersession through revolution. The main European socialist parties in 1914 accepted the doctrines of Marxism. Roberts, p.192 'Socialism before 1914 ... .' to p.197 '... and educate the workers', gives a basic, and perhaps slightly unsympathetic account. He possibly makes too much of the various splinter groups, but note in particular what he says about the relationships between socialism, anarchism, and syndicalism, about the revisionist debates at the turn of the century, about the special features of the British Labour party, about the dominant role of the German Social Democratic party, and about how particular interpretations of socialism (for example, whether it should be revolutionary or reformist) affected the actions and policies of political parties and trade unions. Please now read these pages (192–7) of Roberts.

Feminism

The word scarcely existed. The women's movements, which grew up in the second half of the nineteenth century, had to contend with a widespread acceptance, among women as well as men, that men's was the 'active' sphere, and women's the 'domestic' one; and that it was proper that women should be subordinate to men. However, as a foremost liberal philosopher in Britain, John Stuart Mill, in the 1850s and 1860s, was a proponent of women's rights. 'Suffragist' and 'Suffragette' movements were active in all the main countries.

6   INSTITUTIONAL CIRCUMSTANCES

There is no need to repeat matters focused on in Unit 2. Clearly parliamentary institutions such as existed in France and Britain were more likely to be amenable to change than the inflexible Tsarist system in Russia, or the Prussian-dominated, highly circumscribed, parliamentary system obtaining in Germany. It can be argued too that the Catholic Church in Italy, and to a lesser extent in France, operated as a restraint on change. Trade unions, as potential institutions of change were quite strong in Britain, and fairly strong in Germany. We saw in the previous section how institutional fragmentation in socialist parties rendered them even weaker than they would have been anyway.

7   LEVELS OF SOCIAL AND POLITICAL CHANGE, AND THE POTENTIAL FOR FURTHER CHANGE

In the previous section I tried, in my capacity as teacher, to summarize quite complex material under a series of simple headings. Inevitably such a procedure must seem authoritarian: *I* am telling *you*, without any opportunity for discussion. In the end, all discussion of political values, as of any other historical topic, must be grounded in primary sources. But, as you know, we can't simply go to primary sources 'cold' as it were. The more one knows of the context, the more one can squeeze out of the sources. There is no way in a course of this sort that you are going to be able to read all the important secondary material, let alone seek out all the primary material. Teaching general history is inevitably a compromise. This section is going to take the form of critical, guided reading of three chapters from Roberts, and a discussion of some primary texts. As indicated in its title, there are two aims for this section, both, of course, intimately linked with the overall course aims:

1   to help you to establish what change had already taken place in the different European countries, in order that you will subsequently be in a position to assess the effects of World War I;

2   to help you to assess what further change would have taken place anyway had conditions of peace been maintained (again, obviously, as a basis for subsequent study of the effects of war).

Your main reading now is Roberts Chapters 5 and 6, together with a further quick reading of Chapter 7. We shall have to take the different countries in the order given by Roberts.

Exercise chart   Allocating at least a couple of pages for each country write in, as main headings, the names of the countries discussed by Roberts, deleting Spain, however, but keeping Italy. Then, for each country, and numbering from 1 to 10, list the areas of social change identified in section 2 of this unit. Under each of these headings, and leaving approximately equal space between them, write these two sub-headings: (a) levels of change in 1914; (b) potential for further change. Now before you begin to read Roberts, draw upon what you have already read in this course to fill in what points you can on this 'exercise chart'.

When you come to read Roberts, you'll find that Chapter 7 is not very helpful on topic 7 'Customs and behaviour' – I expect you'll only be able to fill in odd fragments here. Likewise with topic 9 'High and popular culture'. Indeed, if I were writing an essay on, say 'Social and cultural change in Europe on the eve of the Great War', I think I'd apply this heading to the whole of Europe, rather than break it up country by country. None the less, let's stick with the plan and see what we come up with. In the end, the central issues we are leading up to here are: Did World War I affect the development of *modernization*? Did it affect the growth of mass culture? ∎

Before you start your reading I want to make a few comments on the first section of Chapter 5:

• Roberts, in my view, exaggerates the extent to which British society was uniquely different from that of other European countries. In particular, although I disagree with the emphasis of Mayer's interpretation, I think Mayer is right in perceiving a common pattern with respect to the formation of the European upper classes.

• The (correct) figures for numbers of voters which Roberts gives in the second paragraph on p.103 do not in fact suggest the 'democratic mass politics' of which he speaks; in fact, in my view, Roberts greatly overstates the extent to which Britain was a democracy in 1914. In reading Roberts, you should bear in mind that in 1911 only 59 per cent of the adult male population (there were just under 8,000,000 adult males in a total population of 40.8 million) had the vote, and it was clear from the complicated registration procedure that the franchise was still a privilege which a man earned through his respectability and proven value to the community, not a democratic right. As the law stood under the terms of the most recent Reform Act, that of 1884, there were seven different types of franchise, of which the two major ones, accounting for 84 per cent of those registered to vote in 1911, were the occupation and household franchises: the former qualified the occupier, as owner or tenant, of any land or tenement of the clear yearly value of £10; the latter the inhabitant occupier, whether as owner or tenant, of any dwelling defined as a separate dwelling. Half a million among the wealthier sections of the electorate had two or more votes; in the election of January 1910 two especially well-qualified brothers between them cast thirty votes. The principles upon which the system was based were clearly expressed in the rhetorical question posed in the House of Commons in July 1912:

> Is the man who is too illiterate to read his ballot paper, who is too imprudent to support his children, to be placed on the same footing as the man who by industry and capacity has acquired a substantial interest in more than one constituency?

The British franchise in 1914 was not democratic, and was not intended to be.

• On p.107 Roberts refers to 'a mass of legislation' being enacted in the last two decades of the century. Near the top of p.112 he refers to the Liberal government after 1906 'founding the modern welfare state'. Roberts does not make it clear whether this 'founding' differed from the previous 'mass of legislation'. Certainly, Old Age Pensions and National Insurance were new, but my own view is that Roberts exaggerates their significance. We shall look at an extract from the second of these acts shortly.

Exercise   Now start your reading of Chapter 5, reading fairly quickly through to p.110 'resigned in December 1905', but noting down answers to the following two questions, as well as filling in any relevant points in the exercise chart you have already made (if you take this drafting and filling in of the chart seriously you will be giving yourself superb practice in systematic note-taking).

1   What does Roberts say with respect to Mayer's point about the persistence of the old regime?

2   In what quite extensive passage does Roberts set out his views on British political values?

The pages from 110 to the end of the first paragraph on 113 give you the most direct picture of what was happening in Britain immediately before the war. Read this with care, before concluding the section with Roberts's brief account of the Irish crisis. Note further points in your exercise chart, but also answer this question:

3   Roberts makes two very strong pronouncements about political and social reform in this period. What are they?

Now go on to the section on France. Note down relevant points in your exercise chart, paying particular attention to the state of the franchise, and the potential of French socialism as an impetus to change. Also answer this question:

4   What impression does Roberts give of French political values?

Read to the end of the second paragraph on p.129 of the next section, noting the broad contrasts between Spain and Italy, and also the use once again of the word 'structural' at the beginning of the third paragraph on p.128. Now, skipping the detailed material on Spain, move to the beginning of the second paragraph on p.134 'Italy's trials ...'. For your chart, note in particular both the size of the electorate, and whether steady expansion of it was taking place. Read fairly rapidly to near the end of p.140 '... repression would end'. The last few pages give quite a sharp picture of Italy on the eve of the war. Note in particular what is said about Giolitti, the most noteworthy Italian protagonist of the 'liberalism' of which I have already spoken (and, incidentally, the author of Document 1.8 in *Primary Sources 1: World War I*).

5   What phrase does Roberts use to bring out his feelings about the importance of deeply embedded liberal values?

Now read Roberts's section on 'Imperial Russia' in Chapter 6, concentrating especially on p.149 'A more sinister side ...' onwards.

6   Again in keeping with one of his principal arguments, Roberts has a phrase about shared values. What is this?

7   Roberts gives us an example of guided action in the area of economic development. What is this?

8   Compare the extent of extra-parliamentary, or revolutionary, action in Russia with that in Italy, particularly from the point of view of what it achieved, if anything, in either country.

9   Roberts singles out one extremely important social reform just before the outbreak of war. What is that?

10   Turn to *Primary Sources 1: World War I* (I.9). Read this carefully, and bearing in mind the comments of Roberts, say: (a) how this document came into being and what exactly it is; (b) how far it suggests that Russia was now on course for peaceful constitutional development, and how far it suggests the opposite. Now turn to *Primary Sources 1: World War I*

(I.10 and I.11). Read them quickly, and without bothering for the moment about their detailed provisions, say: (c) in the light of Roberts's comments, what hope they offer of reform within the Tsarist system.

Now read the section on 'The Habsburg Monarchy'. In particular note for your exercise chart what is said about the franchise, and what is said about national cohesion.

Now read the section on 'Imperial Germany'. Again, for your chart, note what is said about voting rights, and pay particular attention to the significance of Prussia as a powerful state within the German empire. With regard to 'the abdication of German liberalism' (middle of p.169), remember the comments of Sheehan I quoted earlier.

11   What does Roberts say about German political values?

12   In the second paragraph on p.176 Roberts, given his general point of view, makes a rather surprising pronouncement about the possible achievements of the SPD. What is this?

Finally, read from p.196 'The upshot was disastrous...' to the end of Chapter 7. Make appropriate notes in your chart. ■

Specimen answers and discussion   I shall take the short questions first, giving my version of the exercise chart at the very end.

1   Roberts says that the *ancien régime* was transformed by 1914, with both Prime Minister and Chancellor of the Exchequer men of relatively humble origins. Thus, according to Roberts, significant change in the class structure at the top of society is already taking place. (Personally I think he exaggerates both the extent and the novelty of the change.)

2   The extensive passage comes in the second paragraph on p.100, where he stresses acceptance of the existing system, settled procedures for legislative change, assertion of individual liberties, and dislike of political violence.

3   On p.111 Roberts says 'Radicalism seemed firmly in the saddle at last' and 'It has rightly been called "a landmark in our social history"'.

4   Roberts suggests that after sharp disagreements in the early years of the Third Republic in the nineteenth century, French political values had become pretty settled by 1914 with, he suggests, widespread acceptance of both the Republic and parliamentary government.

5   At the very end of the chapter Roberts comments: 'In the long run, both Spanish and Italian constitutionalism were to fail because the *ideological and social presuppositions of liberal democracy were lacking* [my italics].

6   On p.145 Roberts remarks that: 'Russian society lacked the values and ideas which were the common-places of western capitalism.'

7   In the middle of p.150 he describes the deliberate forced industrialization undertaken by the Russian government at the insistance of Witte at the Ministry of Finance.

8   According to Roberts there was 'a near-revolutionary crisis' in Italy between 1896 and 1900, and he gives a graphic description of this on p.140. The assassination of the king must be taken seriously, but again it

seems to have been an act of revenge rather than a planned take-over of government. For the years up to 1914 Italy, it seems, was relatively stable. In contrast, it was in the middle of these years, in 1905 to be precise, that mass riots, strikes and organized agitation took place in Russia. However, Roberts, on p.152, makes the point that without the crisis of the Russo-Japanese war these would have made little headway. As it was, the combination of agitation and this crisis brought the limited changes described by Roberts on p.153. Great, but apparently somewhat despairing violence continued sporadically in Russia.

9   Stolypin's agrarian reforms which cancelled all arrears of redemption payments (payments dating back to the abolition of serfdom), the abolition of joint family holdings, and the granting of assistance to peasants who wished to buy their own land (p.155–6) – this making possible the emergence of the richer peasants, or 'kulaks', that we will hear so much about later.

10(a) At the height of the revolutionary crisis of 1905, an Imperial Manifesto was issued announcing the setting up of a *Duma* with real legislative powers, the extension of the franchise and the granting of real civil liberties. On the eve of the opening of the *Duma*, this document (I.9), a set of Fundamental Laws, was issued which codified the main constitutional enactments of the preceding months.

(b)   Some basis for future development is provided in the clauses safe-guarding individual rights, that is, clauses 30 to 40, and in the very establishment of the *Duma* (Chapter IV). However, the continued autocratic powers of the Tsar are very clearly marked as are the limitations on the powers of the *Duma*, particularly through the existence of the non-elected State Council.

(c)   The Bolsheviks boycotted the first *Duma* and subsequently were forcibly prevented from playing any active part in Russian government (Roberts, p.154–5). Thus, whatever significance this programme might have for the future, it had no direct effect on Russian policies before 1914. The Kadets (the main voice of the kind of liberalism I have already described) was the majority party in the first *Duma*, but subsequently was effectively excluded from any influence on government policy. Thus this programme too had no direct impact before 1914.

11   Roberts says that despite the fact that many of the assumptions of civilized politics were present in Imperial Germany, it cannot be classed among the constitutional states with widely shared liberal values; there never had been a strong liberal tradition based on respect for individual rights (middle of p.168 and bottom of p.169). There was no acceptance of divergence of political aims within a consensus of agreement about ends (bottom of p.169). Note that Roberts concludes by re-stressing the existence of 'civilized standards'. Recent research has shown that (progressive) liberalism was stronger in some areas of Germany than Roberts allows.

12   Roberts seems to be saying (on pp.176–7) that the SPD could only have 'big'
        achievements if it were positively revolutionary (strange given his obvious
        predilection for constitutionalism). The SPD's problem was that it had
        carved out a comfortable niche for itself and its members (and their families)
        within a system which, according to its 1891 Erfurt Party Programme, it was
        theoretically pledged to overthrow. Actually, it had a big success in winning
        over 30 per cent of the votes in the 1912 *Reichstag* election.

Exercise chart: If you have made a serious effort at this, I think you will have found it a valuable
specimen answer   exercise. Compare your chart with mine. I expect I will have some points that
        you have not thought of. Actually, having one's attention drawn to points which,
        even after conscientious effort, one has omitted, is one of the best ways in the
        world of fixing such points firmly in one's mind. Furthermore, I hope you will
        find my version of the chart a very useful point of reference for your further
        studies. □

UNITED KINGDOM

		Levels of change in 1914	Potential for further change
1	Social geography	Roberts emphasizes decades of 'industry and the growth of cities' (p.98), and 'a growing, ever more tightly packed population' (p.101). He is not very explicit on the growth of suburbs, simply saying that in 1880 'the great shift to suburban areas had not yet taken place' (p.101). In fact this 'great shift' was well under way by 1914. Middle-class families were getting smaller, and the population was growing older.	Further urban and suburban growth is clearly to be expected. Signs of a significant drop in the birthrate ('natural increase', p.101) are not, according to Roberts, apparent in 1914.
2	Economic performance and theory	Wealthiest nation in Europe (in the world, second only to the United States); the world's greatest trading nation. Being overtaken in certain areas by the United States and Germany. The financial centre of the world. Not now as technologically innovative as Germany and the United States or even, with respect to the internal combustion engine, France.	Despite the worries about technology, there was no real reason to believe that Britain could not continue its impressive economic advance, and its dominance of world finance.
3	Social structure	Britain had a clearly articulated, and widely recognized, class structure. In Roberts's view, the bourgeoisie had effectively taken over as the dominant class; in my view, the upper class was still strongly coloured by aristocratic elements, while incorporating the more successful bourgeois elements. A substantial white-collar element had been added to the more traditional professional and business middle classes. The British working class was the oldest and most fully developed in the world. Class divisions were extremely sharp, inequalities gross, and the wage for most working men in employment inadequate to the needs of raising a family.	Liberals, and many Conservatives, were favourable to legislation designed to reduce inequalities; though still very weak, the Labour Party also agitated for such policies. The world's most highly developed trade union movement was an important force in making claims on behalf of the workers. Overall general economic trends had been towards rising living standards for the majority of society; however, in a time of rising prices, wages were static in the years immediately before the war. There was much deference to the existing social structure, and any drastic change in it seemed most unlikely. On the other hand, modest ameliorations could legitimately be expected.
4	National cohesion	Despite modest Home Rule movements in Scotland and Wales, Great Britain was, compared with most continental countries, a remarkably cohesive and homogeneous country. The striking exception, of course, concerns Ireland.	The attitudes of Unionists were threatening, and certainly there was a serious Irish crisis when war broke out; however, it was not necessarily apparent that a peaceful accommodation within the framework of the United Kingdom was out of the question, though, equally, communal tensions between Protestants and Catholics had a long and bitter history.

		Levels of change in 1914	Potential for further change
5	Social reform and welfare policies	A range of social welfare measures had been introduced at the end of the nineteenth century (most particularly in the realms of housing and workmen's compensation), and a further distinctive burst of legislation took place after 1906. Referring to social insurance, Britain had now certainly caught up with Germany, and in most respects was in advance of other European countries. (I should point out to you here that in Book 2, Unit 8, I present a consolidated chart of all social reforms in all countries we are concerned with for the prewar, war, and postwar periods. If you want to get a fuller picture of the prewar situation, have that chart beside you now).	Roberts speaks of the founding of the welfare state, with the obvious implication that further developments gradually extending the welfare state were inevitably on the way. I would be inclined to point to the severe limitations in the post-1906 legislation and suggest that accepted ideas on private enterprise, self-help, and so on, must be a limitation on the expectation that further major reforms would inevitably follow.
6	Material conditions	For the wealthy and much of the middle classes material conditions were extremely good. For the working class, and some of the lower middle class, life was lived at little above a bare subsistence level; there was a large residuum (about a third of the total working class) existing at less than subsistence level.	It is hard to see how any sharp improvement in these conditions was immediately in prospect though, no doubt, given the introduction of old age pensions, and so on, it was not unreasonable to expect gradual amelioration.
7	Customs and behaviour	A general point made by Roberts, which would seem to apply with particular force to Britain, is that 'new economic opportunities and easier communications already [that is, in 1914] made the physical break with the parental home easier' (p.187). Detail, however, is lacking. Other points I picked up were: religion is very much an observance of the middle and lower middle classes, with little impact on the working class; life in the urban slums was often brutal; *but* popular education is spreading – popular newspapers and the cinema have arrived. So, one might add, has the great spectator sport, association football. Roberts suggests that Britain was still a deferential society, though not as deferential as formerly. If you have any acquaintanceship at all with Edwardian photographs you will know that fashions and style of dress very firmly underpinned class distinctions.	Further decline in religious observance, further growth in mass culture might be expected, but the impression is very much not that of a society in which a rapid change in social customs was to be expected.

		Levels of change in 1914	**Potential for further change**
8	Role and status of women	Employment opportunities for women were expanding, as was women's education. Contraception was reducing the burdens of childbearing borne by upper-class and middle-class women. Since 1894 women property owners were able to vote in local elections. Women did not have the parliamentary vote, but very active suffragist and suffragette movements were in being.	Clearly the long-term expansion in women's opportunities was likely to continue. Obviously the women's movement would keep up the pressure, though militant suffragette action had lost the cause a lot of sympathy. Conservative leader Balfour had said that any further extension of the franchise would have to involve women. In fact, in 1914, (apart from the Labour Party) there was no strong support among political leaders for a general extension of the franchise. Resolutions in favour of votes for women had several times passed the House of Commons, but had never received the necessary government support. Finland and Norway already had votes for women, as had several American states. The issue was undoubtedly a major one in 1914. No doubt votes for women would have come some time (though one must note the very strong arguments against made by both men and women), but it does not seem to me that it was an immediate prospect – however, this is a controversial issue and you can only come to a satisfactory conclusion of your own by reading some of the important works on the subject. The beginning in the last quarter of the nineteenth century of the permanent long-run fall in the birth rate and in family size has been singled out as a process with a good claim to be the most important change in women's lives in the whole of history. This, obviously, was a long-term process of change which could be expected to continue.
9	High and popular culture	Even within the élites, modernism was greeted with considerable derision; in the realm of popular culture, cinema and the new popular press were already beginning to establish themselves; religious belief was still strong in the rural areas, but had never been strong in the towns.	Modernism had arrived, and popular culture was expanding, but there was no reason to expect any striking changes and certainly not that cinema would become acceptable to the middle and upper classes.

		Levels of change in 1914	**Potential for further change**
10	Values and institutions	Widely shared liberal values, but the franchise definitely not democratic (two-fifths of men and all women without the vote). Despite the strong Irish Nationalist movement no self-representation for the Irish people. Despite some moves towards collectivism, ideas of private enterprise and *laissez-faire* still strong. The British two-party system tended to produce strong governments capable of carrying through positive social-reform measures. I've commented on religion under other headings. The family was still strong.	Given the series of reform acts and the Liberal commitment to some form of Irish Home Rule, gradual change seemed perfectly likely; on the other hand, as Roberts brings out with regard to Ulster, Conservatives (or Unionists), aided by their entrenched majority in the House of Lords, and their support in the British army, were determined to sabotage any hint of a break-up of the United Kingdom. A slow movement towards collectivist policies was clearly discernible.

FRANCE

1	Social geography	As already noted, France's population, relative to other European countries, was already in decline. The drift from the land was slow.	France's relative population decline was already apparent in 1914 and seemed set to continue. There was no reason to expect any upset or acceleration in the slow change in the balance between town and country.
2	Economic performance and theory	On the world scene, France did not count to the extent that Britain and Germany did; none the less, Roberts (p.115) speaks of 'expansion and growing prosperity'. French technological innovation is exemplified by the Panhard car.	With a strong agricultural sector France, in many respects, had a balanced economy: there was no reason to believe that steady economic expansion would not continue.
3	Social structure	The French social structure, in essence, was not dissimilar to that of Britain. On the whole the upper class neither had the wealth nor the aristocratic tone of the British; within the middle classes there were rather more small businessmen and tradesmen; the French working class was small and ill-organized compared with the British; most critically, France had a very substantial peasant class.	The working class was growing, but there was no real reason to expect substantial changes in the near future.
4	National cohesion	Local loyalties were strong, and many of the inhabitants of rural areas were only slowly beginning to think of themselves as French. Still, compared with Central and East European countries, France was nationally a very cohesive country. The loss of Alsace-Lorraine (taken by the Germans in 1870) was felt quite bitterly.	It was to be expected that France would continue to become a more integrated nation. There seemed little prospect of the regaining of Alsace-Lorraine.

5	Social reform and welfare policies	France's most notable achievement in comparison with Britain was that of the establishment of universal education. For the rest, French individualism, the absence of strong single-party government, and the preoccupation of French 'liberals' with anti-clericalism, militated against extensive social-reform programmes. A more prosperous country, France did not even have the patchy reforms noted in Italy.	Given that there was no sign of effective pressure from the socialists, major social reform seemed unlikely.
6	Material conditions	In general, living standards were lower in France than in Britain, but France did not have the same vast pool of urban misery.	It was to be expected that steady economic expansion would bring a gradual raising of living standards.
7	Customs and behaviour	The key contrasts with Britain which I picked out were that: religious affiliation, or lack of it, counted for a great deal in ordinary life (Roberts, of course, does not say much on Catholic-Protestant clashes in Ireland, or those parts of England and Scotland with large numbers of Irish immigrants; the Chapel traditions of Wales would also be worth noting); that pre-industrial, pre-liberal/ democratic elements were still strong in France. Roberts picks out the telling example of the continuance of public executions in France (abolished in Britain in the 1860s). In general he states (end of last paragraph on p.114): 'France changed less than England or Germany between 1880 and 1914.'	I think we are bound to conclude that any great change in customs and behaviour seemed most unlikely in the France of 1914.
8	Role and status of women	In the world of education and the intellect, opportunities were probably greater for French women than British – note the achievements of Madame Curie mentioned by Roberts on p.198. But the women's movement was not nearly as advanced in France as in Britain – though there was a massive 'Votes for Women' demonstration in Paris in 1914; on the whole, Catholicism stressed women's domestic role even more strongly than was the case in Britain, with its variety of nonconformist faiths. There was no majority for votes for women in the National Assembly, and very strong opposition in the Senate.	Slow advance would undoubtedly continue, but votes for women, despite the Paris demonstration, hardly seemed an immediate prospect.

| 9 | High and popular culture | France, or at least Paris, led the world in the sponsorship and acceptance of modernism. Cinema was at roughly the same stage in France as in Britain, with possibly a greater interest being taken in it by the intellectual middle class. Religion still had a strong hold on popular belief. | Further cultural innovation could confidently be expected in a Paris-dominated France. |
| 10 | Values and institutions | Although liberal values had perhaps been diffused more slowly, the French parliamentary system was democratic in a way that the British was not: all adult males (though, of course, no females) had the vote. | Despite some manifestations of extreme right-wing nationalism, on the whole the trend in France was towards greater stability, and greater acceptance of the system. And there was no good reason to believe that that would not continue. On the other hand, there seemed little likelihood of French socialism influencing high politics in a way that it was possible for the British labour movement to do, since French socialism followed the German example in totally dissociating itself from parliamentary government. |

ITALY

1	Social geography	Italy (Roberts, pp.134–5) was deeply divided geographically and demographically. A fundamental factor was the large and growing class of desperately poor peasants (p.135): the economic and social gap between north and south had 'widened terrifyingly by 1914' (p.135). Italy had a sizable modern industrial base, in the Turin/Milan area.	The expectation could only be that, particularly with further idustrialization in the north, the north-south divide would continue to get worse.
2	Economic performance and theory	In the crisis years of 1896 to 1900 there had been privation and even starvation. Modest economic growth took place thereafter, but the desperate economic plight of the south was not dealt with. About the best that one can say for Italian economic performance is that it was not as bad as that of Spain.	Given Roberts's comments on renewed political instability at the end of the period, and Martin Clark's comments on Italian economic organization and entrepreneurial enterprise which you read in the last unit, steady economic advance in Italy did not look particularly likely.
3	Social structure	The Italian social structure only rather faintly resembled that of France or Britain; you learned from Martin Clark of Italy's lack of a substantial commercial or industrial bourgeoisie and of the very 'undeveloped' nature of its class structure. At the same time, a working class recognizably like that of other countries was steadily developing.	Given the backwardness of large areas, particularly in the south, rapid change in the class structure was not likely.

4	National cohesion	The fundamental divide is that between the north and the south; furthermore, many who now thought of themselves as Italian nationals, were still living under Austrian rule.	There seemed to be no realistic prospect of change. Industrialization in the north simply aggravated the contrast with the south.
5	Social reform and welfare policies	Italy did have workers' social insurance for disability and old age. The other reforms were relatively minor in character. Indeed, Roberts (p.142) suggests that Giolitti's reforms can be interpreted as 'mere tactical expedients'.	I do not think it can be said that Italy was steadily moving forwards in the realm of progressive social reform.
6	Material conditions	Even the petty aristocracy who doubled up as professional workers were not particularly rich. Very widespread poverty and deprivation was a characteristic of Italian society.	The evidence does not indicate the prospect of any rapid improvement.
7	Customs and behaviour	Roberts stresses the pervasive significance of the Catholic Church (p.134). Italy was a country of widespread disorder and violence. It lacked, says Roberts (p.143), 'healthy political *moeurs*', that is, 'customs'. If you know anything of Italian literature (or opera) of the period, you can flesh this out as implying 'primitive' notions of honour and revenge, lack of respect for human life, lack of 'civic virtue'. A majority of Italians might well be included among those 'millions of Europeans' still living in 'a theocentric universe' (referred to by Roberts on p.178).	Apart from the fact that industrialization was advancing in the north, signs of change are notably absent.
8	Role and status of women	Roberts doesn't say much but, reading between the lines, I think we can deduce that the condition and status of women in Italy were considerably lower than in France. Large numbers of men still didn't have the vote. The Catholic church was very strong. But note that the Italian mother was the central figure in the family.	Since the latest franchise reform concerned solely men, it seems unlikely that votes for women was on any short-term political agenda.
9	High and popular culture	Italy was the home of the Futurist movement in painting, irrationally glorifying war, but definitely modernist in style. However, Italian Realism (in literature and opera) was scarcely in the vein of modernism; nor was Italian nationalistic literature. High culture was a political concern (largely, one presumes, because of the importance of tourism). Religion exercised a powerful control over popular belief. In many parts of Italy opera was genuinely a part of popular culture.	If one is required to make some comparative statement about Italy I think it would have to be something like: 'In the eyes of the intellectuals of Paris, Vienna, St Petersburg, Berlin and London, Italy was perceived as having a great past culturally, but little future.'

| 10 | Political institutions and values | Liberal values were not deeply embedded, according to Roberts. The Italian socialist movement seemed too divided to be effective. Throughout most of the period, the franchise was a limited one; however, in 1912 Giolitti introduced universal male suffrage for those over 30. | Certainly Roberts's view is that, given the lack of deep-rooted liberal values, constitutional government was in a very shaky position in Italy. Given the time it had taken to achieve the age-qualified manhood suffrage of 1912 there is no good reason for believing that a move to full democracy was an immediate prospect. |

IMPERIAL RUSSIA

1	Social geography	The essence is contained in the sentence on p.145 beginning 'Most Russians were poverty-stricken peasants... their misery increasing year by year as their numbers grew.'	Yet, by 1912, Stolypin 'had broken the back of the worst problem facing the country' (p.156). But Stolypin was dead, murdered. None the less, says Roberts, 'in 1914 Russia was at last beginning to move into modern history' (p.156). Whether the problem of peasant land hunger had really been solved is open to doubt.
2	Economic performance and theory	This is a crucial matter, and subject for some debate. Roberts stresses Russia's rapid industrial growth and, of course, the guided economic policies of Witte. On pp.144–5 he goes to the core of the matter in stating that 'It is wrong to assume that collapse in revolution was the inevitable fate of Imperial Russia.' Though undoubtedly industrializing rapidly, Russia remained a very inefficient and backward country; however, the weight of expert opinion would in general agree with Roberts's analysis. Technologically, Russia was very dependent upon the inventions of others. She was also very dependent on foreign investment and lacked native entrepreneurs.	From the main argument in the column opposite it can be contended that Russia was already well on the road to economic modernization.
3	Social structure	The Russian upper class were landowners, and the small Russian middle class were also largely landowners. The divide between these on the one side, and the peasants on the other, was greater than could be found in any other European country. There were few institutions through which the middle class could express itself. The working class was small but concentrated into one or two areas. Its conditions and status were very much governed by its peasant origins.	Stolypin's reforms were improving the condition of the peasants; both the middle class and the working class were growing. Growth, however, in 1914 seemed to be suggesting instability and possibly open conflict, rather than the evolution of a stable society – though, arguably, the continuance of economic growth might have provided the conditions for just that.

4	National cohesion	The Russian Empire consisted of a large number of subject nationalities, generally quite firmly repressed. The fundamental laws of 1906 restored autonomy to Finland.	The prospects of self-determination for the subject nationalities did not appear to be great in 1914.
5	Social reform and welfare policies	Any social provision in Russia came through the peasant commune, the very agency that Stolypin was trying to break up. Accident insurance was introduced in 1903; sickness insurance in 1912.	Future developments in social reform would depend upon whether there was any likelihood of liberal elements being brought into government: from the standpoint of 1914 the possibility seems remote though, of course, steady economic advance might have brought a change here.
6	Material conditions	Roberts does not mince words: most of the peasants 'lived in squalor, misery and ignorance' (p.145); 'most Russians grew poorer' (p.150).	Perhaps under Stolypin's reforms, there would have been continuing improvement. In different ways, both the Bolsheviks and the Kadets had plans for social improvements: but, as we have noted, in the normal course of events, the chances of either being in power seemed remote in 1914.
7	Customs and behaviour	There are only hints in Roberts, for example (p.145): 'This huge mass remained an enigma, a vaguely threatening background to the activities of a highly civilized and westernized élite. The peasants seemed inaccessible to progressive influences ... they lived in a tradition of subjection and exploitation ...'	If one believes that a Western model entailing 'progressive influences' is ultimately likely to triumph, then clearly there was much scope for change – though little prospect of it as an immediate reality.
8	Role and status of women	University education (Roberts, pp.198–9) had been long established for women in Russia. However, neither women's rights, nor a strong movement in support of them, are noticeable in that country in 1914.	Both the party programmes which we have studied called for equal rights for both men and women. To that extent, there was the possibility of change in the future. Once, again, as I have said several times, it would depend on whether the opportunity came for such party programmes to be put into practice.
9	High and popular culture	Russian achievements in literature, drama and music were considerable; perhaps as an international centre of high culture Russia was ahead of Britain, but it does have to be noted that the great successes of the Diaghilev ballet took place not in St Petersburg or Moscow, but in Paris. In popular culture Russia was highly traditionalist; the Orthodox church dominated popular belief.	Russia was not seen by contemporaries as being on the threshold of staggering cultural innovations.

| 10 | Values and institutions | Political and individual rights were granted by the fundamental laws of 1906, but the powers of the autocracy were still very great. Because of the general hopelessness of the Russian situation, Russia, the most illiberal of all the countries studied here, had the most convinced revolutionary Marxist movement. | The exclusion from government of the social democrats (Bolsheviks and Mensheviks) was perhaps not altogether unexpected, but the exclusion of the liberal, reformist party, the Kadets, suggests that possibilities of steady constitutional change were not great. |

THE HABSBURG MONARCHY

1	Social geography	Roberts (p.159) brings out very clearly the enormous differences between areas in Hungary 'almost as backward as Russia', or where ' "age-old tribal communism" could still be found', and in Austria, 'virtually untouched by the market economy', on the one hand, and those of urban Bohemia and 'the cultural élite of Vienna or Budapest', on the other.	The existing system appeared well tempered to maintaining these differences.
2	Economic performance and theory	Roberts (going back to p.29) puts Austria-Hungary in his third category of nations, those predominantly agricultural, with a relatively undeveloped industrial base. On the world scene Austria-Hungary was certainly not a major trading power.	Obviously, as is brought out in the extract from Macartney you read in the last unit, economic development was taking place with considerable potential for further growth. But it is debatable whether the monarchy's multi-racial composition, and repression of subject minorities in Hungary, was really compatible with sustained economic growth.
3	Social structure	Class structure is inevitably interrelated with the nationality problem. In many areas the structure is essentially the dichotomous one of landowners and peasants, but Macartney indicated the development of the standard model of the most successful bourgeois elements joining with the aristocracy. The urban working class was still small in 1914, though, as we have seen, capable of supporting socialist organization.	Obviously, following Macartney, social structure was slowly changing, but there were no great signs of a steady modification of the link between nationality and social position.
4	National cohesion	Obviously, the Habsburg monarchy, *par excellence*, was the state without national cohesion. At the same time, despite vigorous nationalist movements, the situation in 1914, did seem to be that, however shakily, and however threatened by such external states as Serbia-backed-by-Russia, the monarchy was managing to hold together its disparate nationalities.	The picture seems to be the rather paradoxical one of rational improvement scarcely seeming possible, while actual collapse was far from imminent.

5	Social reform and welfare policies	Roberts is not very helpful. In fact, Austria (though not Hungary) followed the German social reform programme very closely. The trouble was, the inefficient monarchy was not able to implement it very effectively.	In the light of all that has been said, it is clear that the possibilities for change were not great.
6	Material conditions	Factories could offer wages which were attractive to rural workers. In general living standards throughout the Dual Monarchy were low.	Though working-class organization was growing, prospects for change were small.
7	Customs and behaviour	Little possibility of generalizing: enormous gulfs between 'backward' peasant cultures and sophisticated metropolitan cultures; a multiplicity of national customs.	No major transformation on the horizon.
8	Role and status of women	Obviously in the commitment of Austrian Social Democrats to equal rights for women, we have important signs of change in Austria-Hungry. In general, however, national and religious issues tended to cut across the advocacy of women's rights.	Given that the arguments were being made (ideological circumstances), obviously the potential was there. But, as in the other issues, the position of the 'Dual Monarchy [i.e. Austria-Hungary] as "despotism tempered by slovenliness" ' (Roberts, p.160) must militate against any realistic prospect of change.
9	High and popular culture	In Vienna and Prague the Dual Monarchy had two of the greatest European cultural centres, with Budapest not far behind. Yet it may be that the high culture of Austria (the Strauss family, the paintings of Klimt) exemplify particularly well Mayer's case that the ruling old regime sponsored traditionalist art forms. Against that we have to put the facts that the major works of Freud originated from Vienna and that Kafka came from the Austrian lands. In popular culture and belief, religious and nationalist loyalties are dominant themes.	Who can say? I make this rhetorical question seriously: Vienna, in many ways, may be the declining, decadent city, yet as a cultural centre it rivalled Paris: the conditions of production for high culture are not easily pinned down.
10	Values and institutions	The nationalities problem inevitably intrudes upon that of political rights. Roberts puts matters neatly in the passage from the first paragraph on p.160 to the end of the second paragraph on p.161, when he points out that behind the appearance of liberal attitudes and institutions, the practice throughout the Dual Monarchy was in fact extremely illiberal.	At the very beginning of the third paragraph on p.161 Roberts indicates that the monarchy did not have within itself the powers to carry through reforms.

IMPERIAL GERMANY

1	Social geography	The German birth rate began to fall in 1904, but the population still grew: 'The great flow to the cities ... produced a huge industrial proletariat' (Roberts, p.167).	Everything pointed to the continuance of these trends.
2	Economic performance and theory	The testimony is overwhelming that with respect to economic performance and technological advance Germany is eclipsing all other European countries.	There could be no reason in 1914 to feel that this would not continue.
3	Social structure	The German upper bourgeoisie was doing extremely well, as Berghahn (not that we have to believe him) would seem to suggest. Yet, that fusion between traditional landed elements and the more successful elements from the bourgeoisie, which was already characterizing France and Britain (I would maintain) had not fully taken place in Germany where, as Berghahn points out, traditional lines of social distinction were very strong. To the older middle class was being added the new *Mittelstand* – the developments here, I have suggested, not really being as unique as Kocka suggests. After Britain, Germany had the most fully developed working class in the world. At least adult working-class males had the vote within the German imperial system, more than can be said with respect to the British working class. Yet the German working class, or certainly the German working-class movement, was treated much more obviously as being outside respectable society than was the case in Britain.	The aims of the German Social Democratic party suggest a peaceful way towards transforming this autocratic and sharply divided society. However, it would not be easy to say that, faced with the evidence of 1914, such a transformation was likely in German society.
4	National cohesion	The German Empire was, despite the local differences well identified by Berghahn, nationally a very united entity, despite the existence of national minorities (e.g. the Poles). The problem for the rest of Europe was that the industrious German nation was scattered widely over many other countries outside the ambit of the German Empire. In particular, of course, Germans dominated one part of the Austro-Hungarian Dual Monarchy.	Though Pan-German sentiment (that is, sentiment in favour of a greater Germany including *all* Germans) was quite strong, there were no obvious indications of future change here.

5	Social reform and welfare policies	Because of the policies of Bismarck Germany had the most fully developed social welfare system in Europe, only being equalled and overtaken by the British legislation of the post-1906 period.	Because of the hostility of the established political nation towards the working class, it must be considered a possibility that no further social measures favourable to the working class were likely to be enacted. On the other hand, the tradition was firmly there, and there is, equally, no serious reason for doubting that steady progress might well continue.
6	Material conditions	Material prosperity in Germany was second only to that in Britain.	There was no reason to believe that living standards would not continue to advance.
7	Customs and behaviour	The only hints I could track down in Roberts were: the 'military tone' of German life (p.175); and Germany's consciousness 'of herself as part of a European and Christian civilization' (p.177). The cinema and the popular press, of course, had come to Germany as to Britain and France.	Growth in mass culture, but otherwise no spectacular developments would have seemed a reasonable prediction in 1914.
8	Role and status of women	Educational advances for women at least equalled those of France, and were more strongly marked than those in Britain. Otherwise, the traditionalist, authoritarian attitudes of Prussian-dominated Germany must be seen as inimical to the interests of women.	The existence of a strong Social Democratic party arguing for equality for women must be strong testimony on the other side (again an important 'ideological circumstance'); however, I'd be inclined to extrapolate from what I have just said in the column opposite that the potential for change in the role and status of women was not great.
9	High and popular culture	Germany was Europe's most dynamic nation in 1914 with several traditional cultural centres (Berlin, Munich, Dresden) to rival Paris.	Further developments in both modernism and popular culture seemed highly probable.

10 Values and institutions	Liberalism was not deeply rooted in Germany; in the delicate relationship between nationalism and liberalism, nationalism triumphed. Germany had the largest and best organized Social Democratic party in Europe; it was, on the one hand, committed totally to Marxist theory, but, on the other, against revolutionary action. In the *Reichstag*, the parliament of the German Empire, deputies were elected on the basis of one man one vote. The crucial problem (I hope you spotted this!) was that within the German Empire the individual state of Prussia, because of its enormous military prestige, exercised an overwhelming, and most undemocratic, influence: the voting system for the Prussian parliament was quite undemocratic, and angled towards the traditional elements in Prussian society. The powers of the *Reichstag* were in fact limited; the prestige of the Emperor and of the Prussian military caste very high.	The German Social Democratic party was growing in strength, but since it was effectively excluded from the political nation, and since it did not show the willingness of the British Labour Party to try to influence existing institutions, and since there was a vacuum in Germany where in other countries the parties representative of liberalism existed, the possibilities for steady change in Germany were probably not high.

8   FINAL DISCUSSION OF PRIMARY SOURCES

You will recall my disagreement with Roberts over whether the social policies of the Liberal government in Britain after 1906 amounted to the 'founding of the welfare state'. The two key acts in the Liberal government's social welfare legislation were the Old Age Pensions Act of 1908, and the National Insurance Act of 1911 (Part I dealing with Health Insurance, Part II with Unemployment). Extracts from the second of these two acts are printed in *Primary Sources 1: World War I* (I.12). Turn now to this document and let us work through it together.

National Insurance Act, 16 December 1911: Part II, Unemployment Insurance

Remember that this act is in two parts, the first concerned with insurance against ill health, the second with insurance against unemployment. Roberts may very well be right that the very fact of enacting legislation concerning these two issues can be regarded as 'founding the welfare state'.

With regard to Part II, Unemployment Insurance, I want you now to read the Sixth Schedule, and the third paragraph of the Seventh Schedule.

Exercise   1   The Sixth Schedule seems to present a pretty comprehensive list of working-class occupations. Are there any missing? Why these occupations and not others?

2   With regard to the Seventh Schedule, comment on the length of time for which unemployment benefit may be received. ■

Specimen answers and discussion

1   Manifestly absent are the coal-mining, railway and other transport, textile, and chemical industries.

In fact, to cut a long story short, this is not a comprehensive coverage of working-class occupations, but a concentration on trades where, because of weather conditions or fluctuations in demand (as with the manufacture of ordnance and fire-arms), 'seasonal' unemployment was likely.

2   The maximum coverage is for under four months. Unemployment insurance was intended as a temporary alleviation in trades where temporary interruptions were to be expected. □

To me this is a piecemeal, limited reform, pervaded by nineteenth-century attitudes. This is why I find Roberts's language exaggerated. Note what is at stake here with regard to the main issues of our course. If the pre-1914 legislation is all Roberts says it is (and you will have to make up your own mind), this would probably lead one to downgrade any possible significance attaching to the war in bringing about social reform. If, however, relatively little had been achieved by 1914, then the war might stand out as that much more significant. You see again how initial attitudes can colour later conclusions.

References

Beauvoir, Simone de (1988) *The Second Sex*, Penguin Books (originally published in French, 1948; in English, 1953).

Eisenstadt, S.N. (1966) *Modernization: Protest and Change*, Prentice Hall.

McLeod, Hugh (1997) *Religion and the People of Western Europe 1789–1970*, Oxford University Press.

Sheehan, J.J. (1978) *German Liberalism in the Nineteenth Century*, The University of Chicago Press.

Unit 5 THE ORIGINS OF THE FIRST WORLD WAR

ANNIKA MOMBAUER

Open University students of this unit will need to refer to:

Set book: J.M. Roberts, *Europe 1880–1945*, Longman, 2000
Primary Sources 1: World War I, eds Arthur Marwick and Wendy Simpson, Open University, 2000
Secondary Sources, eds Arthur Marwick and Wendy Simpson, Open University, 2000

Maps Booklet

CHRONOLOGY OF EVENTS

1871	Franco-Prussian War. Wilhelm I becomes first Emperor of the unified Germany. Germany annexes the French provinces of Alsace and Lorraine
1878	Congress of Berlin (attempt to settle Balkan crisis)
1879	Dual Alliance between Germany and Austria-Hungary
1882	Italy joins Germany and Austria-Hungary in Triple Alliance
1888	Wilhelm II becomes German Emperor
1889	Founding of the Second International
1890	Chancellor Otto von Bismarck is dismissed
1894	Franco-Russian Alliance
1898	First German Naval Law
1899	First Peace Conference at The Hague
1902	Anglo-Japanese Alliance
1904	Anglo-French Entente
1904/5	Russo-Japanese War. Attempted revolution in Russia (1905)
1906	First Moroccan Crisis
1907	Second Peace Conference at the Hague. Anglo-Russian Entente concluded
1908	Young Turk revolution
1908	Bosnian Annexation Crisis
1911	Second Moroccan Crisis
1912	First Balkan War (Balkan League of Serbia, Bulgaria, Greece and Montenegro against Turkey)
1913	Second Balkan War (Bulgaria against Serbia, Greece, Romania and Turkey)
1914	Assassination of Austrian Archduke Franz Ferdinand (June)

INTRODUCTION

The origins of the First World War have been debated virtually since war broke out in 1914. Several generations of historians have attempted to explain why the assassination of the Austrian Archduke Franz Ferdinand in June 1914 could have led to the unleashing of a war of unprecedented scale. It soon became evident that the causes of the First World War were not just about an assassination at Sarajevo. However, arriving at an agreement on why the war broke out proved impossible. Unlike the Second World War, which was the result of German aggression, the case was never so straightforward regarding the First World War. Hundreds of books and articles have been published on the subject over the decades, thousands of documents have been unearthed in archives and made available to historians – but nonetheless the issue is still far from resolved. In Philip Bell's words, the search for an explanation of the outbreak of the war has been 'almost obsessive' (Bell, 'Origins of the war of 1914', 1992, p.106). As a result, the task of any history student trying to understand the complex origins of the war is a tricky one. Some historians have concentrated on short-term causes, while others decided that long-term, underlying trends almost inevitably led to war in 1914, and that the question should not be: 'why did war break out in 1914', but 'why was it averted for as long as that?' Some have argued that the policy and intentionality of a particular nation were, above all, the cause of the war, while others have blamed alliance systems and 'old-style diplomacy'.

In this unit, the complex and passionate debates around the origins of the First World War will be outlined and analysed. We will ask why it was so difficult to attribute guilt, and why people cared so much about placing the blame for the outbreak of the war on any particular nation. More than 80 years after the event, we also ask why studying the origins of the war, and the historiographical debate itself, is a worthwhile pursuit today. By looking at some of the pre-war crises and international developments, you will be able to draw your own conclusions about the causes of the First World War.

AIMS

At the end of this unit, you should have:

1 an overview and understanding of the nature of the controversy about the origins of the First World War;

2 an understanding of why certain points of view were advanced by historians at certain times;

3 a knowledge of some of the key arguments advanced during the debate, and familiarity with some of the key documents available to historians;

4 an idea of how the events of the pre-war years, and particularly those of the July Crisis of 1914, brought war ever closer and eventually led to its outbreak in August 1914.

The unit is divided into four main parts. First, we will ask why historians have debated the origins of the war with such passion, and why it might be considered so important to explain why war broke out in 1914. In the second part of the unit, the debate on the origins is investigated in some detail, and you will be able to follow the development of the debate from the Treaty of Versailles to the Fischer controversy and to more recent interpretations. Parts three and four examine both the long- and short-term causes of the war and give you a chance to familiarize yourself with the events and decisions that contributed to an increasingly war-like mood in the years prior to 1914, culminating in the July Crisis and the outbreak of war. By the end of the unit, you will also know how historiography has moved on from the Fischer controversy of the 1960s and how historians today interpret the origins of the First World War.

1   THE OUTBREAK OF THE FIRST WORLD WAR AND THE NEED TO UNDERSTAND ITS ORIGINS

War never seemed far away in the first decade of the twentieth century. Increasing tensions between Europe's great powers meant that an escalation of international conflicts into war had seemed likely on many occasions. It is well known that the trigger for war was provided by an act of terrorism. A Bosnian Serb succeeded in assassinating the Austrian heir to the throne on 28 June 1914, an act of defiance aimed at the Austro-Hungarian state which was seen as suppressing Serbian nationalist aspirations. As a result Russians would soon be fighting alongside French and British soldiers against Austrian, Hungarian and German soldiers, and a localized conflict between Serbia and Austria-Hungary would escalate into over four years of bloody war.

However, such a war had been only narrowly averted during many pre-war diplomatic crises that had created an increasing mood of hostility between the European nations, which were bound into two opposing alliance systems (Germany, Austria-Hungary and Italy formed the Triple Alliance, while France and Russia were joined by Britain in a Triple Entente). Disputes and conflicts had erupted, particularly over colonial matters. Two Moroccan crises had seen German attempts to increase her own influence over the African continent and to assert her great power status. Consequently, her neighbours perceived Germany to be threatening the *status quo* in Europe. As a result of the Anglo-German naval race, Britains and Germans vied with each other over naval supremacy. The French still deeply resented Germany for the annexation of Alsace-Lorraine in 1871 and demands for revenge were regularly voiced. Russia emerged from her war against Japan defeated and weakened by revolution and more than ever in need of her allies. Austrians were suspicious of Russia because of her support for Serbia. Italy and Austria had disputes over territory to which both nations wanted to lay claim, despite being in theory allied to each other. Balkan crises more than once threatened to embroil Europe in war. The potential for conflict was almost endless, and the 'mood of 1914' was certainly increasingly war-like (James Joll, *The Origins of the First World War*, 1966, pp.199ff.). (You might want to refer back to Unit 2, which examines nationalism in some detail. Roberts, pp.200ff. provides useful background information.) There was an underlying expectation and acceptance of war and we should be aware that people did not have the benefit of hindsight following two world wars and therefore did not regard war in the same way as we would today. At the end of the nineteenth century, war was still an entirely legitimate course of action if politics failed to achieve the desired results. Moreover, before 1914, most European governments had ensured that public opinion was primed for the event of war by making certain that the people knew who their likely enemies would be and by emphasizing the defensive nature of their own government's actions. In August 1914, this was how governments ensured that their people rallied, more or less enthusiastically, behind their leaders. Germans and Britains, French and Russians shared the notion that they had been attacked and were acting defensively. It is important to be aware of these attitudes and 'unspoken assumptions' (J.Joll) that informed and influenced people's decisions.

In Unit 2, Section 4, you have already encountered the notion of Social Darwinism and the way it shaped thinking in pre-war Europe. The belief in the 'survival of the fittest' as applied to nations made war appear increasingly likely and even desirable. Nationalist aspirations and militarism often created a mood that was favourable to war, while Socialism and even the relatively widespread peace-movement, which might have tempered the existing bellicose mood, seemed to threaten the established *status quo* so that domestic tensions were added to international ones. As we will see, some governments even deliberately fostered and highlighted international disputes with a view to diverting attention away from domestic problems.

Given these pre-war developments and attitudes, when the long expected war finally became reality, most people felt they knew why they were fighting their neighbours and many were willing to do so. War did not come as a surprise in 1914 and some politicians, statesmen, writers and artists even welcomed its arrival.

Likewise, when the war was over, both victors and vanquished felt that they had fought a justified, defensive war. What had appeared like German aggression to British, French, Belgians and Russians, had been portrayed as justified defensive action to the German people. Germans remembered their Kaiser's speech in the *Reichstag* on 4 August 1914, in which he had emphasized: 'We are not motivated by a desire to conquer', while the Chancellor Bethmann Hollweg had conjured up the image of Germany defending herself against hostile neighbours. All the greater was the outrage with which the defeated Germans greeted the Treaty of Versailles, one of five treaties concluded as part of the victors' Paris peace settlement. Germany's new government had been excluded from the negotiations and been forced to accept the victors' peace conditions under the threat of renewed hostilities in case they refused to sign the treaty. Of its many unpopular provisions, none proved more controversial in Germany than the famous 'war guilt clause', Article 231 of the treaty. It was with the publication of this treaty that the debate on the origins of the First World War began in earnest. Germany was united in the desire to fight Article 231, which was considered unacceptable not just on moral, but also on economic grounds. The controversial war-guilt section read as follows:

> ARTICLE 231: The Allied and Associated Governments affirm and Germany accepts the responsibility of Germany and her allies for causing all the loss and damage to which the Allied and Associated Governments and their nationals have been subjected as a consequence of the war imposed upon them by the aggression of Germany and her allies.

(Further excerpts from the Treaty of Versailles are in *Primary Sources 1: World War I*, Document 1.13.)

Exercise At this point, you should turn to the introduction to James Joll's book *The Origins of the First World War* (reprinted in *Secondary Sources*). Read the first paragraph in which Joll analyses why the outbreak of the First World War has been studied in such detail. What reasons does he give? Why do you think it was considered particularly important to establish the exact causes of the war? ■

Specimen answer and discussion Joll explains that the outbreak of the First World War marked the end of an era and the beginning of a new one. He sees the experiences of the war and in particular the horrors of trench warfare as events that have continued to influence and haunt writers and artists (and one could add the general public, too). Even those born long after the events continue to be fascinated and moved by the terrible suffering the war inflicted upon soldiers and civilians alike. Joll also alerts the reader to the grave consequences of the war: revolution in Russia, political and social upheaval all over Europe, the redrawing of the map of Europe; all of them events that shaped the course of history in the twentieth century. In this sense, the First World War certainly was the seminal event of the twentieth century.

In answer to the second question, you may have speculated that it might have been regarded as important to justify the terrible losses the war inflicted by establishing that the victims died for a 'good cause', or a 'just' one. British Victory Medals, for example, were inscribed with the following legend: *The Great War For Civilization* 1914–1919. The implication is obvious: the sacrifices made by thousands of casualties had not been in vain, but for a just cause. German aggression, in this reading, had threatened civilization, and Britain and her allies had protected and saved it. Obviously, German soldiers and their families felt the need for similarly reassuring knowledge that their suffering had been for a just cause. The hardship and suffering of the post-war years were all the harder to bear because of the assertion of Germany's enemies that German aggression and intent were to blame for the outbreak of the war. Hence the German governments were determined in the 1920s and 30s to correct this apparent misconception. □

2   VERSAILLES: THE DEBATE ON THE ORIGINS OF THE WAR BEGINS

After the war, the revision of the Treaty of Versailles was regarded as imperative in Germany. The intention was not only to remove the guilt attached to Germany, but also to prove that the huge reparations that Germany was compelled to pay were unfair and unjustified (despite the fact that the war-time German government had accepted responsibility for civilian damage, particularly regarding Belgium and France, in a pre-Armistice agreement). For Germany, it became a matter of pride as well as principle that the Versailles' ruling should be shown to have been incorrect. The following section provides an overview of how the debate about the origins of the war developed from the immediate post-war years right through to the 1960s.

Revising the verdict of Versailles

In Germany, reactions to the Treaty of Versailles were hostile. The terms of the 'victors' peace' were considered unacceptable. The state began immediately to try to prove both to the citizens of Germany and to the world at large that the so-called war-guilt paragraph was unjustified. A parliamentary committee was set up with the task of enquiring into the origins of the war. The German Foreign Office established a special war-guilt section for this purpose, the so-called

Kriegsschuldreferat. Under its auspices, the Centre for the Study of the Causes of the War published not only countless studies and documents, but even a journal dedicated solely to the question of war-guilt, entitled *Die Kriegsschuldfrage* (the war-guilt question). These official publications were intended to dispel the view that Germany had caused or wanted the war. This 'revisionist school' of historians was officially subsidised and encouraged by the Weimar governments. The name revisionist stems from the explicit intention behind these accounts of the origins of the First World War to be published within Germany: to revise the Treaty of Versailles. Part of the attempt to disprove the war-guilt ruling was the publication of documents to prove German innocence. The official document collection *Die grosse Politik der Europäischen Kabinette* ('The high politics of the European governments') aimed to establish collective responsibility for the war. Forty volumes of documents were published by the German governments between 1922 and 1927 and to this day they remain an important collection for historians. Based on these carefully selected documents it was argued that no single nation should be made to carry the burden of responsibility for the outbreak of war. Other European nations felt they had to follow suit and publish documents that would likewise prove their own innocence in the events that led to war. All these document collections were necessarily selective and reflect this apologetic intention. The German documents, for example, deliberately omitted uncomfortable facts, such as the 'blank cheque' issued by Berlin to Vienna in the early days of July 1914 (we will investigate this in more detail below). Other important evidence in connection with German decision-making during the July Crisis, or details of the Schlieffen Plan, such as its original intention to violate not only the neutrality of Luxembourg and Belgium, but also neutral Holland, was also kept from the public. It was up to later historians such as, for example, Luigi Albertini and Fritz Fischer to uncover some of the more incriminating evidence that such editions had deliberately excluded. Since the Second World War, many more documents have come to light to inform historians about the events leading up to war in 1914. You will examine some of this primary evidence later in this unit.

It is important to realize that not only German historians were revisionists: in America, for example, revisionist interpretations dominated the inter-war years, partly because the USA had condemned the harsher points of the Versailles Treaty. Sidney Bradshaw Fay and Harry Elmer Barnes are the most important American revisionists of the 1930s. The former argued that no European country had actually wanted war in 1914, and that they all shared the blame for the escalation of the crisis, while the latter completely turned the tables by accusing the Entente powers whilst being an apologist of the central powers.

The new inter-war orthodoxy

In practical political terms, the revisionists failed. The Treaty of Versailles was never revised in the way the revisionists had wanted, although the payment of reparations finally lapsed during the Great Depression, and the peace conditions had already been moderated following the Dawes Plan (1924) and the Young Plan (1929). However, their version of events became predominant in classrooms and in popular accounts of the origins of the war (John Langdon, *July 1914*, 1991, p.4). In that sense, the efforts of the revisionists were rewarded with success, as a new orthodoxy developed in the late 1920s and 1930s. Collective responsibility, rather than the responsibility of one nation, was now emphasized. This new interpretation was summed up by Lloyd George in his war memoirs, when he concluded that 'all the nations slithered over the edge of the boiling cauldron of war in 1914' – this conciliatory view became accepted in most countries. Long-term developments and trends, such as the alliance system and the secret diplomacy of the late nineteenth century, as well as imperial rivalries, were cited as causes of the war. In addition, Marxist interpretations held that the war had been an inevitable outcome of the excesses of capitalism, rather than the design of any particular nation. The British historian G.P. Gooch summed up the thinking of the time: 'The belief that any nation or statesman was the arch criminal in 1914 is no longer held by serious students of history' (quoted in McDonough, 1997, p.25). All the major powers had good reasons to go to war in 1914, he argued, and there could be no question of allocating blame or talking of war guilt.

By the late 1930s, enquiries into the outbreak of the First World War came to be regarded as less important in the face of the threat of a renewed European or World War. In Germany, the Nazi government had deliberately acted in defiance of the Treaty of Versailles and there was no longer a perceived need to revise its hated war-guilt clause. Moreover, in the aftermath of the horrors of the Second World War, there was initially no great concern to investigate the causes of war in 1914, particularly in Germany, which now had more than enough uncomfortable history to come to terms with. In the early 1950s, the pre-war orthodoxy of collective responsibility was still advanced in Germany, as summed up by the German historian Gerhard Ritter in 1951:

> The documents do not permit attributing a premeditated desire for a European war on the part of any government or people in 1914. Distrust was at a peak, ruling circles were dominated by the idea that war was inevitable. Each one accused the other of aggressive intentions; each accepted the risk of war and saw its hope of security in the alliance system and the development of armaments.
>
> (Quoted in McDonough, 1997, p.25)

This comfortable interpretation was challenged by some historians, notably the Italian Luigi Albertini, whose impressive three volume study entitled *The Origins of the First World War* had already been published in Italian during the Second World War, but whose findings only became known to a wider audience in the 1950s, when his work was published in English translation. Albertini pointed the finger at Germany as being the country most responsible for the outbreak of war. Although his seminal work was based on much new primary evidence, the impact of his work was initially very small, especially given the lack of a German translation (to this day!), and particularly in comparison with that of his German colleague, Professor Fritz Fischer, a historian at Hamburg University who presented the first real challenge to the revisionists' orthodoxy in Germany. In Britain, the anti-revisionist position was most effectively supported by A.J.P. Taylor, who saw German policy in 1914 as part of a consistent German tradition from Bismarck to Hitler and who argued, like Albertini, that Hitler had not been an aberration in German history. For the German historical establishment, such claims were unacceptable, particularly when expressed by an insider, like Fischer.

The Fischer school's challenge

Fritz Fischer's publications of the late 1950s and early 1960s have caused one of the most heated and most important historiographical debates of the twentieth century. In particular, his books *Germany's Aims in the First World War* (1967) and *War of Illusions* (1975) (first published in German in 1961 and 1969 respectively) gave cause for disagreement and argument.

In his first major publication, Fischer rocked the boat by suggesting not only that Germany caused the war, but that her policy makers had been motivated by wide-ranging and aggressive foreign policy aims and that there was a continuity in aims from the First to the Second World War. His publication *Griff nach der Weltmacht* in 1961 (literally 'Grab for World Power'), the English edition being entitled less provocatively *Germany's Aims in the First World War*, marked the beginning of the so-called Fischer controversy. It also marked the end of the kind of patriotic self-censorship that German historians had so far practised. The following excerpt gives a flavour of the argument that he advanced:

> [G]iven the tenseness of the world situation in 1914 – a condition for which Germany's world policy, which had already led to three dangerous crises (those of 1905, 1908 and 1911), was in no small measure responsible – any limited or local war in Europe directly involving one great power must inevitably carry with it the imminent danger of a general war. As Germany willed and coveted the Austro-Serbian war and, in her confidence in her military superiority, deliberately faced the risk of a conflict with Russia and France, her leaders must bear a substantial share of the historical responsibility for the outbreak of the general war in 1914.
>
> (Fischer, *Germany's Aims*, 1967, p.88)

In this book, Fischer focused on German war aims, arguing that Germany embarked on the war with clearly defined and wide-ranging foreign policy aims. In his investigation, he focused on diplomatic and military history in order to explain the motivations of Germany's decision-makers. The so-called September Programme of Chancellor Theobald von Bethmann Hollweg was one of the key documents to come to light as a result of his work (see also Unit 6, for a discussion of the September Programme). This document set out the German Chancellor's future vision of Europe following a German victory, detailing plans of annexations of territory, a customs union that would guarantee German economic hegemony and a German colonial empire in Africa. To Fischer, the September Programme was a 'blueprint' for world power. 'It was an expression of German striving for European hegemony, the first step toward "world domination" [...]' (Fischer, *World Power or Decline*, 1974, pp.44–5). His opponents would argue that a memorandum of early September 1914, when Germany was fighting a successful campaign on all fronts, cannot be used as evidence for *pre-war* war aims. Fischer claimed that Germany bore the lion's share of responsibility for the outbreak of the war, due to her expansionist foreign policy aims. According to Fischer, Germany embarked on a 'preventive war'. This did not mean, however, that Germany's decision-makers attempted to prevent an attack by their neighbours, but rather that they wanted to prevent a situation from developing in which Germany would no longer be strong enough to challenge her neighbours – a fine, but important distinction. In Fischer's words, preventive war 'was an attempt to defeat the enemy powers before they became too strong, and to realize Germany's political ambitions, which may be summed up as German hegemony over Europe' (Fischer, *War of Illusions*, 1975, p.470). In addition, Fischer maintained that an aggressive foreign policy had been employed by Germany's ruling élite to detract from domestic problems, an argument that had first been advanced by Eckart Kehr in the early 1930s. The emphasis on the 'primacy of domestic policy', rather than foreign policy motivations, opened up a further aspect of debate for historians about whether domestic concerns were more important in determining the country's policy than external pressures.

Fischer's critics were quick to counter his 'heretical' claims. Gerhard Ritter was Fischer's most critical and outspoken opponent, but he was joined by most members of the German historical profession at the time. Ritter summed up his reaction to the publication of *Griff nach der Weltmacht*: 'I could not put the book down without feeling deep melancholy: melancholy, and anxiety with regard to the coming generation [...]' (cited in Joll, 1966, 'The 1914 Debate Continues', p.31). Fischer's critics accused him and those historians who supported his findings (labelled both the 'Fischer' or 'Hamburg school') of adopting a contradictory approach by focusing on diplomatic and political documents but stressing that German foreign policy was influenced by domestic concerns; they alleged that his focus was too narrowly on Germany and that such an approach ignored the culpability of other nations. Fischer was accused of approaching history with hindsight, particularly in relating Hitler's foreign policy aims to those of Bethmann Hollweg and the Imperial government. The debate became very emotional and in an atmosphere that is almost unfathomable today, Fischer was accused of being a disloyal traitor who was 'soiling his own nest'. He was subjected to professional and personal criticism and accused of secretly being supported by East Germany. Official funding was withdrawn to stop him from embarking on a lecture tour of the US in 1964. In many ways, the Fischer controversy says as much about Germany in the 1960s as it reveals about Imperial Germany. Post-war Germany, after the First as well as after the Second World War, was a place in which historians were expected to put 'national interests' first – and those did not include throwing new and uncomfortable light on the origins of the First World War. Hermann Kantorowicz had summed up this state of affairs in the inter-war years, when his findings about the origins of the war, which did not support the current revisionist orthodoxy, were suppressed by the establishment. He noted:

> For in Germany – and indeed all over the Continent – it is by no means considered sufficient that an historical work should tell the truth in accordance with the convictions of the author. In a work dealing with higher policy it is held without saying that the author should enter upon his investigation in the interests of his own nation and against its antagonists, and that his work shall be 'patriotic', and the outcome of 'national feeling'.
>
> (Cited in John A. Moses, *The Politics of Illusion*, 1975, p. 5)

The German government was as keen as ever to keep the revisionist orthodoxy alive. This is perhaps difficult to understand today, but given the insecure state of Germany in the international arena following the Second World War, any suggestions of a continuity of policy from the First to the Second war threatened to open up a host of uncomfortable questions that one would have to ask of

German history as a whole. In other words, twelve years of National Socialism could less easily be explained away as an aberration if it could be proved that Germany had once before embarked on a war with practically the same foreign policy aims in mind. It was above all this uncomfortable link from Bismarck to Hitler that Fischer's critics could not accept or forgive. It is, however, more easy to understand the defensiveness of the West German government and German historians in the light of the crudeness of such 'from Bismarck to Hitler' arguments which were advanced outside of Germany, and which claimed to be able to prove that a particular type of 'German national character' had been at the heart of the 'German problem'. This, of course, was not something that Fischer had ever maintained.

Fischer followed up his claims about German war aims with a second major study, in which he focused his attention on the immediate pre-war years in Germany. *War of Illusions*, first published in 1969, argued even more forcefully that Germany's leading decision-makers were willing to seize the opportunity offered by a crisis in the Balkans such as the one provoked by Franz Ferdinand's assassination. Another key document was at the centre of this study. Fischer argued that leading decision-makers in Berlin decided as early as December 1912 that they should embark on a war in the not too distant future. We will examine the documents on which this theory is based in some detail later in the unit.

Fischer's new claims provoked further heated discussion, in which his critics and supporters disagreed over the importance of the primacy of foreign or domestic policy and debated the role of individuals in influencing the decision to go to war.

Exercise Now read the rest of the introduction by James Joll from the *Secondary Sources*, which provides you with a useful overview and some further detail about the debate following the Versailles declaration of war-guilt. Some of these motives have not yet been mentioned in my summary of the debate, while others are now already familiar to you. Try to identify the motives behind the different arguments that were being advanced and sketch out briefly the development of the debate. ■

Specimen answer Immediately after the war, the public in France and Britain demanded revenge. There was a particular desire to punish the Kaiser, who was seen as primarily responsible for the events that led to war. Article 227 of the Treaty of Versailles in *Primary Sources 1: World War I*, Document 1.13, addressed the issue of the Kaiser's war guilt. By the 1920s, the mood was less emotive than it had been following the armistice, and the desire for revenge was less pronounced. There was a shift in emphasis, away from wanting to blame individual nations towards blaming the failure of the system of international relations in operation before the war. The war guilt was now attributed to 'old-style-diplomacy' and the development of the alliance system. The League of Nations, whose creation had been an integral part of the peace settlement of 1919, was seen as safeguarding Europe's future against further such 'diplomatic excesses'.

The publication of official document collections helped the advancement of this type of argument. The available evidence seemed to suggest that secret diplomacy had been practised in all countries, as the German official collection of documents was at pains to prove. Other nations had to follow suit and publish their own documents, revealing details of the kind of secret diplomacy that seemed to be at the heart of the origins of the war.

After the Second World War, the causes of the First were generally investigated together with those of the Second. Historians were now more interested in the consequences of the First World War, rather than in just determining its origins. Questions were asked as to the influence of the peace agreement on the collapse of Weimar and the rise of Hitler, and to the continuity of German history from Imperial to Nazi Germany. The question of the origins of the First World War had ceased to occupy minds to the same degree as was the case prior to the Second World War because the issue seemed settled. When this comfortable view of shared responsibility was challenged by Fischer, the violence with which his views were received was partly due to the unacceptability of the theory of continuity from Bismarck to Hitler. If this were true, Hitler and his foreign policy could no longer be explained away as an aberration, but had to be regarded as something quintessentially German. The question of guilt and of national pride was thus firmly on the agenda again. ☐

The debate on the origins of the First World War did not end with Fischer, and we will encounter some more recent and more nuanced interpretations of the origins of the war later in this unit. Recent interpretations have often accepted much of what Fischer and his supporters have argued, although there is continued disagreement over the aims for which Germany went to war in 1914. No historian today would maintain that Europe had slithered into war accidentally, but not all would agree that Germany is more to blame than other nations. Austria-Hungary, in particular, has been the focus of historical investigations, not suprisingly, given the fact that it was Austria's declaration of war on Serbia that began the chain reaction of mobilizations and declarations of war from which the main European powers could not extricate themselves. Britain, too, has been studied with a view to establishing her responsibility for the escalation of the crisis of 1914, while others have concentrated on determining Russia's or France's role in the events leading to war.

Before we turn to some of these interpretations, it is time for you to make up your own mind about the events that led to war in 1914.

3   LONG-TERM CAUSES OF THE FIRST WORLD WAR

Now that we have sketched out the debates and points of dispute among historians, we need to take a closer look at the origins of the war. To help you understand the finer points of the debate, the following section will give you background information on the diplomatic events prior to the outbreak of war and introduce you to some key documents. Historians disagree on when to start looking for the causes for the war, i.e. how far back to go in time. They tend to differentiate between long-term causes, which you might want to call underlying trends, and short-term causes, which one could label triggers of the war. You might already be able to think of some of those based on your reading of Joll. For more background information, you can turn to Roberts, pp.203–19.

Exercise   Jot down what you would consider long-term and short-term causes of the First World War. ■

Specimen answer   You might have come up with a list similar to the following:

Long-term	Short-term
Alliance system	Assassination of Austrian Archduke
'Old-style' diplomacy	International diplomatic crisis
Militarism	Domino effect of mobilizations
Nationalism	Military plans □
Imperial rivalries	
Arms race	

In this section, we will concentrate on some of these long-term causes, before moving on to the events that in the short term triggered the outbreak of war. We will also ask why war was avoided on so many occasions before 1914, despite the many international crises. To help you understand the points of dispute between the various schools of historians, you need to be aware of the diplomatic events and crises in the years leading to war. I have included a chronology of the most important diplomatic developments (at the beginning of the unit). In keeping with the arguments of those historians who look for long-term causes, my list starts in 1870/71. You can also refer to Roberts (pp.203–19) for an overview of the diplomatic developments of the pre-war years.

Exercise   Your task is to read Chapter 4 in the Reader by Samuel Williamson entitled 'The origins of the war'. Read the text once, marking the passages that you consider important, then compile your answers to the following questions after a second reading.

1   Which three major underlying European problems of the pre-war era does Williamson identify?

2   Williamson proceeds to discuss 'additional contextual issues that shaped the framework of international politics' before 1914. He lists alliance alignments, the arms race, Imperialism and economic rivalries as well as virulent nationalism. Note down some more detail on each of these points. What degree of responsibility does Williamson attribute to each of them? ■

Specimen answer   1   Williamson names the following major European problems:

The Eastern question: the disintegration of the Ottoman Empire resulted in loss of her European territory, and the Balkans were still an area of contention in the immediate pre-war years. The Balkan Wars of

1912–13 led to Turkey losing her last possessions in the region, but the area remained contested ground, with Russia, Serbia, Bulgaria and Austria-Hungary still squabbling over the spoils.

The Habsburg monarchy: this multinational, dynastic state was in increasing trouble and looked in danger of disintegration. Its main ally, Germany, was the only country that desperately wanted it to survive.

The German Empire: the recently unified country threatened the European *status quo*. Germany was a growing economic power and a formidable military force, and her aggressive foreign policy was greeted with alarm by her European neighbours. Williamson suggests that Germany's strength led to Britain and France seeking help from Russia to deter German aggression.

2   The alliance system: on the one hand the Triple Alliance of Germany, Austria-Hungary and Italy (with Romania as secret fourth partner), and on the other hand the Triple Entente centred around the Franco-Russian Alliance and the entente partner Britain. According to Williamson, the alliance system as such did not cause the war, but the very existence of a system of two opposing alliance systems ensured that a localized conflict would almost invariably become a European war.

The arms race: Williamson singles out the Anglo-German naval race as a particularly negative influence on the building up of pre-war tensions. Of course, other powers also invested in building battleships at this time to try and match the arming of their neighbours. In terms of military armaments, Williamson points out the sharp increase in military manpower on the continent after 1911. He gives details of the numbers of soldiers each of the European major powers was able to call on in case of war. In total, the Entente and Alliance states could muster approximately 3.6 million men by July 1914.

Imperial and economic rivalry: Late nineteenth-century international politics had been shaped by the scramble for colonies, imperial expansion and economic rivalry. In this context, Williamson mentions the two Moroccan crises and the Bosnian Annexation Crisis, as well as the lingering Eastern question, reinforced by the Italian invasion of Tripoli as sources of tension in Europe.

Nationalism: Williamson identifies nationalism as a dangerous senti-ment in all major European powers. In his words, 'nationalism had turned much of Europe into a veritable box of inflammable tinder'. Of all the major powers, Austria-Hungary was particularly severely affected by tensions resulting from nationalist aspirations, not least because eleven different nationalities were combined within the Dual Monarchy. That nationalism was an important contributing factor to the outbreak of the war is underlined by the fact that the assassination that provided the trigger for war was the result of Serbian nationalists within the Dual Monarchy attempting to assert their claims for independence in order to unite with Serbia. □

Williamson goes on to explore in detail the events of the July Crisis of 1914. We will return to this later, when we examine the short-term causes. At this point, however, the underlying contributing factors that we have identified above, as well as other long-term causes of the war, deserve some closer scrutiny.

Bismarck's alliance system versus Wilhelm II's *Weltpolitik*

Many investigations into the origins of the war start as far back as 1870/71, the time of the founding of the German Empire. We will deal with this only briefly here. It is important background information, but don't be tempted to go into too much detail if you are ever asked to explain the origins of the First World War. In itself, the Bismarckian alliance system does not explain why war broke out in 1914!

German unification occurred as a result of three wars in 1864, 1866 and 1870/1, against Denmark, Austria and France respectively. Following the foundation of the new German Empire, the country's founding father, Chancellor Otto von Bismarck, was keen to avoid further conflict with Germany's neighbours. His complicated alliance system served to ensure that what he considered a 'nightmare of coalitions' against Germany could not threaten the new *status quo*. He declared that Germany was 'satiated' following her recent unification and the annexation of Alsace-Lorraine, and that she sought no further conflict with her neighbours. During his time in office, the complicated alliance system that he created was able to preserve peace and prevent Germany's neighbours from drawing up alliances against her. With the accession to the throne of Wilhelm II,

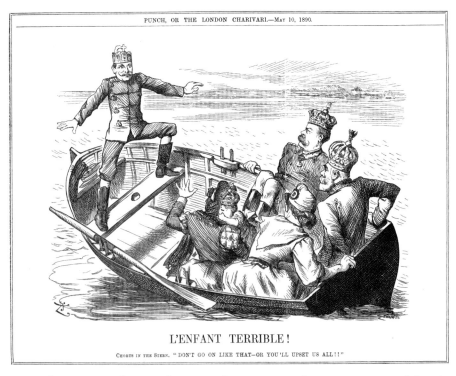

PUNCH, OR THE LONDON CHARIVARI.—MAY 10, 1890.

L'ENFANT TERRIBLE!

CHORUS IN THE STERN. "DON'T GO ON LIKE THAT—OR YOU'LL UPSET US ALL!!"

A Punch *cartoon of 1890 depicting the Kaiser and representatives of Russia, Austria-Hungary, France and Britain.* Source: *Punch,* vol. 98, January–June, 1890.

Source: *Punch*, vol.98, January–June, 1890.

however, and particularly following Bismarck's dismissal in 1890, German foreign policy became more erratic and began to threaten the European balance of power that had developed since 1871.

Exercise   Comment on the Punch cartoon from 1890. Who is depicted, and what point is the picture trying to make? ■

Specimen answer   In the picture, Wilhelm II is standing on one side of a small and unstable-looking boat, quite literally rocking the boat and upsetting the balance (of power, by implication). In the stern of the boat, representing Great Britain, Russia, Austria-Hungary and France respectively, are the frightened-looking Queen Victoria, Tsar Alexander III, Emperor Franz Joseph and, symbolizing the French state, Marianne. The caption of the cartoon sums up what must have been the contemporary opinion: with his policy-making and provocations, Wilhelm II would end up upsetting all the major European powers. The cartoonist was right in almost every respect: Wilhelm was able to keep the old ally Austria-Hungary on his side until 1914, but crossed and upset every other nation represented. In many ways, the 1890 cartoon anticipated with uncanny foresight what the future held. □

After Bismarck's dismissal, his carefully constructed alliance system began to crumble. Germany entered a new era, in which her newly gained position of economic might was to be reflected in achieving a position of world power. It was alleged that Germany had missed out when other European nations had acquired their imperial possessions. Germany wanted her 'place in the sun', her 'rightful share', given her economic predominance on the continent and her population size.

   Under Wilhelm II's erratic leadership and in pursuit of the goal of becoming a *Weltmacht* (world power), the powerful new Germany at the centre of Europe soon began to challenge her neighbours, who were quick to react to the perceived threat emanating from Imperial Germany by forming defensive alliances. Germany refused to renew the so-called Reinsurance Treaty with Russia, leaving her feeling vulnerable and in need of allies. France and Russia started the process of alliance-forming in 1894 with the conclusion of a military alliance that would from now on give rise to a feeling of 'encirclement' in Germany. Due to her geographic situation, Germany now faced potential enemies both in the West and the East, inspiring a fear that, in the not too distant future, Russia or France might attack. However, Germany's politicians and leaders were unable or unwilling to admit that their own actions had helped to lead to this perceived 'encirclement'.

Exercise   Comment on the following excerpt from Prince von Bülow's speech in the German Reichstag on 11 December 1899. Bülow was Foreign Secretary from 1897–1900, and then became German Chancellor until 1909, when he was replaced by Theobald von Bethmann Hollweg. What are the key themes of this speech, and what do you think its purpose might have been? What do you think Bülow meant when he said that Germany would have to be 'either the hammer or the anvil' in the coming century?

Gentlemen, recent decades have brought to Germany great good fortune and power and prosperity. Good fortune and growing prosperity in one quarter are not always greeted in others with pure satisfaction; they may awaken envy. Envy plays a great part in the life of individuals and in the life of nations. There is a great deal of envy of us in the world, political envy and economic envy ... [T]hose past days in which [...] foreigners looked down on us in political and economic respects [...], those times of political impotence and economic and political insignificance must not return. We do not intend again to be [...] the bondmen of humanity. The one condition, however, on which alone we shall maintain our position is that we realize that without power, without a strong army and a strong navy, there can be no welfare for us. The means of fighting the battle for existence in this world without strong armaments on land and water, for a nation soon to count sixty millions, living in the centre of Europe and at the same time stretching out its economic feelers in all directions, have not yet been found. In the coming century the German nation will be either the hammer or the anvil.

(Prince von Bülow, *Memoirs*, vol. 2, 1897–1908, p.353) ∎

Specimen answer and discussion

Bülow is addressing the Reichstag in an attempt to convince his audience of the necessity of army and navy increases for Germany. He conjures up an image of a Germany whose newly found strength and prosperity have provoked hostility and envy among her neighbours. Note how often he repeats the word envy to emphasize his point. He urges the members of the Reichstag to consider that Germany, due to her precarious geographical position and due to her neighbours' misgivings, might face a 'battle for existence' in the future. Strong armaments were the only way to ensure that Germany would be able to defend herself against her envious neighbours. Bülow's often quoted metaphor of the hammer or anvil was intended as a powerful argument to persuade the Reichstag to vote in favour of army increases. At the heart of Bülow's reasoning lay the belief that a future conflict was almost a foregone conclusion. At the same time, his speech summed up the principle of *Weltpolitik*: to maintain Germany's strong position, to be a nation expanding in population size and economic and industrial power at home while at the same time 'stretching out its economic feelers in all directions'. □

Two years previously, in December 1897, Bülow had supported the acquisition of Kiaochow in the Reichstag, and had justified Germany's embarking on *Weltpolitik*. He had stressed the importance of cultivating German shipping, trade and industry and had put Germany's demands for imperial influence quite bluntly: 'we don't want to put anyone in the shade, but we demand our place in the sun, too'.

You might want to think back to Unit 2 at this point, where you have already examined the economic background to the development of pre-war rivalries. Appendices 1 and 2 in Roberts (pp.488–90) confirm Bülow's view of a Germany increasing in population size and industrial importance. The figures also show that in Europe Germany's sudden rise to economic predominance challenged one nation in particular: Britain. The developing antagonism between Germany and Britain was a major contributing factor to the rising tensions of the pre-war years.

The development of two opposing alliance systems

Germany's aggressive foreign policy following Bismarck's dismissal led to the establishment of two rival alliance systems. On the one hand, Germany had been allied to Austria-Hungary since 1879, and Italy had joined them in 1882, forming the Triple Alliance. The Franco-Russian alliance of 1894 was followed by the conclusion of the *Entente Cordiale* between France and Britain; a loose arrangement of the two powers that was strengthened as a result of the first Moroccan Crisis, during which Germany attempted to break up the new allies. In effect, this entente allied Britain and Russia, too, via their shared ally France. Britain had given up her position of 'splendid isolation' in 1902 when she had become allied to Japan, but it was the conclusion of the entente with France that signalled to Germany that Britain would be found on the side of Germany's enemies in any future European conflict. In 1907, Britain and Russia concluded an entente, settling their major differences in Asia and India. The system of two major opposing alliances was now in place. Germany had stirred Britain into a position of hostility towards her by deliberately and openly challenging her naval supremacy with the building programme for a great navy that would, in time, be able to hold its own against the British navy. Britain took up the challenge and responded in 1906 with the construction of the first *Dreadnought* – an 'all gun ship' whose supremacy could not be matched by the new German navy. The main result of this Anglo-German naval race was enmity and suspicion in the governments and populations of both countries. In Britian it was regarded, quite rightly, as one of the ways in which Germany was attempting to improve her international position and challenge her rivals. The worsening of Anglo-German relations has often been stressed as playing a major part in leading to a general deterioration of the relations between the great powers, and thus as a contributing factor leading to an increasingly war-like mood before 1914. Although there were some attempts to come to amicable agreements between Berlin and London, for example the 1912 Haldane mission to Germany, none came to fruition. The main reason for this failure was Germany's insistence on building a strong navy, and the threat that German foreign policy seemed to pose for the European *status quo*.

Exercise   Document 1.14 in *Primary Sources 1: World War I* gives the views of a British diplomat on Germany's foreign policy in the pre-war years. Sir Eyre Crowe was a senior clerk in the Foreign Office from 1906–1912, and despite his German connections (he had been born in Germany and both his mother and wife were German), was part of an anti-German group in the Foreign Office. His views were thus not those of an outsider. His statement on German policy dates from 1907.

Read Document 1.14 and summarize how Sir Eyre Crowe evaluated German policy in 1907. How does he think that Germany might pose a threat to Britain then and in the near future? Remember that this is the time which saw the climax of the Anglo-German naval race, to which Britain had reacted with the introduction of the *Dreadnought*. You might also want to compare this document to Bülow's speech of 1899. ∎

Specimen answer   Crowe begins his summary by making reference to Prussia's/Germany's 'blood and iron' history, and the fact that what he calls a 'Prussian spirit' had permeated Germany following the events of 1871. Germany had fought her way to great power status in Europe. It was when Germany attempted to widen her influence overseas, Crowe asserts, that it became obvious that other nations, and Britain in particular (note how Crowe uses 'England' when he means Britain!), were colonial great powers while Germany, despite her power on the continent, had no great role to play on the colonial stage.

German patriotic pride demanded that she, too, would become a world power, and so she set about acquiring her own 'place in the sun' by amassing colonial territory 'of somewhat doubtful value'. According to Crowe, Germany's colonial and maritime ambitions posed a direct threat to British interests, either in the long run, almost accidentally and without actual design to threaten British supremacy or, more likely in his opinion, in the short-term as a result of Germany's aims of political hegemony and maritime supremacy. In either case, Germany posed a danger to Britain. Crowe's anti-German views need to be seen in the context of his Francophile views. He was strongly in favour of the Anglo-French Entente, and wanted to avoid any closer links being forged with Germany. In the wake of the Moroccan Crisis, his words would undoubtedly have found some approval in the Foreign Office. □

It is interesting to compare this document to Bülow's views of the envious neighbours, who begrudged Germany her place in the sun and her ascendancy to the position of world power status, which we have encountered earlier. In a way, both Bülow and Crowe are quite near the truth in how they sum up the other country's aims and motivations, and the documents give a sense of the way a perceived outside threat could be used to justify foreign policy strategies.

International crises and the threat of war before 1914

The Russo-Japanese War, First Moroccan Crisis, Balkan Wars and the Second Moroccan Crisis have already been mentioned briefly in the introduction to this unit. In this section, we will examine how these crises contributed to the worsening of great power relations to the point of war breaking out in 1914. We will also ask why a European war was averted at all these junctures.

The Russo-Japanese War and the First Moroccan Crisis

Exercise   Read Roberts' account of the Russo-Japanese War and the First Moroccan Crisis, pp.206–10, and answer the following questions. You should also draw on any relevant other reading you might already have done on the subject to give as broad an answer as possible.

1   In what ways was the Russo-Japanese war an important juncture in the years before the outbreak of the First World War?

2   How are the Russo-Japanese War and the First Moroccan Crisis connected?

3   What were the real motivations behind Germany's policy in the First Moroccan Crisis? ■

Specimen answer   1   The Russo-Japanese war involved land battles of almost unprecedented
and discussion   scale, and provided in that sense a taste of things to come. Much to
                          everyone's surprise, a European 'white' country was being defeated by a

'non-white' race – this is how the events appeared to many commentators at the time. The most important result was a significant change in the balance of power in Europe, following Russia's defeat and the revolution of 1905. Japan had emerged as a force to be reckoned with, and the renewal and extension of the Anglo-Japanese Alliance just before the peace agreement of Portsmouth has to be seen in this light. Russia, on the other hand, was for the time being so weakened that she could almost be discounted as a great power. The lost war spelt the end of Russia's expansionist aspirations in the Far East. Any future expansion would have to look towards Europe. France had managed to escape getting embroiled in a war between Russia and Great Britain, which could have resulted from the hostilities between Russia and Japan, but in the aftermath of the lost war, Russia could be of no support to her French ally in the Moroccan Crisis. Moreover, Russia's weakened state encouraged Germany to provoke a crisis over Morocco, based on the assumption that Russia would be unable to come to her ally's aid, thus heightening Germany's chances of achieving a diplomatic victory. At the same time, as we will see later, Germany's military planners developed a new and daring deployment plan (the so-called Schlieffen Plan), based on the fact that the recently defeated Russia would not pose a real threat to Germany in the East.

2   In a sense, we have already answered the second question as to the connection between the war and the Moroccan Crisis. It was the fact that Russia was militarily weakened that led Germany to feel she could provoke a crisis, considering that the risk of such a crisis escalating into a war in which Russia would support her ally France was almost non-existent.

3   Germany's policy in 1905 was about Morocco on the surface only. Her reaction was provoked by the Anglo-French agreement over the territory of Morocco. Although Germany had some economic interests in Morocco, these were only cited as a pretext. In reality, Germany's decision-makers felt slighted by not having been consulted, and wanted to demonstrate that a great power such as Germany could not simply be passed over when such important decisions were made. As Roberts emphasizes, Germany did not object on economic grounds, but for reasons of prestige. German policy aimed at demonstrating that France could not rely on her new Entente partner Britain, and that Russia was too weak to support her in an international crisis. At the heart of the Moroccan Crisis was Germany's desire to show up the newly formed Entente as useless, to split the Entente partners before they had a chance to consolidate their bond, and to intimidate the French. Rather than a war, Germany's leaders aimed at a diplomatic victory that would demonstrate to her European neighbours the importance of the German Empire. Unfortunately for Germany, this aim was not achieved. On the contrary, the newly formed Entente between Britain and France emerged strengthened from the crisis, with both countries realizing the benefits to be had from such a coalition, while the international conference at Algeciras, which was the result of Germany's demands, amounted only to

a pyrrhic victory for Germany. Germany found herself isolated, with support only from her ally Austria-Hungary, and had revealed to the rest of Europe her aggressive foreign policy aims. In Roberts' words, 'a revolution in European affairs had occurred'. □

The 'Balkan Issue'

Just as it was no real surprise that war would eventually break out between Europe's major powers, it was equally no surprise that a Balkan crisis would provide the trigger for such a war. The years before 1914 saw frequent Balkan crises which threatened to escalate, and war was only narrowly avoided on many occasions. It was with the disintegration of the Ottoman Empire that the *status quo* in the Balkans changed considerably. Austria-Hungary had as much interest in the area as Russia, and the smaller Balkan states were keen to expand their area of influence, thus posing a direct threat to Austrian ambitions. Serbia, Austria-Hungary's main Balkan enemy, received material and moral support from Russia, who considered herself the guardian of the pan-Slav movement. There were disputes over access to the sea, over control of the Straits of Constantinople, providing vital access to the Black Sea, and simply over territorial possessions. For Austria-Hungary, the matter was made worse by the fact that the Dual Monarchy united several disparate nationalities in one state, many of whom wanted to establish their independence. In the case of Serbian and Romanian nationals, the threat was heightened by the fact that these subjects felt an allegiance to a sovereign state outside of Austria-Hungary. In many ways the Balkans, then as now, were an area of conflict for which no easy solutions could be found, as nationalist aspirations and the desire for territorial expansion resulted in repeated conflict. The Bosnian Annexation Crisis was one such serious dispute, which threatened to bring war to Europe as early as 1908.

Exercise   Read Roberts' section on the re-emergence of Balkan issues, pp. 210–13, keeping the following questions in mind:

What were the intentions of Austria-Hungary in 1908, and how did Russia, France and Germany react?

What was the result of the Annexation Crisis, and how would you assess its importance in leading Europe closer to war? ■

Specimen answers   Following the Austro-Russian Entente of 1897, when the two powers had come
and discussion   to an agreement over the Balkans, relations between the countries had been amicable. The Balkan issue only reappeared after Russia's disastrous experience in the Far East, when her interest in the Balkans was reawakened. Revolution in Turkey by the 'Young Turks'[1] in 1908 led to a change of government and policy, and the previously assumed disintegration of the Ottoman Empire seemed to be halted – a threatening development for those European countries that had an interest in Turkey's decline and had welcomed it. The Balkan *status quo*, on which Austro-Russian cooperation was based, was affected by these developments, but Austria and Russia were still cooperating by the time Aehrenthal became foreign minister in 1906. Aehrenthal decided that domestic

---

[1] 'Young Turks' was the name given to a liberal reform movement in Turkey. The revolution of 1908 led to the establishment of constitutional rule in Turkey.

problems should take precedence over the preservation of the *status quo* in the Balkans. The multi-national state of Austria-Hungary faced numerous internal threats due to the nationalist aspirations of its many minorities, and Aehrenthal's policy aimed at diverting domestic discontent with the help of an aggressive foreign policy. On the back of the 'Young Turks' revolution, and in the light of Russia's relative weakness following the Russo-Japanese war, Aehrenthal decided to annex the provinces of Bosnia and Herzegovina, which Austria had occupied following the Treaty of Berlin in 1878, but which had formally remained under Turkish suzerainty.

Russia, too, hoped to gain from the instability in the Balkans, and the Russian foreign minister Izvolsky and Aehrenthal came to a secret agreement in 1908. Austria would be allowed to go ahead with the annexation, and in turn was expected to support Russian interests in the Bosphorus and Dardanelles. However, Aehrenthal proceeded with the annexation on 5 October 1908 before Izvolsky had time to get diplomatic support from other European capitals. Izvolsky felt betrayed by Austria, and denounced the secret agreement. Serbia was ready to go to war over the annexation, but in the event was not supported by Russia, who was still too weak following the war against Japan. Given the fact that Germany gave unconditional support to Austria-Hungary over this Balkan matter, it was primarily Russia's moderating influence on Serbia that prevented a war on this occasion.

Germany's open and unconditional support of her ally had significantly changed what had so far been a purely defensive alliance agreement between her and Austria-Hungary. From now on, Austria's leaders knew they could count on Germany even if Austria provoked a crisis. The Bosnian Annexation Crisis marked an important juncture in this respect. In future, Serbia, humiliated in 1909, would be keen to redress her status in the Balkans, while Russia was now suspicious of German interests in the Balkans and more determined than ever to regain her military power. Russia and Serbia had to back down on this occasion, but they were unlikely to do so again in future. □

The Agadir Crisis and the Balkan Wars

In 1911, Germany tried again to assert her claim as a great power who could not simply be ignored in colonial affairs. In a move that was contrary to international agreements, the French sent troops to Morocco to put down a revolt in that country (and thus, by implication, to extend their influence over Morocco). Germany's decision-makers dispatched the gun-boat *Panther* to the port of Agadir to provoke and intimidate the French, demanding the French Congo as compensation for the extension of French influence in Morocco. However, as during the First Moroccan Crisis, France received support from Britain and the links between the two Entente partners were only further strengthened in the light of German aggression. Britain let Germany know in no uncertain terms that she intended to stand by France, and David Lloyd George's famous 'Mansion House Speech' of 21 July 1911, threatening to fight on France's side against Germany if the need arose, caused great indignation in Germany. Although the crisis was resolved peacefully, and Germany was given part of the French Congo as compensation, the affair was in fact a diplomatic defeat for Germany, whose leaders were becoming increasingly worried that their foreign policy adventures did not lead to the breaking-up of alliances against her.

Soon after the Agadir Crisis, the Balkans once again demanded the attention of Europe's statesmen. Following the humiliation of 1909, Serbia had set about creating a coalition of Balkan states, and in 1912 Bulgaria, Greece, Montenegro and Serbia formed the Balkan League. In October 1912, the League declared war on Turkey. The latter was quickly defeated and driven out of most of the Balkans, but in the aftermath of the war, the victors fell out over the spoils, and ended up fighting each other in the Second Balkan War of 1913. As a result of the wars, Serbia doubled her territory, and now posed an even greater threat to Austria-Hungary. This is essential background for understanding Austria's reaction to the Serbian-supported assassination of the heir to the Austro-Hungarian throne. Given the long-standing Balkan crisis, and Serbia's many provocations, this was a challenge that she could not ignore.

Military origins of the war

With war seemingly always just around the corner, military preparations were of the utmost importance. In Germany, military planning even began to influence political decisions, as an examination of Germany's famous deployment plan, the Schlieffen Plan, reveals. Germany's narrow military planning was certainly one reason why war could not be averted at the last minute in July 1914.

The Schlieffen Plan

Anyone who has ever studied this period of European history has come across the name of Germany's military deployment plan, taking its name from the long-serving Chief of the General Staff, Alfred Count von Schlieffen. The international background to the development of the Schlieffen plan is significant in trying to understand its genesis and the reasoning behind it. We have already seen that as a result of the Russo-Japanese war Russia was eliminated as a serious threat to the European *status quo* for the foreseeable future. She would first of all have to recover from a lost war and from revolution. For those who feared Russia as a potential future enemy, in particular Germany and Austria-Hungary, this was a perfect time to consider 'preventive war', unleashed while Germany still had a chance to defeat Russia. In the not too distant future, Germany's military planners predicted, Russia would become invincible. The military decision-makers in Berlin advocated a 'preventive war' at that time to avoid such a development. However, in 1906, they were unable to convince the German Chancellor or the Kaiser to support their plans.

The Entente between Britain and France was only just being shown to be effective following the First Moroccan Crisis. As a result of the Crisis Germany began to feel the full effects of her own expansionist foreign policy. To Germany, British involvement in a future war now seemed almost certain, and as a consequence Italy, allied to Germany and Austria since 1882, became a less reliable ally, for she would be unable to defend her long coastlines from a hostile Britain and might therefore opt to stay neutral in a future war. The international events of 1905–6 marked the beginning of Germany's perceived 'encirclement' by alliances of possible future enemies against her. Between this time and the outbreak of war in 1914, the General Staff became more and more concerned about the increasing military strength of Germany's enemies, without ever realizing that they were largely *reacting* to German provocation.

Schlieffen saw Germany's best chance of victory in a swift offensive in the West, against France, while in the East, the German army was initially to be on the defensive. Russia would be dealt with after France had been delivered a decisive blow. In effect, Schlieffen aimed to turn a two-front war into two one-front wars. The plan further entailed that Germany would have to attack France in such a way as to avoid the heavy fortifications along the Franco-German border. Instead of a 'head-on' engagement, which would lead to position warfare of inestimable length, the opponent should be enveloped and its armies attacked on the flanks and rear. Moving through Switzerland would have been impractical, whereas in the North, Luxembourg had no army at all, and the weak Belgian army was expected to retreat to its fortifications. Schlieffen decided to concentrate all German effort on the right wing, even if the French decided on offensive action along another part of the long common border and even at the risk of allowing the French temporarily to reclaim Alsace-Lorraine.

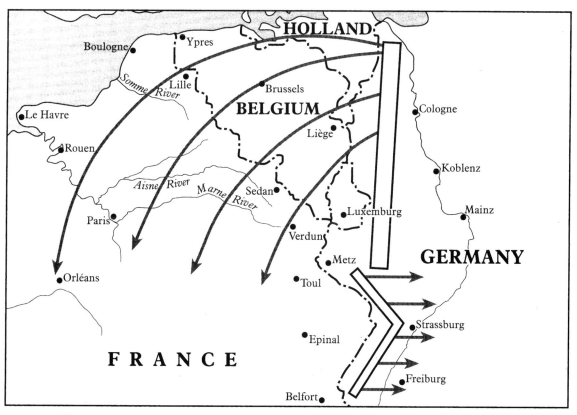

The Schlieffen Plan

Source: R. Chickering (1998), *Imperial Germany and the Great War, 1914–1918*, Cambridge University Press.

In his planning, Schlieffen counted on two things – that German victory in the West would be quick (he estimated this to take about six weeks), and that Russian mobilization would be slow, so that a small German defensive force would suffice to hold back Russia (regarded as the 'clay-footed colossus') until

France was beaten. After a swift victory in the West, the full force of the German army would be directed eastwards. Russia would be beaten in turn. This was the recipe for victory, the certain way out of Germany's encirclement.

The plan was first put to paper in 1905/6, and was adapted to changing international circumstances by Schlieffen's successor, the younger Helmuth von Moltke in the years before the First World War, but the underlying principle remained the same until August 1914, when it was put into action. The plan imposed severe restrictions on the possibility of finding a last minute diplomatic solution to the July Crisis because of its narrow time-frame for the initial deployment of troops. The escalation of the crisis to full-scale war was in no small measure due to Germany's war plans, which also impeded Austria-Hungary's deployment. Germany and Austria-Hungary had failed to coordinate their strategies, and when war began, Austria-Hungary regarded Serbia as the main emeny against whom to mobilize, while Germany expected the Austrian troops to be deployed in the East against Russia.

Germany's neighbours developed their own military strategy in the face of the threat that Germany posed. Following the agreements France had reached with her former colonial rival Britain, France was able to concentrate her military planning on the German neighbour. Her war plan, 'Plan XVII', envisaged a powerful offensive in the South of Germany, into Lorraine and Alsace. French military leaders, like their German counterparts, believed in the offensive as the only strategy worth pursuing, despite the fact that, as the course of the First World War would show, modern fire power would actually give advantage to defensive warfare. Britain's plan for a future war on the continent was much more limited. A force of 150 000 men was to be dispatched to assist the Entente partner against a German offensive. Britain and France had finalized their plans regarding the deployment of the British Expeditionary Force following the Agadir Crisis, in the face of Germany's continual aggressive posturing.

The arms race

Fear of the military potential of one's neighbours as well as the need to be as strong as possible for the war that was generally expected to be 'just around the corner' led to an increasing desire for armaments. As one country expanded its military and naval potential, others immediately followed suit, and the resulting arms race in Europe was regarded by some contemporaries as one of the main reasons why war broke out. Thus, Sir Edward Grey wrote in 1925:

> The enormous growth of armaments in Europe, the sense of insecurity and fear caused by them – it was these that made war inevitable. This, it seems to me, it the truest reading of history, and the lesson that the present should be learning from the past in the interests of future peace, the warning to be handed on to those who come after us. This is the real and final account of the origins of the Great War.
>
> (Cited in Stevenson, *Armaments*, 1996, p.1)

Table 5.1 National construction budgets of the European powers, 1900–1913 (£mn, current prices)

	Britain	France	Russia	Austria-Hungary	Germany	Italy
1900	11.2	4.6	3.1	0.6	3.2	1.5
1901	11.1	4.5	3.1	0.8	5.3	1.2
1902	10.7	4.6	2.6	0.9	5.5	0.9
1903	13.9	4.8	3.3	1.0	5.3	1.2
1904	14.1	4.7	4.1	1.1	5.1	1.4
1905	12.1	4.8	4.1	2.6	5.3	1.0
1906	11.1	4.9	4.3	1.2	5.8	1.7
1907	10.6	4.4	2.6	1.2	6.6	2.1
1908	9.4	4.8	2.2	0.8	9.0	2.4
1909	11.2	4.6	1.4	0.8	11.5	2.2
1910	16.7	5.3	1.8	1.8	12.7	2.2
1911	18.9	6.7	3.2	3.1	13.1	3.5
1912	17.3	6.2	6.2	3.6	12.2	4.3
1913	17.1	7.0	11.1	4.4	11.4	–

Table 5.2 Army expenditure of the European powers, 1900–1913 (£mn, current prices)

	Britain	France	Russia	Austria-Hungary	Germany	Italy
1900	91.5	26.8	35.1	15.2	–	–
1901	92.3	29.0	35.4	16.4	33.2	9.8
1902	69.4	29.2	36.3	16.9	38.0	10.0
1903	36.7	28.1	37.1	17.2	37.6	11.3
1904	29.2	28.0	39.4	17.6	36.6	9.7
1905	28.9	28.5	40.0	17.4	39.7	10.1
1906	27.8	34.2	41.5	17.4	41.5	10.1
1907	27.1	32.7	42.9	18.5	46.0	10.3
1908	26.8	33.3	54.4	21.1	47.0	10.9
1909	27.2	34.7	57.9	27.4	49.0	12.0
1910	27.4	36.4	56.6	24.2	47.3	13.5
1911	27.6	40.5	58.1	22.4	46.9	14.7
1912	28.1	43.4	67.6	25.4	52.1	18.7
1913	28.3	–	75.8	34.4	78.3	25.3

(Tables taken from Stevenson, *Armaments*, p.8)

Tables 5.1 and 5.2 show the staggering amounts of army and naval budgets, particularly in Germany and Russia, each of whom was racing in a desperate bid to keep its armed forces and armaments ahead of the other's. Throughout this period, an army bill in one country would invariably lead to army increases in the other.

France, too, responded to German armament increases with her own, particularly following Germany's 1913 army law. France depended on Russia for a successful military strategy, and both France and Russia substantially increased their armies in terms of numbers of soldiers, equipment, armaments, railway lines and so on. This, in turn, led to increased fear in Germany, and further demands for army increases. It was an arms race that seemed bound to lead to conflict. In Germany in particular, the fear of the future strength of Russia and France led to demands for preventive war. An example of such a demand, and at the same time an example of the way historians have debated the evidence and come to different conclusions about it, is the so-called 'War Council' of 1912. We will examine the evidence in the next section. While you do this, try to keep at the back of your mind the idea of 'preventive war', and ask yourself what exactly was meant by this in pre-war Germany.

The War Council of December 1912

An example of the way war was advocated by certain influential individuals in Berlin in the pre-war years is the war council meeting of 8 December 1912. Historians have debated the importance of this meeting of the German Kaiser and his closest military advisers with the same passion that is part and parcel of so much of the debate on the origins of the war. Depending on their own theory of the origins of the war, historians have differed even in their interpretations of the same documents, as the example of the war council will show. The controversy was sparked by Fischer's second major book, *War of Illusions*, in which he published documents about the meeting.

Exercise   Now read Document 1.15 in *Primary Sources 1: World War I*, which is an excerpt from the diary of Admiral von Müller, the Chief of the Kaiser's Naval Cabinet, who recorded the events of that day.

This is quite a complicated document which you will probably have to read closely several times. Pay attention in particular to the background to the meeting, the people present, the events mentioned, and the importance of the document when assessing the origins of the First World War. Ask yourself: who is present at the meeting? What is the reason for having it? What is being discussed? How might historians have used this document to explain the origins of the war? ■

Specimen answer   First of all, you should mention that the document in question is a diary entry,
and discussion   written by Admiral von Müller who, as you already know, was the Chief of the German Kaiser's Naval Cabinet, and as such a close confidant of the monarch. The fact that these are not the official minutes of the meeting, but a personal account, is significant. No minutes were recorded for the meeting, which was called by the Kaiser on Sunday, 8 December 1912. Apart from Müller and the Kaiser, three other people were present: Alfred von Tirpitz, the head of the Naval Office, Vice Admiral von Heeringen and Helmuth von Moltke, the Chief of the General Staff. No civilians were present at the meeting.

The background to the meeting is obviously important to understanding its importance. The date should suggest to you that the 'political situation' referred to in the document is that created by the Balkan Wars. The Kaiser had just been told by Germany's ambassador to London, Prince Lichnowsky, that in case of a

European war breaking out because of the current Balkan problem, Britain would not stay neutral if Germany attacked France, but support her ally against Germany.

The Kaiser, with characteristic over-reaction, received this information with great outrage. He recommended that Austria adopt a tough stance *vis-à-vis* the Serbs, and that, if Russia came to Serbia's aid, Germany would then support Austria in the impending war. The Kaiser expected the navy to be prepared for war against Britain, and was supported in his bellicose demands by Moltke, who considered it 'unavoidable'. Moltke suggested that the German people needed to be 'prepared' for a war against Russia, and recommended a campaign in the press to achieve this aim. Müller recorded that he initiated this by writing to the Chancellor that afternoon.

Tirpitz advised that the navy was not yet ready, and recommended postponing 'the great fight' for one and a half years. Moltke, rather scathingly, pointed out that the navy would not even be completed then, while time was running out for the army, which would be in an increasingly weak position. Müller summed up the result of the conference disappointedly as 'zero': although Moltke advocated war 'the sooner the better', he did not suggest what Müller considered to be the logical step: to issue an ultimatum to Russia and France 'which would unleash the war with right on our side'.

In trying to establish the causes of the First World War, this document could obviously be of importance. After all, the postponement of the 'great fight' that is being advocated in December 1912 would mean having that fight in the summer of 1914. To some historians, this seems too much of a coincidence. Certainly, the document demonstrates the wide acceptance and even desire for a war in the near future at the highest level of decision-making in Imperial Germany. Such evidence was used by Fischer, among others, to make his case for German responsibility for the outbreak of war. □

Exercise   Now that you have read the document closely, turn to the articles in the *Secondary Sources* by Wolfgang Mommsen and John Röhl. Then answer the following questions:

How do Mommsen and Röhl differ in their views about the war council, and what further evidence is cited by Röhl that was not available when Mommsen wrote his critique of the Fischer thesis?

What does John Röhl name as the most important conclusion to be drawn from the evidence about the war council meeting? ∎

Specimen answers   1   Wolfgang Mommsen dismisses the importance of the meeting, arguing,
and discussion   for example, that no civilian statesmen were present, which would have been the case if the meeting had been considered important. He also claims that the Chancellor was not informed about the meeting until a week later, and that there is no evidence that the Kaiser's demands for a press campaign were followed up by any action.

John Röhl points out that the Müller diary excerpt about the war council had originally been published in a 'deliberately distorted and mutilated form'. The last sentences of the diary entry, following Müller's remark that the result of the meeting was 'almost 0' had been omitted, giving the document a very different ring. In addition to the Müller diary, other evidence about the war council meeting is now available: a report by the Saxon military plenipotentiary Leuckart von Weissdorf to the Saxon Minister of War, a similar account by the Bavarian military plenipotentiary Wenninger, a diary entry by the Naval Captain Albert Hopman who had found out about the secret meeting from his masseur (!) Schulz. According to Röhl, the evidence we have about the meeting is thus 'unusually abundant'. Nonetheless, as Röhl asserts, the meeting 'cannot be separated from the emotive controversy' on the causes of the war. He argues that many historians are reluctant to accept that war might have been decided on by Germany's decision-makers one and a half years before it broke out. Until even more evidence has been found which directly links the meeting of December 1912 with the outbreak of war, the wider question of the historical significance of the war council must be left unanswered.

Mommsen could only have made his dismissive claims on the basis of the incomplete Müller diary, for Müller clearly stated that he wrote to the Chancellor about influencing the press later that afternoon. Based on the new evidence cited by John Röhl, these arguments can no longer be supported. The meeting did result in a press campaign, and also had influence on the forthcoming army increases, and the Chancellor was informed about the events in the Kaiser's castle on the same day.

2   Whatever conclusions one might draw from the meeting, Röhl asserts that 'no other event is capable of illuminating so clearly the military-political decision-making process in the Kaiserreich on the eve of the First World War'. The men present at the Schloss were the same men who would make decisions regarding Germany's foreign policy in July 1914. The evidence about the meeting reveals the important role played by military leaders in Imperial Germany and the marginal role allocated to civilians by a Kaiser who preferred to make decisions with the help of his military advisers. It also demonstrates the acceptance in Berlin of a war in the near future, and the willingness to wage a 'preventive war' before Germany's potential enemies would become invincible. This, as you will remember, was also Fischer's definition of 'preventive war'. □

In the long term, it seemed as if the position of the Entente powers could only improve with time, while that of the Central Powers seemed to be deteriorating steadily. Soon, it was feared, war would no longer be an option for Germany's policy makers; soon, Germany's enemies would be invincible, and the 'encircled' Germany would be at the mercy of her envious neighbours and rivals. Only in the short term did a solution seem to offer itself. A crisis would have to be found which would provide a perfect trigger for war, preferably a Balkan Crisis, so that Austria-Hungary's support could be relied upon in Germany. Such a short-term cause of the war would eventually be provided in June 1914. It is to the short-term causes of the war that we now turn.

4   SHORT-TERM CAUSES OF THE FIRST WORLD WAR

Chronology of short-term causes of the war

28 June 1914	Assassination of Archduke Franz Ferdinand and his wife.
5–6 July	Count Hoyos's mission to Berlin to establish level of German support for Austrian action against Serbia. Germany issues 'blank cheque', promising unconditional support to the ally.
7 July	Austro-Hungarian Ministerial Council convenes and decides on (deliberately unacceptable) ultimatum to Serbia to iniate military action or Serbia's humiliation. Decision to deliver ulimatum only after the French premier had returned from his planned trip to St. Petersburg.
20–23 July	French state visit to Russia.
23 July	Austria's ultimatum to Serbia.
25 July	Serbia replies to the ultimatum and mobilizes. Austria-Hungary breaks off diplomatic relations.
26 July	Britain proposes mediation conference.
28 July	Austria-Hungary declares war on Serbia. Wilhelm II proposes 'Halt in Belgrade'
28 July	Russia orders partial mobilization.
29–30 July	Bethmann Hollweg attempts to restrain Austria-Hungary.
30 July	French attempts to restrain Russia. Nicholas II authorizes general mobilization for the next day.
31 July	Germany declares state of 'impending danger of war' and sends ultimata to Russia and France. Russia begins mobilization.
1 August	Germany declares war on Russia. France and Germany begin general mobilization.
2 August	Germany invades Luxembourg. German ultimatum to Belgium. British cabinet approves protection of French coast and of Belgian neutrality.
3 August	Germany invades Belgium and declares war on France. Italy decides to stay neutral.
4 August	Britain declares war on Germany.
6 August	Austria-Hungary declares war on Russia.

The July Crisis and the outbreak of war

Given all the tensions and underlying hostilities of the pre-war years, it is not surprising that war would eventually result from these international rivalries. However, a trigger was needed to spark off such a final conflict, and that trigger was provided by the assassination of Archduke Franz Ferdinand and his wife in Sarajevo. Most non-historians you might ask about the origins of the First World War would probably answer that the war broke out because Franz Ferdinand was shot on 28 June 1914. You already know better than that. War had been looming for over a decade, and the assassination was no more than the spark that would set light to a Europe that was riddled by international rivalries and tensions. However, even in July 1914 war was not inevitable. Right until the last moment there were people who wanted to stop it from breaking out, and others who did everything in their power to make it happen. That war finally resulted was far less the product of bad fortune than the result of intention. In order to understand why the crisis escalated into full-scale war, we must look at Vienna and Berlin, for it was here that war was consciously risked. France, Russia and Britain entered the stage much later in July 1914, when most decisions had already been taken.

In Vienna, the reaction to the assassination was officially one of outrage, although behind the scenes there were some pleased voices, because Franz Ferdinand had not been universally popular. The Chief of the Austrian General Staff, Franz Conrad von Hötzendorf, was keen to have an excuse for a war with Serbia. He still regretted what he had considered the 'missed opportunity' of a 'reckoning with Serbia' in 1909. In Berlin, the possibility of a Balkan crisis was greeted favourably, for such a crisis would ensure that Austria would definitely become involved in a resulting conflict. Most historians would today agree that Berlin put substantial pressure on Vienna to demand retribution from Serbia, and that Berlin was happy to take the risk that an Austro-Serbian conflict might escalate into a European war. When the Austrian envoy Count Hoyos arrived in Berlin to ascertain the ally's position in case Austria demanded recompense from Serbia, he was assured that Germany would support Austria all the way, even if she chose to go to war over the assassination and even if such a war were to turn into a European war. This was the so-called 'blank cheque'.

Exercise   Read Document 1.16 from *Primary Sources 1: World War I*, the Kaiser's 'blank cheque' to Austria. Apart from giving Austria a completely free hand in dealing with the Serbs, what else do you notice that is important to know about the document? ■

Specimen answer   You might have noticed that the Kaiser spoke without having consulted the Chancellor, Bethmann Hollweg, whose approval he simply took for granted. Because the Chancellor depended on the Kaiser's good will for his position, it was indeed unlikely that he would contradict the monarch, even on such important matters. Wilhelm II not only actively encouraged Austria to take action against Serbia, but even insisted that such action must not be delayed. He clearly expected Russia to adopt a hostile attitude, but felt that she was ill prepared for war 'at the present time' and might therefore perhaps not take up arms. The Kaiser urged Austria to 'make use of the present moment', which he considered to be very favourable.

While the political decision-makers in Berlin did not actually *want* a European war, they were certainly willing to risk it. They had been encouraged to do so by Germany's military advisers who, as we have seen, had advocated war 'the sooner the better' on many occasions and had assured the politicians that

Germany still stood a good chance of defeating her enemies. Implicit in this document is the attitude of the military leaders, who had been conjuring up the image of a Russia that could still be defeated by Germany at this time, but that in future would be too strong to be taken on successfully. You might have remembered that we have already encountered this argument in the discussion of Fritz Fischer's views. □

Armed with such reassurance from Germany, the Austro-Hungarian ministerial council decided on 7 July that the best step would be to issue an ultimatum to Serbia. This was to be deliberately unacceptable, so that a Serbian non-compliance would lead to the outbreak of war with right on Austria's side. (Although later in the crisis Germany was prepared to violate neutral Belgium in defiance of the Treaty of London of 1839, thus helping Britain to unite against Germany with right on Britain's side.) However, much time would go by before the ultimatum was finally delivered to Belgrade: first the harvest had to be completed, for which most soldiers of the Dual Monarchy were away on harvest leave. Moreover, it was decided to wait until the state visit of Raymond Poincaré, the French president, to Russia was over, so that the two allies would not have a chance to coordinate their response to Austria's ultimatum. While all this was plotted behind the scenes, both Vienna and Berlin gave the impression of calm to the outside world, even sending their main decision-makers on holiday to keep up this illusion. It is due to this deception that the other major powers did not play a role in the July Crisis until 23 July, the day when the ultimatum was finally delivered to Belgrade. They were simply unaware of the secret plotting in Vienna and Berlin.

The Serbian response to the 'unacceptable' ultimatum astonished everyone. In all but one point the government agreed to accept it, making Austria's predetermined decision to turn down Belgrade's response look suspicious in the eyes of those European powers who wanted to try to preserve the peace. Even the Kaiser now decided that there was no longer any reason to go to war, much to the dismay of his military advisers. Britain suggested that the issue could be resolved at the conference table, but her mediation proposals and attempts to preserve the peace were not taken up by Vienna or Berlin. Only at the very last minute, when it was clear that Britain, too, would become involved if war broke out, did the German Chancellor try to restrain the Austrians – but his mediation proposals arrived too late and were in any case not forceful enough. Austria declared war on Serbia on 28 July, and thus set in motion a domino-effect of mobilization orders and declarations of war by Europe's major powers. By the time Britain had declared war on Germany at 11 pm on 4 August, following Germany's invasion of neutral Luxembourg and Belgium, the Alliance powers (without Italy, who had decided to stay neutral) faced the Entente powers in the 'great fight' that had been anticipated for such a long time. The war, which was commonly expected to be 'over by Christmas', did not go to plan. Unit 6 in Book 2 will deal in detail with the nature of the war whose origins we have tried to unravel.

Exercise   Turn to Michael Gordon's essay 'Domestic conflict and the origins of the First World War' in the *Secondary Sources*. Read the essay with the following questions in mind:

1   How does Gordon evaluate German and British foreign policy in the period just before and during July 1914?

2   What were German aims during the July Crisis?

3   What charge could be made of Sir Edward Grey's policy during the crisis?

These issues are addressed in Section II of the article. ∎

Specimen answer   German policy was shaped by a readiness to accept the risk of war, either a localized one between Austria-Hungary and Serbia, or a European war, in which Russia, Germany and France would become involved. Either case would serve German interests: a successful localized war would perhaps break up the entente between France and Russia, it would restore Austria-Hungary's prestige and would clear the way in central Europe for German *Weltpolitik*. A victorious continental war, on the other hand, would achieve these aims to an even greater degree. Germany did not aim for a world war, but hoped for British neutrality, although German decision-makers thought a British intervention likely. By accepting this implicit risk, Gordon asserts, the German government was responsible for the ensuing world war. Although they were aware of the possible repercussions resulting from a war between Austria and Serbia, they nonetheless went ahead in encouraging their ally, and they were prepared to fight on Austria-Hungary's side against Russia.

As far as Grey's foreign policy is concerned, Gordon argues that he did not pursue as active and decisive a policy as he could have. Instead, he wavered between backing France and Russia on the one hand, and making mediation proposals on the other. According to Gordon, British influence in July 1914 could have been much more pronounced, given her status as a great power. ☐

A similar argument is advanced by Niall Ferguson in the following excerpt:

> From the outset Grey was extremely reluctant to give any indication of how Britain might respond to an escalation of the conflict. He knew that if Austria pressed extreme demands on Belgrade with German backing, and Russia mobilized in defence of Serbia, then France might well become involved – such was the nature of the Franco-Russian entente and German military strategy, so far as it was known in London. Part of Grey's strategy in trying to turn the ententes with France and Russia into quasi-alliances had been to deter Germany from risking war. However, now he feared that too strong a signal of support for France and Russia [...] might encourage the Russians to do just that. He found himself in a cleft stick: how to deter Austria and Germany without encouraging France and Russia [...].
>
> (Ferguson, *The Pity of War*, 1998, p.155)

This is a good summary of Grey's predicament in July 1914. It certainly is worth speculating that Bethmann Hollweg's mediation proposal to Vienna would have been delivered sooner and more forcefully, if the Chancellor had known earlier of Britain's definite resolve to come to France's aid in a European war. When Grey made Britain's position clear, preparations for war had already gone too far in Germany (see Document 1.17 in *Primary Sources 1: World War I*). However, the ambivalence of Grey's policy cannot be seen as a cause of the war. After all, this hesitant attitude was motivated by the desire to avoid an escalation of the crisis, while German and Austro-Hungarian decisions were based on the explicit desire to provoke a conflict. As the former ambassador to London, Prince Lichnowsky, summed up in January 1915:

> On our side nothing, absolutely nothing, was done to preserve peace, and when we at last decided to do what I had advocated from the first, it was too late. By then Russia, as a result of our harsh attitude and that of Count Berchtold, had lost all confidence and mobilised. The war party gained the upper hand. [...] Such a policy is comprehensible only if war was our aim, not otherwise.
>
> (See *Primary Sources 1: World War I*, Document 1.18, for Lichnowsky's memorandum)

CONCLUSION

The debate on the origins of the war: is there a consensus?

The Fischer controversy of the 1960s has itself become history, but disagreements continue to exist to this day about the origins of the First World War. In David Stevenson's words, 'the "Fischer controversy" overturned the orthodoxy of the 1950s without any one view replacing it' (*The Outbreak of the First World War*, 1997, p.12). Some consensus has been reached, and most historians today would no longer support Lloyd George's dictum of the European nations slithering into war accidentally. Many would agree that Germany must bear the main share of responsibility for the war that started in 1914. Although, as we have seen, her decision-makers did not want the world war that the conflict turned into, they were nonetheless willing to risk an escalation of a localized crisis into a European war, because they felt reasonably confident of winning in such a scenario. The original outrage provoked by the allegations of the Fischer school can only be understood in the context of the time in which they were advanced. The late 1950s and 1960s in Germany were characterized by insecurity, the result of being a divided nation that had to come to terms with a terrible past, of finding its position at the centre of a divided world, etc. Today, passions run less high, but disagreements continue to exist about the origins of the First World War.

Studies of individual countries show different levels of culpability – depending on the point of view or focal point of the historian, different countries appear more or less prominently involved or guilty. There are those who believe that Germany bore the main share of responsibility for the outbreak of the war, and most historians would probably agree on this, although they might differ over just how big that share really was. Certainly it is the interpretation that I have advanced in this unit. However, the Balkan tensions that 'plagued' Europe in the pre-war years clearly are also of crucial importance, as are the decisions taken by the individual governments in July 1914. The following excerpts demonstrate the diversity of opinions among historians in interpreting the origins of the war. Clearly, the issue is still far from resolved, as historians continue to unearth new documentary evidence and continue to differ in their interpretations of the source material.

Niall Ferguson, *The Pity of War,* 1998

The German decision to risk a European war in 1914 was not based on hubris: there was no bid for world power. Rather, Germany's leaders acted out of a sense of weakness. In the first instance, this was based on their inability to win either the naval or the land arms race. [...] Paradoxically, if Germany had been as militarist in practice as France and Russia, she would have had less reason to feel insecure and to gamble on a pre-emptive strike 'while [she] could more or less still pass the test', in Moltke's telling phrase.

(pp.442–3)

Samuel R Williamson, Jr., *Austria-Hungary and the Origins of the First World War,* 1991

[...] In Vienna in July 1914 a set of leaders experienced in statecraft, power and crisis management consciously risked a general war to fight a local war. Battered during the Balkan Wars by Serbian expansion, Russian activism and now by the loss of Franz Ferdinand, the Habsburg leaders desperately desired to shape their future, rather than let events destroy them. The fear of domestic disintegration made war an acceptable policy option. The Habsburg decision, backed by the Germans, gave the July crisis a momentum that rendered peace an early casualty.

(pp.215f.)

John Röhl, 'Imperial Germany. The riddle of 1914', 1990

To me personally, [...] the conclusion seems more and more inescapable that at the end of the nineteenth century, Imperial Germany under Kaiser Wilhelm II embarked on a long-term bid to secure 'world power' status [...]. By about 1909, however, it was becoming clear that this gigantic 'bid for world power' was failing. The British were outbuilding and outmanoeuvring Tirpitz at sea, the Triple Entente had been formed to 'contain', 'encircle' or 'isolate' Germany internationally, and the tide of Democracy and Socialism at home was threatening to sweep away the very pillars on which the Prusso-German military monarchy was based. Most menacing of all, the multi-national Austro-Hungarian Empire, the German Reich's only serious ally, was in a state of rapid and terminal decline.

In this situation Germany's hopelessly irrational governmental system, in which the Kaiser, his Court and above all his Generals played a bigger role than the civilian Chancellor and his civilian Foreign Secretary, opted for what they called 'preventive war' [...]. So great was the faith in the Generals and their [War] Plan that the civilian statesmen did not feel impelled to seek a political or diplomatic solution to Germany's grave problems at home and abroad. Her military and civilian leaders appear to have agreed that in starting a war they had to make it seem as if Russia were the aggressor, and that a Balkan crisis involving Austria – perhaps coupled with an ultimatum to 'unleash the war with right on our side' – was the best way to achieve that.

(*Modern History Review,* vol.2, no.1, September, 1990, pp.11f.)

Mark Cornwall, 'Serbia', 1995

For Serbia, most of the uncertainty of the crisis ended when Austria-Hungary declared war on 28 July. The evidence suggests that during the previous month Serbia was far more independent and obstinate than historians have previously imagined. [...] Above all, Serbia throughout July 1914 was prepared to refuse Austrian demands incompatible with its status as a sovereign and 'civilized' state and, like the Great Powers, it would even risk war at this time to defend its status. This obstinacy stemmed partly from Serbia's new confidence after its expansion in the Balkan Wars [...]. As a result the government produced (from its own point of view) a very conciliatory reply, but one still hedged with reservations and still resistant over the vital points: despite Serbia's military weakness and near-isolation diplomatically, the kingdom was prepared on 25 July to run the risk of a localized war with Austria-Hungary. [...] By the end of July 1914, Pašic [Serbia's Prime Minister and Foreign Minister] knew that if Greater Serbia materialized, it would be out of the fires of a full European war. Serbia itself had helped to create this war because during the July crisis it was not prepared to return to the status of an Austro-Hungarian satellite.

(*Decisions for War, 1914*, ed. Keith Wilson, 1995, pp.83f.)

Was war unavoidable in 1914?

Given the horrors of the First World War, and given its poisonous political legacy, it is tempting to ask what, if anything, could have been done to avert war in 1914, as it had been averted on so many previous occasions. Was pre-war Europe really a place in which governments and people were bent on war and eager to fight it to prove themselves or better their positions? While the desire for war clearly was present, it would be wrong to see the period before the First World War as one in which only belligerence and militarism existed. Pacifism was a term that was coined in 1901, and although it was 'one of the early twentieth century's least successful political movements' (Ferguson, *The Pity of War*, 1998, p.20), its existence is nonetheless important to keep in mind. There were influential voices who advocated limitations to arms races, and there was a substantial peace-movement that attempted to avoid a war in future. The two international peace conferences at The Hague in 1899 and 1907, convened at the behest of the Russian Tsar, demonstrate the fact that there was a real desire to try to limit the excesses of the armaments race. The steady advance that Socialism had made gave a further influential voice to those who advocated peace. A general strike in response to war had been decided on at the Second International, although in the event, only a few individual socialists opposed the war (such as Keir Hardie, Rosa Luxemburg and Karl Liebknecht, as well as the Bolsheviks in Russia). It is not surprising that one of the main concerns of governments was to ensure that their people would understand the need to go to war and that they would support such a venture. Recent research into the so-called 'spirit of 1914' has shown that the apparent enthusiasm with which 'ordinary people' greeted the declarations of war has in fact been exaggerated. Of course, the rallies and demonstrations of patriotic fervour that we associate with the outbreak of the war did occur, and they were as common in Germany as they were in France, Russia or Britain, but to focus on them to the exclusion of other sentiments is to paint a one-sided picture. Many people were far from enthusiastic, but rather frightened of what the future would hold, and reluctant to fight in a war whose purpose and alleged benefit they failed to see. Often, the news of the outbreak of war was greeted by reluctance and fatalism, rather than enthusiasm (cf. Roger Chickering, *Imperial Germany*, pp.13ff.).

However, if the people of Europe were not belligerent, their governments certainly were to a greater or lesser extent. In the final analysis, war could only have been avoided in 1914 if the governments in Berlin and Vienna first and foremost had been willing to accept mediation of a problem that could have been solved at the conference table. Those mediation proposals, made with the honest desire to preserve peace by the government in London, were deliberately turned down because it was deemed high time to 'deal energetically with the Slavs'. Once this decision was made, the opposing alliances made an escalation of the war almost unavoidable. Of course, even the government in Berlin did not want the world war of unprecedented scale and destructiveness that developed as a result of the events of July 1914, nor could they have foreseen its full horrors. However, they were willing to risk an escalation of a localized war into a European war because they felt able to win and improve their position in such a war. War could only have been avoided in 1914 if all the governments involved had acted openly and with an honest desire for peace. Underestimating the war that they would unleash, and overestimating their own abilities, German and Austrian decision-makers did not have such a desire for peace. The war that broke out in August 1914 would spell the end to their ambitions, for by the end of it, the empires of the pre-war era had ceased to exist. It is not surprising that the origins of this devastating war would be discussed with such passion and it is testimony to the general war-like mood of the pre-war years that attributing the blame for the outbreak of the war has been such a difficult undertaking.

References

Albertini, Luigi, (1964) *The Origins of the War of 1914*, 3 vols, Oxford University Press.

Bell, Philip (1992) 'Origins of the war of 1914' in Paul Hayes (ed.), *Themes in Modern European History 1890–1945*, Routledge.

Prince von Bülow, (1931) *Memoirs*, vol. 2, 1897–1903, Putnam.

Chickering, Roger (1998) *Imperial Germany and the Great War, 1914–1918*, Cambridge University Press.

Ferguson, Niall (1998) *The Pity of War*, Penguin.

Fischer, Fritz (1967) *Germany's Aims in the First World War*, Chatto & Windus.

Fischer, Fritz (1974) *World Power or Decline: The Controversy over Germany's Aims in the First World War*, trans. L.L. Farrar, Robert Kimber and Rita Kimber, Weidenfeld & Nicholson.

Fischer, Fritz (1975) *War of Illusions: German Politics from 1911 to 1914*, trans. Marian Jackson, Chatto & Windus.

Geiss, Imanuel (1967) *July 1914. Selected Documents*, Batsford.

Joll, James (1966) 'The 1914 debate continues: Fritz Fischer and his critics', in H.W.Koch (ed.), *The Origins of the First World War*, second edition, Macmillan, 1984.

Joll, James (1992) *The Origins of the First World War*, second edition, Longman.

Koch, H.W. (ed.) (1984) *The Origins of the First World War*, second edition, Macmillan.

Langdon, John W. (1991) *July 1914. The Long Debate, 1918–1990*, Berg.

McDonough, Frank (1997) *The Origins of the First and Second World Wars*, Cambridge.

Moses, John A. (1975) *The Politics of Illusion. The Fischer Controversy in German Historiography*, Georg Prior Publishers.

Röhl, John (ed.) (1970) *From Bismarck to Hitler. Continuities in German History*, Longman.

Röhl, John (1990) 'Imperial Germany. The riddle of 1914', *Modern History Review*, vol.2, no.1, September.

Stevenson, David (1996) *Armaments and the Coming of War. Europe, 1904–1914*, Clarendon Press.

Stevenson, David (1997) *The Outbreak of the First World War. 1914 in Perspective*, Macmillan.

Strachan, Hew (ed.) (1998) *The Oxford Illustrated History of the First World War*, Oxford University Press.

Turner, L.C.F. (1970) *Origins of the First World War*, Arnold.

Williamson, Samuel R Jr. (1991) *Austria-Hungary and the Origins of the First World War*, Macmillan.

Wilson, Keith (ed.) (1995) *Decisions for War, 1914*, UCL Press.

Further reading

Herwig, Holger H. (ed.) (1991) *The Outbreak of the First World War. Causes and Responsibilities*, sixth edition, Houghton Mifflin (a useful collection of articles from authors who have contributed to the debate).

Langdon, John W. (1991) *July 1914. The Long Debate, 1918–1990*, Berg (an excellent summary of the debate).

Mombauer, Annika (2001) *The Debate on the Origins of the First World War*, Longman (traces the development of the debate from 1914 to the 1990s).

Stevenson, David (1997) *The Outbreak of the First World War. 1914 in Perspective*, Macmillan (contains a useful chronology and an excellent bibliography).

Index